*Chocolate Pudding*
*and Other Approaches to*
*Intensive Multiple-Family Therapy*

# Chocolate Pudding

## and Other Approaches to INTENSIVE MULTIPLE-FAMILY THERAPY

By Ruth McClendon and Leslie B. Kadis

SCIENCE AND BEHAVIOR BOOKS
PALO ALTO, CALIFORNIA

To Bob and Mary Goulding
whose wisdom and friendship
have provided continuous support

To the families in this book
whose courage and willingness to change
provides the validation for what we do

Library of Congress Number 83–060321

ISBN 0–8314–0066–8

Printed in the United States of America

# Contents

# Preface

As psychotherapists, we love to devise new structures for doing therapy, particularly structures where we work with the entire family.

In 1972, Ruth created this structure for Intensive Multiple-Family Therapy that combines elements from individual, group and family therapies. It was originally designed to fill a specific need: families from out of the area could come to California, work with Ruth, and get therapy in a brief time. Ruth and George McClendon actually conducted the first workshop in the fall of 1972. In later years Ruth, with a new partner, Les Kadis, developed the model further as they continued the work.

The workshop we describe here combines two actual workshops that we, Les and Ruth, conducted during the summer of 1979. We selected four families (from the nine who actually participated) in order to provide a cross-section of individuals and problems. *Chocolate Pudding* conveys the experience of family members, trainees, and primary therapists.

These are not fictitious families: The people (with the exception of one person) and their problems are real. With their permission, we recorded their sessions. Transcriptions of these video and audio tapes provided the material for this book. Although we changed names, identities, dates, and locations to maintain confidentiality, we have reported dialogue and events with extreme accuracy, or as much as the printed medium will allow. In the one instance in which we changed a real person to a fictitious character, that character bears no resemblance to the actual person. (Much of our communication is nonverbal, especially in therapy situations. We have at times expanded slightly on taped conversations to catch nuance or where a too literal transcription would have falsified the experience.) In all cases, we have remained true to the spirit of the workshop.

Sections of this book can be read separately. For the reader who is interested in the families, the stories are moving and complete. Those interested in more detail on how we work with the families will find the introduction useful. It contains a general overview of our theories and the structure of the workshops. The final chapter contains the bulk of theoretical information.

By sharing the workshop experience, we hope to help the reader know what we do; and how to apply our ideas to their own practices and even how to participate in therapy. Our most important message to the reader, however, is that: *Change is possible and even fun along the way.*

# Acknowledgments

This book would never have been started, and certainly not completed, without the encouragement and support of many people.

Bob and Mary Goulding were two of our most important teachers. We can acknowledge our debt in no better way than to dedicate our book to them.

George McClendon was instrumental in many of the workshops that took place before this book. He helped develop some of the structure and the therapy method and has continued to be very supportive of this book project. Chris Hatcher encouraged us from the beginning. His enthusiasm gave great impetus to our project. He has continued to support us by reading parts of the manuscript and making valuable contributions.

Paul McCormick was present at both of the workshops. He helped us formulate some of the ideas for the structure of the book and was involved with commenting on some of the early drafts.

Kitty Dautoff, the Kitty of this book, has a unique ability to connect with and understand kids. Her insights and suggestions have always been invaluable. Her contributions are most evident in our successes.

Our staff during these and other workshops consisted of friends who were in training. Kay Bartlett, a public health nurse supervisor, was our general manager. Without her we would not have survived. Lauren Crux, a therapist in private practice, was our video expert and chief housekeeper. She did an incredible job. Barbara Steen, also a therapist, fed us all in a grand and healthy manner. We shall never forget her homemade muffins and chocolate mousse. Laura, Christina (Pam), and Heidi cheered us on and helped with everything.

Finally, we have three very special acknowledgments. Joan Minninger, respected colleague and friend, deserves a special place in the history of this book. She is a "writing therapist" who created the environment that made this book possible. Her intuition and skill in helping us "talk" the book provided the feedback, encouragement, and structure that ultimately led to these pages. Connie Casey is a writer and editor who, working with Joan, gave the first form and substance to our spoken words. Her skill helped us make the transition from the spoken word to the written word. Thanks for her perseverance, discernment, and intelligence. Peggie Deane typed the entire manuscript. But more than that, her excitement about the families—as their stories unfolded under her devoted fingers—was continual, positive reinforcement for us. Without her feedback, we would have stopped more than once.

# _Introduction_

This book tells the stories of four families who were in pain and whose pain has been relieved.

In the pages that follow we take you session by session through an Intensive Multiple-Family Therapy workshop. In the telling, we demonstrate how each family discovers the roots of their current problems and then reintegrates into a new structure to become a more supportive and autonomous family unit. In addition to their stories, we share our own experiences as therapists: We demonstrate the excitement and effectiveness of doing intensive multiple-family therapy with four families who live together for one week.

## WHERE WE WORK

We work in a pleasant vacation place: Pajaro Dunes on the California coast, Snowmass in the Rockies, or Lake Tahoe in the Sierra Nevada mountains. Living together in a place away from home concentrates family resolve and orients them toward their goal. No one leaves at night to go home to habitual living environments, distractions, and supports that maintain the family status quo. Because the environment is new families group together for support. The interactions between people are free and immediate, as if we were all on a boat or a wilderness trek together.

# HOW WE WORK

Our time structure for the week is simple: On Sunday evening we meet the families, help them settle into their living accommodations, and allow them to become acquainted with the area. On Monday through Saturday we meet for morning and afternoon therapy sessions. Throughout the week we eat, rest, and play together.

Workshop sessions are intense, exciting, and fun. People of all ages as well as toys and cuddling things are available. We encourage movement and interaction. We aim to bring information to life. If someone has been or is being affected by a person not present, we ask that workshop member to imagine that person in the room and to speak directly to him or her. We encourage people to give information about the past by picturing it in the present. After one family member does this work for himself or herself, we move on to someone else. As they see other families and persons work, people very quickly become confident that they themselves can look at their own problems productively. Group members support and confront each other as friends and as equals. They comment on similarities in life situations, point out discrepancies and incongruities that are more obvious to the listener, and when applicable, they cheer other group members on. This interaction is sometimes more valuable than comment or direction from a therapist, because group members often invest the leaders with the cloak of their parents or other important people from the past and react to them by overadapting or rebelling. As they do this, the opinions and judgments of other group members become more valued.

Members do silent work on their own problems as they observe someone else working on similar difficulties. Although they are not active at the moment, these members use the work that the active member is doing to stimulate new thoughts on their own difficulties. We also utilize the resources of all the possible subgroups such as male, female, parents' and kids' groups. Dividing the group into smaller units allows individuals to explore different role identifications and to examine their relationships from different perspectives. (We will discuss and demonstrate this later.)

After years of experience with intensive multiple-family therapy, as well as more traditional family therapy, we've found that the model presented in this book works best. It is an effective, quick, and exciting approach that offers many, many elements (such as those mentioned above) never available in the single-family, weekly treatment models. It combines some of the best elements of family, group, individual, and marathon therapy.

# AN INTRODUCTION TO OUR THINKING

In the study of genetics, we see that diversity increases a species' chance for survival. This is also true of families: Having a variety of ways to behave under stress increases the chances for a workable, enduring family structure. To say this in reverse: Families get into trouble because they cannot maintain a broad repertoire of responses in the face of stress, internal or external. If one or more family members retreat from a healthy variety of behaviors to a few "safe" (that is, familiar) old responses, they will encounter danger particularly if this retreat is to primitive or frightening emotions, such as extreme anger, depression, or suicide attempts. When reading these stories, you will notice that each family and each individual has a repertoire of behaviors they are familiar with and ready to perform—a singer with a set of songs.

What we have just said is that every family has operating patterns that have developed out of the combination of each member's experiences. In families that do not work well, these patterns are few and rigid; in families that do, numerous and flexible.

Unfortunately, not only the present patterns or repertoires are a problem. As you will see, the past and the present are intimately connected: The family, as a unit, has a history; each of its members has one, too. People who operate presently in ways that do not get the results they want are frequently reacting to images from the past. We help people separate the past from the present. By so doing, we enable them to release their energies, skills, and creativity.

Families and individuals in trouble are like a record with a scratch completely across it. If you move the needle only a little bit, it always travels back to the place where it gets stuck. In this book we'll help each family member to change the internal pictures of himself or herself and others so that the individual does not return to the same old groove. This relationship between the present and the past is the core concept around which we organize the data derived from our observations of the family and our ideas about how to help the family change.

People limit their options in their present circumstances because they hold antiquated ideas about how their families "should be." These ideas were learned in their families of origin. People impose these antiquated pictures on other family members so that each person acts like a supporting actor or actress in another family member's life script. Severing the connection between the past and the present, for individual family members as well as for the family as a whole, allows the current family to rewrite its script in order to account for current realities.

Our job as therapists is first to learn as much as possible about how the family operates in the present. We then search out the connections between present and the past for each of the family members. For some, that connection is a thick rubber band; for others, a delicate filament. We help hack away at the connection. Once the connection is severed, we have successfully interfered with the automatic snap back to the past that prevents people from acting effectively.

The instantaneous cocky reaction Dominic Dellapietra shows whenever challenged, the way Bette Sarnon tightens her whole body when another woman approaches, and the immediate lapse in the thinking process that Berenice Barker suffers when anyone disagrees with her definitions are all examples of this rubber-band phenomenon. Their response was so quick, so automatic that none of these people were aware of it, not the stimuli, not the internal process, not the behavior. When we mentioned the reaction, each person recognized it was true of him or herself. Each had a vague sense of discomfort and all wanted to change.

This is the focus of our work: placing the past in its proper perspective so that present interactions are based on present rather than past realities.

## OUR MODEL FOR THERAPY

Our therapy is a combination of Family Systems, Transactional Analysis, and Gestalt theories. We call this approach Redecision Family Therapy. RDFT integrates the approaches of family systems theory and Redecision therapy (a development of transactional analysis and gestalt therapy) into one three-stage model.

### Stage One—Systems

In this stage, we observe, evaluate, and intervene in the system. We focus on present interactions between family members. As you will see, we actively intervene in the family process to restructure family boundaries, to reframe interpersonal issues, and to stop destructive behavior.

### Stage Two—Redecisions

Because we have interrupted the old system each person needs to redecide how to get his or her needs met. Individuals' early decisions are based on the only information available to them back then. Such information was the sum of internal processes, together with each individual's perceptions of the availability and trustworthiness of other persons in his or her environment.

In second-stage Redecision work, we take an individual's present and relate it to his or her past. We point out characteristic responses, trace the roots of those responses and facilitate redecision. Using gestalt techniques brings these early issues to the foreground, allowing the person to "redecide" about these early issues.

### Stage Three—Reintegration

Here we help the family practice its new system of interacting. Planning for the future, rehearsing, and role-playing prepares them for cooperating in new ways.

This stage is a future-oriented, reintegration stage. We facilitate the forming of a new family system with a new and different structure and more flexible family rules. The family's interactive process moves to a new level of organization. The present becomes a choice, not an echo of the past, or of the parents' individual histories.

The final chapter of this book, which may be read separately, explains our thinking structure. It explains this flexible combination of therapy techniques, how we developed it, and the beliefs that underlie our interventions and goals in treatment.

# THE INTENSIVE MULTIPLE-FAMILY FORMAT

People often ask us why we do these intensive workshops. Our answer is simple: it works best this way—it's quick, complete, and fun. We continue to experiment with different treatment models but always come back to the residential, away-from-it-all environment as our first choice. We provide the comforts, the safety to work, and the care needed when someone is opening up and facing himself or herself. Group members are removed from school problems, job problems, housekeeping, buying groceries, cleaning house, and picking up suits at the cleaners. They have already overcome many of their own resistances. We know that distance from pressure works. By creating a complete, protected environment we can observe families in detail. This detail most therapists are never lucky enough to see. We can watch how family members act at meals—how they talk to each other while they're eating. We know who comes to meals, who doesn't, and who comes late every morning to breakfast and still expects to get served. We listen to who tells whom where to sit. We watch who cuts the children's food and who responds when the milk is spilled. The first time we see the Barkers sit down to a meal, we notice that everyone eats off everyone else's plate. The lack of boundaries in regard to food turns out to be an important clue to an excessive entanglement in other areas.

We can also see who drinks what. Gerry Barker, who says, "I'm not drinking anymore," sits down and finishes off six glasses of wine with his first dinner.

We have a no-smoking policy in the public and eating areas. It's interesting to watch the way people break the no-smoking rule and to see their reactions to our responses.

Between sessions families come and go as they choose. People go into town, hike, or walk by the lake. We get to play with them as well as work. We get to know each other in widely different settings.

### Some Practical Considerations

The workshop we will describe takes place on the shore of Lake Tahoe in the High Sierras of California. We rented a cluster of condominiums for the week. It is July. The days are warm and the nights crisp. The air is always clear and full of good mountain smells.

Over the years we have learned that attention to a myriad of details is essential to the success of the workshop. These are a few principles we follow in planning the workshop.

The environment must invite people to feel comfortable and cared for, without being too plush.

The environment must be childproof. Children must be able to roam free without danger of their being physically hurt. This allows the family members to concentrate on their work without concern for the physical safety of other family members or other things, and at the same time we can watch the family's protective tendencies and abilities and evaluate these tendencies in relation to real dangers.

The living environment must have as little external structure as possible, so that people can interact freely and we can observe them outside of the sheltered therapy room. We use large common rooms for meeting and eating, serve meals buffet style, and encourage social interactions between everyone in the workshop—participants, trainees and ourselves. The most important part of our data is often derived from observations and experiences made during these nontherapy times.

We choose the location and dates of the workshop long in advance, often more than a year. This allows members to make reservations and to make certain that the workshop does not conflict with school schedules or other important events. Soon after we set the place and the date, people call for details—the workshop begins to take shape. The composition of the group will change many times during the next few months as the circumstances change for any one family in particular.

The first families to commit themselves to the workshop determine which families we will accept later on. If, for example, the first two families have early-adolescent children, we will look for additional families with children of similar age. (We channel other families to different workshops.)

We contact the professional who refers each family to us to give us the background of the problem, the course of therapy thus far, and resources available for the end of the workshop.

We keep records of transactions between us and the family prior to the workshop: who contacts us, why, and how; how our responses are received; how the family handles money and other day-to-day transactions; and how it handles the anxiety of taking part in this workshop. These are all carefully recorded and become part of the saga that culminates in the workshop itself.

People often express concern about the cost of the workshop: what will it cost; is it covered by insurance. Such details must be carefully explored and resolved before the workshop begins.

Through this attention to detail we learn a lot about how the family copes with day-to-day problems of the real world and often have more than sufficient information to begin therapy before we have actually met the family.

We bring our own cook to provide big healthy, meals. We eat meats once a day. The dietary emphasis is on lots of fresh vegetables, fruits, and freshly made bread. Jars of peanut butter and jelly are always around for the kids. We have an infinite supply of fruit, raisins, coffee, tea, and juice available. (One curious detail: The first two days the families go through loads of food. The cooks, who are veterans of the workshops, double the recipes for these days. By the fourth day the cooks reduce the meals and cut back the heavy snacks. People, including us, tend to eat heavily when they're uncertain and nervous; they eat less after they become comfortable with the environment and absorbed in the work they're doing.)

The meeting rooms where the therapy sessions are held are open to the outside and views of the lake or mountains. The dining room and the working rooms have fireplaces, giving a cosy heart to a room that is airy, expansive, and fresh.

There is some maid service, but group members make their own beds and clean up after themselves. We, Ruth and Les, do not check the wastebaskets or inspect for bathtub rings, but we learn some more about a family's private life if rooms are particularly messy or if furniture is broken. We do most of the cleaning up at the end of the week.

Sometimes someone will get angry with us for not having the right thing to eat, or enough towels, or something special. We need to know whether the angry comment is appropriate (sometimes we find we have goofed) or whether it is out of proportion to the facts. We use this information to confirm or reject previous hypotheses. It also allows us to watch the family operate in an environment other than the sessions. We worked with one family in which kids were tightly controlled during sessions but not within their own four walls.

### Of Course It's Artificial

Fellow therapists have questioned the advantage of an intense week of living together, saying that the atmosphere is artificial and likely to encourage unusual behavior.

Of course it's artificial. We are therapists, not anthropologists. It is our job to intervene as well as to observe. As to the idea that people in a strange, though very pleasant, setting will behave in unusual wys, the time and space concentration at the workshop encourages people to an intensification, but not distortion, of their usual daily behavior—or so we observe.

(We also use structures other than the week long in residence model for doing intensive multiple family therapy. Many of these do not require the families to be in residence, and therefore cost less while allowing work and school to continue. The Family Development Center, our training center, sponsors workshops that are one week long and families live at home or find their own accomodations. Other models are structured around one weekend followed by two evenings each week for five to six weeks: three successive weekends with one midweek evening session; or one Friday night and all day Saturday for four weeks in a row. Each of these has its own advantage. It is too soon to decide which one works best. We lean toward the week-long live-in model because of the feeling of community and family, and the nurturing environment that we experience.) However other models are easier to set up and sometimes easier for families to commit to.

## THE FAMILIES

What kinds of families take a drastic step like this—scheduling a week out of their lives, traveling a long way from home and investing considerable funds?* First, families in severe trouble. These families are referred usually by another psychotherapist who knows of our work. Second, families who are already in therapy, but who are not changing quickly enough and decide to come to an intensive multiple-family therapy workshop. Third, families of therapists who have been in training with us. Finally, many, many families who want to learn more about themselves, to grow, and change. These families often refer themselves.

The families you will read about have trouble in their present lives. The Barkers have multiple problems: an imminent divorce, a suicidal mother, a son who has had serious trouble with the law, a young adolescent girl who drinks and the recent death of a second son for whom the family still grieves. The Sarnons worry about Bill's rage and about Nick's school work. The Dellapietras are dealing with Dom's alcoholism and two young kids who run wild. The Quinns have come because David has school trouble and his brother Robin is on the verge of major emotional difficulties.

Each of the families has already struggled on their own to solve their problems, and these struggles have become an additional source of difficulties. Two families have been or currently were in therapy.

### Uncertain Beginnings
When families first arrive, most are uncertain, some are scared, others defensive. The family unit reacts to the uncertainty in whatever way is characteristic of it. The Barkers huddle closely together as a group, the Sarnons, initially quiet, became even more so, the Quinns act as if they are going on vacation rather than to therapy, and the Dellapietras, initially rambunctious, became even more so.

What helps these families is that they have already committed considerable time, energy, and money to get to the workshop. This determination and commitment counterbalance some of the anxiety. Also, there is little

---

*The cost of a 1980 workshop was $425.00/person including room and board. Insurances cover the therapy costs of the workshop, to their usual degree.

here that will act as a target for displaced anxiety: The accommodations are pleasant, the food good, and the overall environment inviting. Most important, there are other families present: The young people connect with each other almost instantly. The sharing of commitment, commonality of experience, and the children's openness help the group to cohere.

### The First Session

At the very first session we continue to build on this early commonality. We shift the emphasis from a social group to a working therapy group. We start with simple, getting-to-know-you, person-to-person exercises that encourage trust. These exercises help people identify other group members to whom they might later turn for support. To start, we ask people simply to tell basic information about themselves: who they are, what they do, how they feel about being here. Then we ask people to select, based on what they've just heard, someone outside of their family who they would like to get to know. People then talk with each other about what they like about themselves. In this way, we start to loosen some of the boundaries that circumscribe and contain the family.

Next, we shift from the group to the families and work with them as units. In order to reinforce the notion that a family is here to work as a family, we ask them to talk together as a unit. Many families come to the workshop focused on an identified "patient," one family member who has all the symptoms and all the problems. We are interested in the family's idea of why they are here, but more important is the process of how they interact. We develop some structure and then, at the first opportunity, observe how the family works on a particular task. We help them show us themselves as we help them formulate their goals for the week. What they want for themselves as a family and as individuals, plus our understanding of what needs to change so they can function together successfully, become the basis for what we call the contract.

### Contract for Change

We ask the family to define what they want to change in terms of their behavior so that the end point of therapy is clear to them and to us. Success is readily apparent when contracts are clear; the pleasure of positive achievement acts as a positive reinforcement. The contract is completed after we assess the dysfunctions in the family's patterns of interaction, draw the connections between each individual's early decisions and his present behaviors, and get agreement with each individual on resolving this particular difficulty. (We will describe this process in more detail later.)

Throughout our work we are active, even playful where possible, encouraging participation of all group members. Successful short-term work requires lots of energy and action rather than drawn-out talk and intellectualization. Most people will not be reached in a short time by simply talking about things; some people will never be reached. For many of us talking structures are defense structures. Because language is a representational medium and therefore removed from reality, talking is often a way to avoid showing feelings.

During the first day, we are occupied with building the group, creating a safe environment, and getting the initial contracts. After the first session, we take a long break to permit the families to back off a little. Some family members have laid themselves bare in the morning, and their defensiveness rises with their anxiety level. Lunch and free time take up part of the break; the other part, filling out questionnaires. These questionnaires give us additional information about the way family members see themselves as individuals, each other, and their families as a unit.* Different questionnaires are completed at the workshop. Work with these questionnaires takes about an hour and a half. Helped a bit by trainees,** even children of four, such as Marco Dellapietra, can give pertinent replies to the questions.

---

*Some of the questionnaires take time to fill out and require gathering information about the family's history through three generations. We mail these ahead and ask members to complete them before the workshop.

**Trainees (that is, therapists in training) who are there as observers are additional resource people for us and for family members. They notice what is happening outside of group sessions. They support, comfort, and confront members outside of group sessions when that is part of the strategy. Each trainee is assigned to one family throughout the week and helps with particular tasks and requests. (See Trainees.)

**Making Predictions**

We, Ruth and Les, use this long break to sit alone and review our initial observations of people and families in the workshop. We begin to plan how we will proceed. We discuss intervention strategies: where we predict we will make the easiest contact, where we will meet resistance, where we might get into trouble. The latter is particularly important because a stumbling block with one family, a failure to respond to unspoken fear, anger, or hostility, may impede the progress of all the families and the entire workshop.

# THE WORK BEGINS

We often split the group into subunits that reflect our most current assessment of the dominant themes. This makes it easier for people to experience themselves and their family differently and to explore and to work on the problem more productively. In this workshop we decide on Monday afternoon to split the families into two groups. Two families go with Ruth; two with Les. Each family gets more individual attention, quickly opens up more in the smaller setting, and develops an increased sense of closeness to the other family it is working with. Furthermore, this split-family structure often is used to implement an intervention for change. In this case, we divide the Barker family into two parts to help them become less entwined.

We also further the group process by some physical work. For instance, we begin by helping Robin Quinn create a sculpture, a living tableau of his family, using members of other families. Using this technique early in the workshop serves many purposes. First, sculpting shifts the inactive "talking about" to the active "show me" mode. Second, it energizes as well as involves group members who personally are not working at this time. Third, those who portray members of other families often have two distinct reactions. They may play a role that relates to their place in their own families. Then, after playing the role and sensing the character they are portraying, they may ask themselves what the sculptor saw in them that led to their choice.

Finally, the sculpture facilitates group interaction.

Nothing builds bonds like playing someone's mother or father. and giving feedback on how you feel in that role. Much later, people frequently will begin contact with statements such as "when I was your mother. . . ."

By the end of the first day, we have clearly determined that the parent/child separation has been maintained poorly between Paula and her sons Robin and David in the Quinn family; between Bette and her son Nicholas in the Sarnon family; and in the entire Dellapietra and Barker families. Therefore, on the next day we divide the groups into a parents' group and a young people's group. We are also anxious to know if there will be a teen-age peer group; if Nicholas and Melissa will connect with David and Robin. Will David discuss his father and that loss? Will Nicholas be more open about his anger at his mother? Will Angela and Dom talk about their marital difficulties in the parents' group? Will Bette talk about her sense of failure as a mother?

Another very important grouping is the division into the men's group and the women's group. This division focuses on same-sex identification and same-sex relationships, such as father and son. This generates new awarenesses, new connections, and new sources of strength. Several times during the week we use this group to build a sense of personal identity that is different from family-role identity.

This is the way we think about the intensive multiple-family group and the structure and flow of the workshop. We consider what is happening with each family, what needs to happen next, and how to best accomplish that next step. We organize each succeeding working session to incorporate these plans.

### Specialized Techniques—Chocolate Pudding and Others

We believe that effective therapy requires an affective, or emotional, experience with cognitive grounding. We are constantly developing ways of involving people. Molding a family sculpture, drawing family pictures, games, dramatizations, and even chocolate pudding are all techniques for this.

The chocolate-pudding group is play-therapy for adults and children working together—an easy channel for people to let out angry feelings that they wouldn't dare express in a more adult fashion. We usually start the pudding group when people either seem to move slowly or act restrictedly.

There is a slightly impish quality to the way we set up the group. We invite people to participate, making a special event—almost like a party. Usually we select very neat, grown-up people. Bill and Bette Sarnon and Angela Dellapietra are in the Tuesday-afternoon pudding group because of their restricted range of affect, their extreme sense of neatness, and their external control.

It is a bright, warm day and everyone is sitting outside on the grass—seven people, including Ruth. Everyone is wearing bathing suits or old clothes, and each person has a big bowl of chocolate pudding (gallons of it were made from Jello instant pudding mix) and a couple of pieces of paper. The only directions given are to explore the pudding by yourself and with others. People start off on their own using the pudding as fingerpaint on the paper. However, chocolate pudding being what it is, they soon are tasting it and touching one another with it. It takes only a little encouragement from Ruth for a lot of fun and revealing nonverbal interplay. We include Paula Quinn because we want to see what will happen if she loosens up. We wonder how Paula reacts to unstructured situations that allow for regression to childlike behavior. Robin Quinn is included in the group because we want to see if we can get something different going between him and his mother—an exception to our usual way of choosing people. (Robin is not overly neat or grownup.) Whenever Robin gets playful, angry, or anxious, Paula stares at him. Robin freezes and becomes more anxious. We want to see if we can help them to interact differently by radically changing the setting.

We also use other energy-generating techniques, such as encounter bats. An encounter bat is a three-foot-long, canvas-covered, foam cylinder. It may be used safely for hitting pillows, chairs, and other people. It is, of course, important to follow the rules: (1) no hitting the head, breasts, or genitals; (2) stop when either party, or the appointed observer, says "stop"; and (3) express verbally what you feel each time you hit. (This rule is sometimes suspended.) Using encounter bats stimulates energy, presents diagnostic information, confronts fantasies of one's omnipotence and limits, encourages safe contact, and awakens associations from the past.

## More Details: Trainees

The workshop is exciting and challenging, but draining. We experience much pressure to help people get what they came for, to go home with a plan to build on, and to carry out what they have learned. To do all of this requires that we, as leaders, bring to the workshop all of our experience and all of ourselves. It also requires that we have some help. We include eight to twelve trainees and one play therapist. Trainees are professional therapists, many of whom have spent at least two years in practice. Many referring therapists come with the families they have been treating.

Participating in the workshop gives a trainee an intense learning experience: observing the families every day of the week and being involved in the planning and process of therapy. Also, because we have four or five families at the workshop, trainees have contact with a wide variety of family and individual problems.

We meet with the trainees each morning and each night of the workshop to review the day's work and plan the intervention strategies for the next day. We frequently design roles for trainees to play in a session or, more frequently, out of a session. Each trainee is assigned to one family. This focuses his or her learning and provides us with resource people who help plan and carry out treatment.

The advantages of trainees to the family members are many: extra support, contact, fun, and professional input and energy. Family members usually find someone else they can go to when they're having trouble with us. One example is the work of one trainee, Claudette, with Bette Sarnon. Claudette reports that she has the impression that Bette is covering up a lot of sadness, perhaps about her distant mother and evasive twin sister. Bette is able to admit to Claudette that everything is not fine and that she has been keeping up a cheerful front, especially with Ruth. A short while after her talk with Claudette, Bette is able to talk more openly in the sessions.

Bethany, another trainee, is the first person to talk to Melissa Barker about her boyfriend and her womanly feelings—Melissa shies away from talking about herself in the young people's group. Barbara teaches magic tricks to David Quinn. It is a completely new experience for David to see any kind of learning as fun. Concentrating on the task of learning card tricks outside of sessions is a release for David. Barbara contributes greatly to his growth. Don is a trainee who helps immensely with talking to Dom about Alcoholics Anonymous. Terry is instrumental with Berenice.

We frequently get follow-up letters from trainees after workshops. They write to say they have integrated what they learned at the workshop into their own practice. We often see them again. Sometimes they return as trainees for another workshop, sometimes they come back as clients with their own families.

When children below five to seven years participate, we employ a play therapist. Kitty, our play therapist, has worked with us for many years. Because of her familiarity with our model and facility with young kids, she is often able to provide us with invaluable information. Marco Dellapietra showed his anger in his play with Kitty. He kicked her, teased her, and acted overtly sexual toward her, attempting to fondle her and play under her dress. This behavior was a reflection of his feelings toward his mother. Kitty was able to relate to Angela what she saw in the in the play groups.

## *Videotape*

With advance permission,* we use videotape for many purposes: to check on our work and as a teaching aid for trainees. Sometimes we get caught up in the emotional struggle of the family and are not as objective as we need to be. Reviewing the videotapes gives us a different perspective on the family and on our own interaction with the family. Trainees can question us and validate their own perspectives.

The videotape is also an effective therapeutic aid. Operating the camera can give a workshop member a different perspective on him- or herself. It gives the

---

*In this workshop, for example, families knew before they arrived that we would record the sessions for teaching and training purposes. Formal releases were obtained on arrival. In these documents, we further spelled out our intentions. Occasionally, a family or an individual does not want their work shown publicly. We honor this wish. No one has ever refused to be videotaped.

remaining group a chance to get more distance from the emotion-laden scene and to interact differently with the on-camera member. We invite people to review these tapes with us, trainees, or other family members present. Videotape will be invaluable in helping Berenice Barker and Bette Sarnon see themselves.

As we mentioned earlier, the video and audio tapes enabled us to write this book. Using the tapes, we followed each family through session by session, word by word, action by action. Later, we spent hundreds of hours transcribing each family's week of therapy. What follows are the actual stories, told in the participants' own words.

# 1

# Meeting All the Families

The *Sarnons* are a three-member family: a wife, her second husband, and her son from the first marriage. This family suffers noticeably from the common problems of a stepfather having difficulty with his teenaged stepson. By the middle of the week, we find the husband has long-buried skeletons that, until he unburdens himself, prevent him from moving on with the rest of his life.

The *Quinns* are a three-member family headed by a single parent, an indomitable single mother struggling to get things right for her two children. The Quinns also illustrate how the symptomatic behavior of one family member—in this case a highly anxious teenaged son who compulsively repeats actions while counting—can help throw a family out of balance.

The *Barkers* are the largest and most complex family. There are three generations. Six individuals have come to Tahoe, but there are two important offstage characters: a grandmother (the matriarch), and a dead son. The Barkers are like a family dynasty in a television drama. It's hard to see the people underneath the problems. As they tell us later, they are constantly involved in one major life catastrophe or another.

The *Dellapietras* exemplify the "normal" family setup: two parents, two children. Though these parents look glamourous, casual, and carefree at first glance, they have individual problems that interfere with being effective parents and close to each other.

In this chapter we will introduce all of these families as we met them—four at a gulp. We will then follow each family separately through the week, Monday to Friday.

## THE BARKERS

Edgar Barker, 50: Bald, plump business executive for his mother-in-law's Arizona company.

Berenice Mackay Barker, 46: Blonde, girlish wife of Edgar. Married 30 years. Dropped out of nursing school at age 20.

Melissa Barker, 14: Third child of Berenice and Edgar. Long, tawny hair and curvy body. Intelligent, but doing badly in school, partly because of her alcohol and drug involvement.

Edgar Barker, Jr., 28 at his death three years ago. Known as "Rusty." Served 18 months in prison for possession of cocaine. Died in a car accident.

Gerald Barker, 26: Berenice and Edgar's second child. Dropped out of college at age 20 to work in his grandmother's company. Married four years.

Margaret Ann Barker, 29: Wife of Gerald. Secretary to the attorney for the grandmother's company. Her parents also worked for the company until recently.

Gerald Barker, Jr., 3: Called "Little Gerry," son of Gerald and Margaret Ann. Active child with straight, blond hair and round, sweet face.

The most important member of the Barker family, the person to whom all threads can be traced back, did not come to the workshop, although her daughter, her son-in-law, her grandchildren, and her great-grandchild did. This is Gertrude Mackay, mother of Berenice Mackay Barker and employer of Berenice's husband, Edgar Barker. Gertrude and her husband inherited a family manufacturing business in the twenties. They weathered the Depression together. After her husband shot and killed himself, Gertrude took over, doubling the business's capacity and tripling its profits. Gertrude's daughter Berenice met Edgar when he was working as a salesman for the business. Their second son, Gerry, met his wife through the family business. Her parents worked for Gertrude.

Berenice and Edgar Barker's recent history is filled with disturbing and tragic events. But it is the family web that entangles the Barkers, rather than these events. We realize early on that our primary job is not to find the reasons for a suicide, an accidental death, or drinking and drug problems, but to help disentangle each Barker from the family network.

Berenice and Edgar have three children, two living, one dead. Edgar, Jr., known as "Rusty," died three years before our workshop. Rusty had been using and dealing in drugs. He was killed when his car missed a curve on a freeway ramp. Gerald, the second and surviving son, is married to Margaret Ann. Berenice takes care of Gerry, Jr., after nursery school, while Margaret Ann works.

Berenice and Edgar's third child, and only daughter, is Melissa. Her mother tells us that Melissa often drinks up to a pint of vodka a day and smokes marijuana before school. Physically precocious, with wavy, tawny hair, Melissa looks and acts as if she is twenty-one years old rather than fourteen. She is involved with a thirty-three-year-old man who keeps her supplied with vodka. Berenice is worried because Melissa is doing terribly in school. She is terrified that Melissa will die like Rusty in a fatal accident.

It takes us a full day to begin to separate the Barkers from each other in our minds. One family member begins a sentence and another family member finishes it. Their emotions overlap: Melissa says she is sad, and Berenice cries.

Berenice is most insistent that something is seriously wrong with her family. It is she who sought help. She is a slight, scattered-looking, blonde woman who looks and often acts much younger than her age. A nervous, girlish smile takes up half her face, and her voice is tinged with self-pity. We do not suspect that she is capable of the resolve she will show by the end of the week.

Berenice's husband Edgar seems much older than his age. His words say he is concerned but his voice is monotonous and emotionless. He is in the most difficult emotional situation. He separated from Berenice and moved out three months before the workshop. He has already made the decision that he does not want to be part of this family, but he wants to help them. He senses that the family is too entwined. The only response he knows is to split off, but he believes he cannot finally leave until his wife and his two remaining children are better.

Gerry, blond, affable, and handsome, takes after his mother. Unlike her, he often speaks forcibly as spokesman for the family. He drinks a lot. Until a recent year of group therapy, he liked to risk arrest by drinking too much, stealing small things, driving too fast, or breaking store windows. Three times, Margaret Ann has answered the front door to find the police asking for her husband. We find ourselves wondering why Margaret Ann, pretty, confident, and warm, married Gerry, a man who is frequently in trouble. Part of the answer, apparently, is that she admires Gerry's vitality and his dramatic love for life. She also feels a debt to repay because her parents have been helped by Gertrude.

The birth of Little Gerry, Gerry and Margaret Ann's first child, reinforced the family's interconnectedness. Before the birth of her grandson, Berenice responded to the family chaos by returning to nursing school to get a good job. In actuality, she never wanted to go to school or to work. When Margaret Ann went back to work (because she and Gerry needed money), Berenice promptly quit her classes. She picks up little Gerry after nursery school, and cares for him every weekday afternoon. That Little Gerry was born only a month after her son Rusty was killed is significant for Berenice. The family believes in replacement. They act as if children can make up for the deficits of the previous generation.

Rusty had spent 18 months in jail for the sale of marijuana and possession of cocaine before he died. Melissa's dearest memory is of the times she visited her brother in prison. She writes, "My best experience as a child was getting to see my brother Rusty every other Sunday up at prison. Rusty would let me ride on his shoulders and he'd get me a candy bar. He could wiggle his ears. I thought he was super neat!"

Melissa believes that her brother's death was not an accident or a suicide; she thinks that people with whom he had been dealing drugs killed him in revenge for being shortchanged. Berenice is afraid that Melissa idolizes Rusty. She also fears that Melissa thinks she can only leave the family through some violent rebellion.

Melissa alternates between brooding sulkiness and overt seductiveness. She wears brief tops and short shorts to show off her full bust and shapely thighs. A solid, but not unattractive, roll of baby fat pokes out at her midriff, giving away that she is close to being a little girl.

There seems to be a history of separating from the family through self-destructive methods. Berenice's father, whom she describes as "intelligent, creative, and alcoholic," shot himself not long after divorcing her mother, when Berenice was five. The senior Edgar's parents and grandparents had bitter divorces. His mother was an alcoholic with severe liver disease.

Berenice reacts to any challenge by becoming very emotional. (This complicates our job.) We ask Edgar and Berenice, "How did your parents respond to your choice of partner?" We learn that resorting to emotional outbursts is a trait of Gertrude's as well. Edgar says that his mother and father, business partners with Gertrude, were pleased that he was accepted as a son-in-law by the grand old lady. But Berenice says her mother was so upset that her sixteen-year-old daughter planned to marry Edgar that she got a gun and threatened to shoot him. "She is delighted now that we're separated," Berenice says. "It's what she has wanted for the past 30 years. I'm sure I stayed married because I didn't want to let her know she was right."

Berenice says she married Edgar in order to find a protector. She still sees herself as incompetent and even crippled. That is not so far-fetched. She has a barely noticeable deformity of the foot and a limp, stemming from a childhood accident. When Berenice was two, a horse stepped on her foot at her paternal grandfather's. At two-and-a-half, she spent almost a year in the hospital to reconstruct the crushed bones.

Gertrude never forgave her husband or his father for Berenice's accident. She lived with her daughter in the hospital, an unusual occurrence in the 1930s. Berenice remembers this as the only time that her mother was with her for any amount of time.

Berenice was born prematurely as a twin and weighed only three pounds. Her twin brother, born dead, was never named. According to family legend, the doctor said, "Do what you can for the mother. The baby won't survive the night." Two myths developed around the story of Berenice's birth. First: She is someone who must always struggle against predictions of a bad outcome, but she comes through. Second: She is responsible for her twin's death. He should have been the one to survive because her parents wanted a boy. (Berenice alone believes this.)

"I should have died" is a theme that continues throughout her life. "I would have died to keep him alive," she says of her dead son. "I should be dead," Berenice says again on the first day of the workshop, causing her son Gerry to dash across the room to care for her. Berenice's verbal threats are given credibility by her father's suicide. They help to keep the family enmeshed.

The Barker family has come from their home in Arizona, all piled into one rented car. We know that they have been in group therapy together for the past year. We have to resist being distracted by the extremely dramatic facts of the family history.

The Barkers tumble over each other when they talk. They all talk about their recent therapy, about Rusty's death, about Gertrude and Gertrude's business. Our first reaction is that it will be tough to work with this family. (It did turn out to take a terrific effort to free each individual member of the Barker family from the web in which they were all tangled. The effort was worth it.)

## THE QUINNS

Paula Quinn, 49: Dark-haired and thin, geriatric nurse and recovering alcoholic. Divorced from her first husband (two children). Second husband dead (one child). She lives in a small town in Nevada.

Robin Goerner, 18: Paula's second son from her first marriage. He now goes to a local college part-time, after a becoming extremely anxious and withdrawing from an out-of-town school. He has a long, tan body, awkward except on the tennis court.

David Quinn, 10: Eager, appealing boy with brown hair. Son of Paula and her second husband. His father died when he was three. Going on 11, but reading at first-grade level.

Paula Quinn is a woman of grim determination. After two unhappy marriages (one ending in divorce, the other in widowhood) and a long period of alcoholism, she is determined to make a better life for herself and her two children. Unfortunately, the sternness of her resolve may defeat her purpose. Paula is a thin, neatly dressed woman with a sad, tense face. The only visible evidence of her years of alcoholism is a slight pouchiness under the eyes. She has a deep, coarse voice that is never soft. Her most noticeable feature is the severe expression in her eyes. When Paula goes stone-faced and glares at her teenaged son Robin, he becomes increasingly anxious. David, 10, reacts to his mother's glare by acting babyish.

Paula and David Quinn, who live in Nevada, have arrived at Tahoe by Greyhound bus. They were referred by a social worker in their town. Last spring Paula traveled twice by bus to see Ruth in California. Robin Goerner, already at Tahoe, arrived on his motorbike two days earlier. He is staying in a house with four of our staff. Paula has paid for the workshop out of her salary, in installments of $20 a month.

Paula first saw Ruth when Robin had to come home from school because he developed a set of ritualistic behaviors that severely limited his ability to operate on a day-to-day basis. He was attempting to control his anxiety of being away from home by redoing everything he had done to the point of incapacitation. He checked the front door to see if it was locked so many times, for example, that he failed to get to his appointments and sometimes even failed to get to meals. This and similar other behaviors progressively limited his action to the point where the school psychiatrist recommended he go home and consider hospitalization. Seeing her son so incapacitated galvanized Paula. Two years before, she had been unemployed and became severely depressed. During her depression, Paula lived on social security. Her first husband, Robin's father, contributes nothing to his son's support, although he is a high-salaried executive at a Texas-based international oil company after "dropping out" for several years when Robin was 11. Paula was married to him at the age of 20. The marriage lasted 14 years. He had been married before and had one son, Drake, who sometimes lived with him and Paula until Robin was born. He then became a permanent part of the household.

Paula met her second husband at an alcoholic-rehabilitation clinic. She was a patient and he was a counselor. She describes him as a proud, possessive, self-made man. She was 36 when they married and 40 when he died. She was left with their son David.

The Quinn family's other major problem is David's severe reading problems. He cannot read a page without losing his place repeatedly; he is unable to recognize familiar words or to sound them out; and he cannot follow directions that have more than one step. He has spent a large part of his time in school being tested. The conclusion of the barrage of tests is not very helpful: David has learning difficulties of unknown origin.

Paula's history was sad, Robin's was awful, and David's problems are a mystery to us. Paula was born at the beginning of the Depression and her family had to move wherever her father could find work. Sometimes they moved more than once a year. The worst part of her childhood, she says, was constantly making new friends in new schools. Her best experience was going to junior high school in her home town. People did not know her, but they remembered having heard her name. She appreciated even that.

Robin is a tall, slim young man. He has thick blond hair and a sharp but rugged face. He moves awkwardly and speaks rapidly in a loud voice. Robin quickly takes offense and becomes agitated, hyperventilating and wringing his hands. He had gone to a small college in Indiana thinking that he could manage in that "homey" environment and was surprised to learn that he was scared, having trouble making friends and not keeping up with the work.

Robin thinks that Paula was constantly drunk when she was pregnant with him, and almost miscarried. It was at that time that Robin's parents separated and subsequently divorced. For the first three years of Robin's life, his mother was a severe alcoholic. When Robin was two, Paula left home for a residential alcoholic-rehabilitation center. From age 2 to 11, Robin lived with his father and brother. He idolized his brother Drake, but often fought with him. When the fights worsened, he withdrew into fantasy and spent hours in his bedroom telling himself stories.

At age 6, Robin began to visit his mother, who had remarried. Asked for his worst childhood memory, Robin

replies: "I was 7. I was petrified when my stepfather beat
up on my mom. When I tried to stop him from beating up
my Mom, he hit me. She was pregnant with David."
Because of these incidents, Robin has seen himself as
David's protector. He even fantasizes that he is David's
father.

When Robin was 11, his father "dropped out." He quit
his job and went to live "in the country." Robin arrived on
his mother's doorstep and has had no personal contact with
his father since then except for an occasional postcard. His
brother, Drake, went to live with his own mother and
Robin has no contact with him either.

Robin has difficulty keeping his family situation
straight. He believes he has three families. In spite of the
lack of contact he believes one family consists of his father,
himself, and his older brother Drake. The second is Paula,
David, and himself. His third family is made up of his
parents reunited with their children and David. Robin is
tense because of and confused by his three-layer family. He
sees himself as the bridge between the scattered elements.

David will have his eleventh birthday during the
workshop. Everyone looks forward to it. The coming
birthday will be intimately connected to his treatment.
David is a bright, engaging boy who speaks readily in a
sharp, clear voice. We know that his father died when he
was three and he has moments of deep depression. We also
know, from Ruth's previous work with Paula, that his
father reverted to alcoholism and David's parents had been
separated several times before his father died of cancer.
Paula thinks David knows nothing of this.

David, Robin, and Paula still live in the house in which
David remembers living with his father. David can identify
the last place he sat with his father. He has found nails
that he and his father pounded into the fence.

Just before the workshop, Paula has gotten a better job,
and the family is planning a move to a nearby town. Before
he would agree to move, David made his mother promise
that they would visit the house once a week. He wants to
ensure that the family renting the house will not change
anything he associates with his father.

We suspect that Paula and Robin encourage David to
remember his father as a marvelous man. David's
unresolved feelings for his father are a significant clue to
us as we watch him slip back easily to childishness. As an
eleven-year-old, David is wonderful. As his younger self, he

is a pain. He will not take responsibility for cleaning after himself. He slips into baby talk. Our hunch is that he causes some of his own reading difficulties. We suspect that he does not want to learn anything beyond the level he learned by age three, the year his father died.

David adores his brother Robin, but it is clear that he does not want him as a father. He does not understand Robin's behavior. He does understand that Robin is intruding and wants him to stop.

## THE SARNONS

Bill Sarnon, 46: Successful pathologist with his own lab in Madison, Wisconsin. Married 20 years, divorced. Remarried for two years. Bill has a daughter in her twenties from his previous marriage. She is not part of the workshop.

Bette Sarnon, 43: Bill's second wife. A part-time reading teacher and competitive runner. Married 12 years, divorced. Remarried for two years.

Nicholas Grumbach, 15: High school basketball star. Bette's son from her first marriage to Mort Grumbach, an unsuccessful businessman.

Bill and Bette Sarnon are extremely calm and unruffled on the surface, as is Bette's fifteen-year-old son Nicholas. All three are dressed in collegiate clothes: freshly pressed button-down shirts, crisp khakis, polished loafers.

Bette is almost too neat and thin. She has many awards to her credit as a runner. Bill was an equally good athlete until an accident two years ago. He excelled in both running and tennis. He now uses a cane, and he grimaces when he walks.

The drama in the Sarnon's work comes from the slow exposure of one family member's burden and terrible secret. But the Sarnons came to us for a different reason—a jeep accident that left Bill filled with potentially explosive rage. Six months before their marriage, Bette and Bill were passengers riding on a mountain road. The driver, recklessly horsing around, tried a manuever that flipped the jeep, throwing Bill over a cliff.

Bill spent six months in the hospital, undergoing a series of knee-reconstruction operations. Shut off from his work and exercise, Bill built up a head of anger. He concluded that the driver's carelessness had caused his accident, and he talked about killing him.

The Sarnons came to our workshop on the advice of a lawyer friend who was afraid Bill would actually take revenge. We discovered that it was characteristic of the family for Bette and Nicholas to team up to control Bill's anger. (Nicholas all too willingly forms a team with his mother.)

The second problem that brought the Sarnons to therapy was that Bill and Nicholas were not getting along well. When Bill first came into the family, he tried very hard to make contact with Nicholas. At that time, Nicholas was hostile and rejected his new stepfather. Later, Nicholas tried to get to know him, but Bill had become unreachable, wrapped up in his anger about the accident. Bill and Nicholas do not fight now; they are almost too civil, too cool.

The third reason that Bette gives for coming to the workshop is her wish for Nicholas to do better in school. Yet, Nicholas' records show that he performs very well academically. To most mothers, his work would be a source of pride.

Significantly, Bette outlines what she wants from the workshop for Bill, what she wants for Bill and Nicholas, and what she wants for Nicholas. But it is not at all clear what she wants for herself.

It is important to Bette that she present the *correct* image at all times: never a hair out of place, a stiff off-putting smile. She is attractive in an all-American way: clean features, a slim figure in tailored sports clothes, and only the slightest hint of sexuality.

Bette strives to present the correct image in her marriage as well. She and Bill seem to adore each other. Bette always sits near Bill with a hand on his leg, a gesture that strikes us as at once as protective and worshipful. One unusual answer on Bette's questionnaire alerts us to the extent of her devotion to her husband. She believes in reincarnation. There is no mention of her own future life, but she writes that in Bill's final reincarnated stage he will sit at the right hand of God.

We learn that Bette has been very respectful of men in her life. She routinely follows their advice. Bette's father was an Army intelligence officer who spent much time in the Far East when Bette was young. She describes this often-absent man-in-uniform: "My Dad was perfect, except for his drinking." We asked Bette to think of something her father commonly might have said to his children. "Keep a flat stomach," she said. Bette has a very flat stomach. She trains daily by running and swimming. She always did everything she was told to do, particularly if the orders came from her father.

Bette's mother was an overweight woman who, despite a near addiction to diet pills, got fatter and fatter. She was, however, capable in her intellectual life. After her four children were born, Bette's mother went back to school, finishing her doctorate at the age of 55. As Bette describes it, her mother had a kind of truce with her father: "You don't talk about my overeating, and I won't talk about your drinking."

An important factor in Bette's childhood is that she was a twin. Her nonidentical twin Barbara, a very pretty girl, was their mother's favorite. Their mother was busy, studying for college and later for graduate school. In her rare free hours, Barbara was her favored companion. Bette was ignored. As a result, she favored her two brothers and idolized her father.

At first Bette wanted to be like her twin, but two very bad childhood incidents detached her from Barbara. The first was a fight during which Bette heaved a chair at Barbara. "I suddenly realized I could really hurt her," she remembers. "I could even kill her." The second event Bette recalls is the day Barbara took a rope and laid it down the middle of their bedroom, telling Bette, "Don't ever come on my side again." Anger, competition, and separation are themes that will emerge over and over again with Bette.

Bette stopped competing for her mother's attention because the odds appeared to be against her from the start. Instead she pursued her father's attention and her brothers' companionship. She still keeps herself neat, perfect, and polished, playing down her soft, feminine aspects that might have led to sexual feelings in the relationship between herself and her father and brothers. These feelings can be frightening. She wanted to avoid them by being more like her brothers.

Bill struck us both as being sincere and unaffected. He speaks in a very low voice, his shoulders are stooped, he communicates a sense of weary sadness. Yet, when you talk to Bill, you sense that he is interested in you and wants to connect.

Bette adores Bill; Bill idolizes Bette. Because she is athletic and takes good care of things and of him, Bill considers her the perfect woman. An important part of their relationship is that Bill feels indebted to Bette. He believes that Bette saved his life in the jeep accident. She managed Bill's rescue, telling the others what to do.

The women in Bill's past were not as calm and collected as Bette. Bill's mother was severely depressed. One of his two sisters is also severely disturbed and has spent the last 26 years in a mental hospital. Bill's father and his only brother drink heavily. Asked for three adjectives to describe his father, Bill volunteers, "Responsible, depressed, passive." For himself Bill chooses, "Responsible, depressed, restless." He repeats the first two adjectives in describing his healthy sister: "Responsible, depressed, independent." When asked to imagine the end of his life, Bill says, "I am any age from 50 to 79. I died from an accident or suicide."

Asked for his worst childhood experience, Bill presents us with a Norman Rockwell bad memory, a socially acceptable shame. He writes, "Sent to store to buy some food during Depression. Neither my mother or father would go because the bill was so big they didn't think they would be allowed to charge. Presumed store owner wouldn't turn a child down, and he didn't. Felt ashamed and embarrassed."

Fifteen-year-old Nicholas is a tall, lean, good-looking boy who speaks in a very loud voice. As we get to know him, it is clear that he is struggling to love his mother and to try to be the son she wants. Yet, he realizes that it would be very unhealthy for him to be exactly what she wants.

Bette idolizes Nicholas at least as much as she does Bill. She sees Nicholas as her gift to her father: Nicholas makes up for her not having been a boy. When Bette and Barbara were born, the family story goes, their father repeatedly asked the nurses if they were sure the twin girls were his. Weren't his children the twin boys who had been born the same day?

"I had to have a boy for Dad," Bette writes on her questionnaire. "Nicholas came as a surprise. We were waiting for the right time. I was on birth control, but Nicholas was strong enough to be conceived in spite of it." Nicholas was 11 when his parents divorced. He lives with his father in Milwaukee for three months every year.

We have almost no information about Nicholas's natural father. He decided to end the marriage after becoming involved with one of Bette's friends. Throughout the marriage, which lasted 12 years, he was often away on business trips. Bette took solace in sports. One reason she is now so attached to Nicholas is that she feels guilt over leaving him alone when he was little. It was common, she says, for her to take him on sunny days to a lakeside near their house. She would ask a child playing there to care for Nicholas for several hours while she ran.

When Nicholas was first born, Bette stopped working as a teacher. She was determined not to be distracted from her child, as her mother had been. "I was so excited to have a boy," she said, "I talked to him all the time from the first moment he was alive. People asked me if I thought he could understand. Of course he could." She managed the loneliness of her first marriage by alternately being overinvolved with Nicholas and abandoning him for her athletic training.

Nicholas says his greatest pleasure comes from scoring in school sports: He feels the excitement and gratitude of his coach and teammates. His mother, who once pushed him to success at sports, now nags him about academic work.

A classic picture of the Sarnons is: Bill sits in a chair, stooped over with head down; Bette sits at his side with her hand on him as if taking care of or restraining him; Nicholas sits on the floor between them. The family always looks posed.

As we first meet them, we have not a clue how dramatic the situation will become. Bill is amazingly quiet. He moves unobtrusively and agrees with everything Bette says. Why does he think that he will die by accident or suicide? Bette sticks rigidly to three themes: Bill's anger, Nicholas's coolness with Bill, and Nicholas's disappointing academic performance. She smiles broadly but dismisses the suggestion that anything else is an issue.

As we talk alone together on Monday, Ruth says, "This is a sweatless family." Their calm alerts us. We begin to wonder if there is energy being spent trying to divert our attention from something. Our first question is, "Where's the problem?"

# THE DELLAPIETRAS

Domenic Dellapietra, 33: Ex-singer and rock guitarist, now running his family's trucking company. Short and fair, he has been a heavy drinker since age 13. First married at age 20, then divorced. Married 10 years to second wife.

Angela Dellapietra, 30: Domenic's second wife. Elegant and slight. She worked as a television actress for eight years. Married first at 18, divorced after a year.

Maria Dellapietra, 6: Dark haired like her mother, noisy, over-active.

Marco Dellapietra, 4: Blond, robust, excessively babyish. Successful heart surgery at three months.

Domenic Dellapietra, known as Dom, runs his family's trucking company in Los Angeles. At age 33, Dom is a millionaire and an alcoholic. At age 13, he was an alcoholic. Dom's wife Angela is an occasionally employed television actress. Both have had previous marriages, without children. They have two children together, Maria and Marco.

Dom is an athletic-looking man with a swagger in his walk and cocky way of talking. Angela is very pretty, with straight black hair and pale skin. She appears very quiet and shy. Both Dellapietras wear expensive casual clothes. Maria, age 6, is a sometimes irritating, clingy little girl with very dark hair like her mother's. She often seems confused about how to act. Marco, 4, is a pink-cheeked, affectionate little boy who acts younger than he is, often retreating to thumb-sucking and babytalk.

Dom was first married at 20 to a woman who was eight years older. Angela's first husband, whom she married at 18, was a drug dealer who threatened to kill her if she did not join in drug peddling. She turned him over to the police. The marriage was annulled after one year.

Dom and Angela met when Angela was only 16. She was baby-sitting for the children of Dom's first wife. They had an affair, but it didn't last because he was married. They reunited after Angela's brief first marriage. She was twenty and living at home with her mother.

At the time of his first marriage, Dom's mother was married to her fifth husband. Dom's parents had divorced when he was nine. Dom lived with his mother and many stepfathers, all of whom were drunks. Dom's worst childhood memory is of walking down the street with his mother and a new stepfather (whom he barely knew). When he met a neighbor, he was expected to treat the stepfather like a real father. He felt humiliated, angry, and dishonest. This happened again and again.

Dom's contacts with his real father centered around business and booze. Even as a boy, Dom spent time in bars with his father, getting him home when he was drunk.

Dom has had stomach ulcers since the age of 14. After seven years of playing the guitar in a successful rock band, Dom (in his late twenties) joined the trucking business his great-grandfather started. The men in the business could only communicate when they were drinking. Drinking was a source of pride in the family. "Dellapietra men have been this way for seven generations," Dom's father would say.

Dom and Angela have come to the workshop because Angela has had enough of Dom's drinking. After she threatened to divorce him, Dom's lawyer referred them to us. Angela lived away from home for a week. During this time, she had a short affair with a man she met at an exercise studio. When Angela moved out, Dom called her mother and asked her to intervene. He threatened to kill the man Angela was involved with. Then he threatened to commit suicide in front of the children. Angela returned after that last and worst threat.

Calling Angela's mother was a particularly hostile act on Dom's part because Angela feels that her mother is an enemy. Angela's father left her mother when Angela was 12—the week after Angela's sister, then 15, came home pregnant. From that moment, Angela has had frequent, violent fights with her mother. When Angela and Dom married, Angela felt that he rescued her from her mother, the way Angela had always prayed her father would.

Dom is not the ideal rescuer. Drinking is not his only problem. During the first two years of their marriage Angela and he traveled with the rock band. Dom took LSD and was on amphetamines almost constantly. He was also taking cocaine several times a month as well as drinking at his usual rate. Angela does not drink, but she used cocaine often in the years Dom was on the road. She still uses it occasionally and smokes marijuana two or three times a week. Drugs constitute their social life. Angela and Dom have few sustained friendships. It is almost as if drugs take the place of people in their world.

For a fragile-looking woman, Angela has survived much knocking around. Her mother went back to work as a legal secretary a week after Angela was born, leaving her with a woman named Nell. From what Angela says, it seems to us that Nell was responsible for bringing out Angela's positive side—warmth and a capacity for attachment. Nell left when Angela was 9. Her father left when she was 12. After this time Angela and her mother, an alcoholic, started having such fierce fights that it was not unusual for one or the other to end up in an emergency room. The fights would start when Angela defended her father against her mother's bitter attacks. Angela was the only family member to maintain any relationship with him. (She is a middle child and has an older sister and a younger brother.) She thinks that he only saw her because he was too embarassed to push her away.

During the years that she fought with her mother, Angela had several stays in a California Juvenile Detention Center—charged with being "out of control." After Nell left, the grown-ups in Angela's life said she was bad. She was hauled off to juvenile court after a fight. Her mother was never taken to jail.

Angela repeatedly threatened to run away from home. Sometimes she called the police. They would say they could not do anything, or they would take her home. Her mother would punish her after they left. Angela remembers feeling fearful for her little brother's safety. He would hide in a closet while his mother and sister fought. As the workshop progresses, we note that Angela has a habit of defending men. We notice this pattern in her relationship with the men at the workshop and in her family. Though Dom is an alcoholic (as is her mother), Angela defends him when he has a confrontation with anyone else just like she defends her father. We also notice that Angela continually retreats to the position of the one to blame—a position from which you expect someone else to punish you.

"My father was right to leave," Angela says even today. "My mother was a witch and his children were bad." She defends her father by saying that he was a sensitive man who could never show it. The one time she saw him cry was devastating to her. Her father fell between a boat and a dock, breaking an arm. He was crying, she recalls, but screamed at her to go away so that she would not see him cry. She believes she caused the accident by not holding the rope tightly enough.

Angela describes herself as "insecure, sensitive, determined." After one day with her, we have the sense of two opposing sides that do not fit together. She is insecure, shy, and withdrawn: she acts like someone who scares easily. Yet she emerges determined from a tumultuous history of physical danger and personal misery. Without emotional support from her husband, she has managed to care for two children and carve a career in the competitive field of television acting. (She has three or four jobs a year, small parts in a detective series.) Angela attacks everything, including the workshop, from the position that she will have a tough time, but she will get through it successfully.

Dom treats the workshop as a threat. He and Angela are here because his lawyer says they need to be. This creates a special problem for us. Under the threat that his wife is going to walk out, he has an interest in making things look good. He believes that, if he and Angela open up, we will see how bad things are—perhaps, how bad he is. To gloss over unpleasant things, Dom often makes a joke. For example, the circumstances around his birth were painful, but he laughs about them. "It took an extremely long time for Mom to get pregnant," he says, "because Dad was drunk all the time."

Another childhood memory of Dom's is of waiting for his father to take him to a father-son dinner. He was to get an award for a musical performance. When Dom's father finally arrived, he was too drunk to stand and they could not go to the dinner. Dom jokes about trying to pull the old man to the car.

We ask Dom what adjectives he would use to describe his father. "Hard-worker and what-the-hell attitude," Dom replied. For himself? "Easy-going, hard worker." How can you be a hard worker, we thought, if you don't give a damn? For the Dellapietras, not giving a damn is an essential, manly attribute; the way to show the world you do not care is to drink a lot. The Dellapietra men have managed somehow to combine excessive drinking with business success.

On the questionnaire, Dom makes a meaningful mistake. Asked to list himself and his siblings, he lists instead himself and his two children. In the next few days, we find out that is indeed how the family operates—Angela is the mother, Dom one of the children.

Dom jokes about Maria's conception. His daughter seems to have a feeling that she was not wanted. Angela had an abortion, of Dom's child, before they married. They planned not to have children. Dom, horsing around, threw away Angela's birth control pills. Maria behaves as if she knows this, approaching her mother in a desperate way that can be irritating. Maria never simply sits next to her mother, allowing an easy flow of affection. Instead, she hangs on her. Maria's nervous, but tight, relationship with her father is also expressed physically. She sits next to him much of the time and rubs his leg while Dom strokes her head.

Angela withdraws in response to Maria's pushy appeal for affection. This strengthens the ties between father and daughter. As in Angela's family, father and daughter band together and leave the mother out.

On the first day of the workshop, we ask Maria how she could solve the problems she has. "To be good," she responded without hesitation—a reasonable answer for a six-year-old worried about fitting in. But some confusion about what it means to be good comes out in a later question. If things go the way you want them to go, Maria, how will you end up? Her answer is chilling, "I will be good. I fell over a cliff. I meant to be good." Does she imagine that being good is so hard that the only way you can really be good is to kill yourself?

Marco was born when Maria was two. He is named for Dom's great grandfather, who began the family business. Marco was born with an enlarged heart. At the age of three months, he spent several weeks in the hospital for heart surgery. Because the doctors were not sure the baby would live, Angela held back from forming an attachment to him. (While his son was in the hospital, Dom was away starting a new line of the trucking business.) When it became clear that Marco would survive, Angela became intensely attached to him. This attachment is now part of Maria's distress. At age four, Marco alternates between acting like a two-year-old and more grown-up to please the adults.

Throughout the first days, Angela and Dom insist that their problems primarily involve the children. The difficulty with this view is that it obscures their marital difficulties and Dom's tremendous individual difficulties.

Both Angela and Dom are pessimistic about the workshop. Angela says she does not believe that Dom is ever going to change: "He doesn't have a tough bone in his body," she says.

Still, they stay, and they do change because they want to be better parents.

"I feel separate. I feel different. I feel like a grown-up son. I am a man."

—Gerry Barker

## 2

# The Barkers

## MONDAY MORNING

## FAMILY GROUP—LES SPEAKING

*Both Ruth and I are working with all four families in the main meeting room.*

*The Barkers are all huddled together on the floor pillows. I have little sense of who is who, even though I met them yesterday. New members usually sit up very straight, look around at other people, and wonder how to behave and what is going to happen. The Barkers look already settled in. As we are to find out shortly, they are all too familiar with the techniques of therapy.*

*I ask each family to talk amongst themselves about what they want to get from the workshop. I didn't even have time to finish asking the Barkers before Gerry jumped in with an answer.*

**Gerry** *(very animated)*: We won't move into the center, because we're already here. Now, for the past five years, different members of our family have been involved in different types of therapy. I would go; my wife and I would go; my Mom would go; and then my Dad would go. We were all members of a therapeutic community. We've learned a lot about how to solve problems, but we haven't been able to change.

As soon as we solve one problem, another one crops up and—

**Les** *(interrupting Gerry, who has started to sound like an after dinner speaker)*: Talk to the other members of your family about what you would like to change.

*(Gerry looks miffed, and again begins to address the whole room.)*

**Ruth:** Gerry, talk to your family about your idea that you have problem after problem. Tell them what you think is going on. Find out what they think.

**Berenice:** We are never without a problem. If we don't have a problem, someone in this family will make one up.

**Gerry:** If my problems are done with for the moment, my sister steps in and creates one. Melissa can come up with something at anytime.

**Ruth:** Continue and talk, amongst yourselves, about each of your ideas of the current problem.

*It is again necessary to repeat our instructions. We note that Berenice takes over for Gerry; Gerry takes over for everyone. Nothing is specific or tangible. They seem to be making a speech or report.*

**Gerry:** Right now, Margaret Ann and I have our own place. Dad is not living with my mother and little sister. The separation—whether their marriage stays together or not—is the current problem.

**Berenice:** I think, over the years, we had so many problems with you, Gerry, and with Rusty, and with Melissa, that we didn't have time for our own.

**Gerry:** Some clarification is needed. I had an older brother, Rusty, who was killed three years ago.

**Les** *(to Ruth)*: Let's give up for now. We'll just find out how they will present things. Let's also get the data we need.

**Ruth** *(turning back)*: Will any of you tell us how Rusty was killed?

**Gerry:** It was a car accident. He missed a turn and went off a freeway ramp.

**Berenice:** It might have been a suicide.

**Melissa:** He might have been killed.

*The information is startling to us. So is their manner of presentation. No one agrees on what happened. They compete for whose view is correct.*

**Berenice** *(from her central floor position)*: When Rusty was alive, Edgar and I had to pull together to keep him alive. We went to see psychiatrist after psychiatrist. When Rusty was killed, we all pulled together over that—at least, sort of.

*(Turning:)* Gerry, it is my belief that we then had to work to keep you from destroying yourself. Then you got yourself into therapy and got straightened out. That was when Melissa started drinking and began having a bad time at school.

*(Turning now to us:)* I didn't see Melissa's actions as self-destructive at first. Now I think they are. Her being angry and sick kept us focused for awhile. Then Melissa did some therapy, too, and she felt better. Finally, there was no kid trying to kill him- or herself to worry about anymore.

*(Turning, now to Edgar:)* Edgar, you and I never learned how to relate to each other. We saw that when Melissa calmed down. Then you moved out of the house. The problem, now, is whether we will continue to live as man and wife. I agree as Gerry said it, the system is: let's get the kids in trouble, so then we don't have to face our problems.

*Berenice follows our directions in a very controlling way. She talks to everyone and declares how it is.*

**Edgar** *(to me)*: That's true. Whether I live at home or not is the question.

**Les:** So this is also your sense of what should be answered this week?

**Edgar:** The problem I see in our family is that of always having to have a problem in order to exist. Nothing is ever right. There's always got to be something wrong for us to be a family. I don't choose to live this way. I believe there are times when things aren't wrong, times when there is a rainbow in the sky.

**Ruth:** Are you saying you want to clear up the way things work in your family and work towards getting back together with Berenice? You didn't really answer Les.

**Edgar:** My goal is either to get back together with Berenice, or not get together. I want to have a good line of communication open to her in either case.

**Ruth:** I understand now. I experience a sense of relief as you talk about having had all the kids in the middle and now wanting that over. My relief is for Melissa. It is really good for her not to be caught in the middle, acting out serious life and death issues for herself.

*The family makes a contract to not create a problem in order to keep the parents together. This makes sense to us. We are still aware of the correctness of their presentation.*

**Les** *(to Margaret Ann)*: Where do you fit into the picture?

**Margaret Ann:** I have some things to work on with Gerry and Little Gerry. I think that the two of them compete for my attention. Also, I want to stay out of the middle of Edgar's and Berenice's disagreements. I like both Edgar and Berenice. I hope they'll be happy together or not together.

**Ruth:** In the midst of this, how do you get what you need for yourself?

**Margaret Ann:** When Gerry is available to our family, we have a lot of fun together. He gives me what I need.

**Ruth:** I'm glad to know that. *(Turning:)* Les, I'm still not clear about how we're going to begin. The words sound clear. Yet, it doesn't seem clear at all.

**Les:** I have a sense of fog or a cloud in the middle, and everyone seems to be connected through that cloud. I wonder how any person in this family can get out and go their own way.

**Ruth:** Maybe some more of the facts will help us with the fog.

*(Turning:)* Gerry, you mentioned you have lots of problems. Will you tell us about them?

**Gerry:** I have several different ways of living an exciting life. None of these ways are legal. This has caused some problems.

**Les:** Will you be specific about these ways? I think not being specific contributes to the fog.

**Gerry:** Stealing, fighting, psychopathic things would leave me on the outskirts of the law. Because I'm smart, I could get away with things. It was lots of fun.

In a twenty-day workshop on scripting, I was able to turn things around and not have to do something illegal to get excitement.

I'm more open now. Everyday I don't have to worry there's going to be a phone call or a knock at the door, with someone there to arrest me.

*We again learn that this family has put a lot of time and energy into therapy. The word "psychopathic" isn't helpful. It is frequently used to distance and con others.*

**Ruth:** Margaret Ann, were the two of you together when Gerry was getting into all this trouble?
*(Gerry starts to answer for Margaret Ann. She gently puts her hand on his knee, to stop him.)*
**Margaret Ann:** Part of the time, Gerry was away. For the last two or three incidents, he wasn't living at home.
**Ruth:** So you have had some periods of separation?
**Margaret Ann:** Yes, months.
**Ruth:** I need some more facts, from any of you. You've talked about Rusty and his troubles. What were they?
**Gerry:** He was sentenced, from 6 months to 5 years for possession of marijuana. Rusty was in prison, off and on, for a total of 20 months.
One of his times out of prison, he broke his neck in a car crash. Another time, he had two motorcycle accidents.
**Berenice:** No, Gerry. Rusty was arrested for marijuana and served 6 months. The second time it was cocaine. He served a year and a half in the state penitentiary.
He was in the hospital with a broken jaw from one motorcycle accident. As soon as he got out, he rode his motorcycle off a bridge.
The final incident was when he drove his car off the ramp and killed himself.

*Whenever Rusty's name comes up, there seems to be an openess about things. But no one agrees on the facts about him. Edgar, Rusty's father, remains silent. Berenice and Gerry correct and recorrect each other. Things remain unclear.*

**Margaret Ann:** There is something else you ought to know. My family and the Barkers worked together for many years. Gerry and I have known each other since we were small. Edgar and Berenice have known me since I was three—Little Gerry's age.
**Les** *(turning)*: What was your trouble, Melissa?

**Melissa** *(with a flirtatious smile and coquettish voice)*: I got my first "F," and I got into some other kinds of trouble.

**Les:** What do you mean other kinds of trouble?

**Melissa:** Before school every day, I would go over to my friend's house, and we would smoke some joints. Sometimes, we would drink quarts of vodka.

**Les:** Have you stopped doing that now?

**Melissa:** Yes.

**Les:** How long since you have stopped?

**Melissa:** Since about March.

**Les:** So recently you've been getting yourself together?

**Melissa:** Well . . . But, also recently I've been in a lot of trouble.

**Les:** Is there any more for right now, Ruth? I still experience the fog. I need to get some distance, for awhile, so I can tell the forest from the trees.

**Ruth:** Yes, there is more. I have a special assignment for all of you. Each one of you, write down—without showing it to anyone else in the family—what you want to change here. What you want different about yourself and about each other person in your family.

Write it in words that Little Gerry could understand. I don't think he knows words like "therapeutic community" or "psychopathic behavior." Write it down for reading to your grandson, or your nephew, or your son.

*Ruth has two goals. She wants something that will keep each person's thinking distinct and private. Also, she wants them to state the problem simply. She explicitly points out their separate roles in relation to Little Gerry—as grandparents, parents, aunt.*

*(As the next family is talking, Little Gerry goes back and forth, between his mother's lap and his grandmother's lap. His skittishness about where to sit is the only disturbing part we have noticed with this charming and engaging young boy. Little Gerry is wearing a T-shirt with a picture of Donald Duck on a roller coaster. The caption reads, "I keep going up and down."*

*(After a break, we initiate an exercise for the whole group. We organize three groups: one for first and only children, one for middle children, and one for last or younger children. We ask everyone to join one of these groups, depending on their birth position in their family of*

*origin. We ask each person to talk about the experience of being in his or her family position. Gerry began in the group of oldest children. He then moved over to the group of middle children. Finally, he went to the youngest-child group. Then, half jokingly, he sprawled across the floor, between the group of oldest children and the one of middle children. His father, Edgar, never joined any group. Everyone is sprawled out all over the meeting room. People from different families have made good contacts during this exercise.)*

**Les** *(loudly, pointing his finger, from standing position):* One of the things I noticed is that you, Gerry, started over here, moved over there, and then there. You act as if you belong in all three of the groups.

Edgar, I also noticed that you never joined any group. It seemed hard for you to claim any position.

**Edgar:** I think that's right.

**Ruth:** Is there any way, in this family, that a person can have his own space without moving out?

**Edgar:** No. When I was filling out the questionnaire, there was one group of questions, "How would your mother solve the problem you have?" My answer was, "She wouldn't." My father's solution would be to run away.

*Both Ruth and I are struck by the interweaving of the family patterns. At the break, we decided to initially treat Rusty's death as a suicide. Berenice's father hung himself. Rusty is dead. Edgar's father ran away. Now, Edgar is moving out. Leaving and separation are major issues with this family.*

**Ruth:** What is it like, for you, to have to leave in order to have a place for yourself?

**Edgar:** Anything I've wanted, I didn't get. I didn't get it, in part, because I didn't ask. I didn't ask, because I thought I wouldn't get it.

**Ruth:** You didn't answer my question. What I think I heard you say is that you can't be yourself and get what you need here.

**Edgar:** I can't be myself, get what I need, and live with my family. It was my belief that everything and everyone else was more important than me.

*This is a most important belief. It seems to be Melissa's position, also.*

**Gerry** *(intensely, and shifting things to himself)*: Here's how I got messed up on that exercise. I am a middle-born child. But I couldn't identify with what the other middle people were saying. From 0 to 13, I was a youngest son, so I moved over to the youngest group. Then, my mother just said, "You're now an oldest son." So I moved there, and finally didn't know where to be.

**Ruth:** So it was your mother who beckoned you over to that group?

**Gerry:** I spent more time being my older brother's little brother than anything else. What I want to change most is to find space for me.

*Gerry didn't answer Ruth's question. He operates from his own track, with little attention to others. He covers this up with his good-guy, right-answer, conning manner.*

**Ruth** *(loudly, to Les)*: The women seem to do the leading in this family.

*Ruth has decided to confront.*

**Margaret Ann** *(quickly and directly)*: It makes me angry to hear you say that. Berenice and I are not the same. I don't lead the family, either. Sometimes I wish I could. We'd sure go differently.

**Ruth:** It sounds real important that you not be lumped with Berenice.

**Margaret Ann** *(loudly)*: I don't want to be lumped with anybody, much less her. If what you said was true, I wouldn't like it. Suddenly, I feel scared.

**Les:** About what? Tell Ruth what you're scared about right now.

**Margaret Ann:** I don't know. I just know that, all of a sudden, I'm shaking and upset.

**Ruth:** Make a guess about what is happening with you.

**Margaret Ann:** I just don't have an answer right now. I'll continue to see if I can figure it out.

**Les:** I like your willingness to define yourself clearly.

**Ruth:** Melissa, what is going on with you?

**Melissa** (*very quiet, looking down*): I've always been lumped with somebody else.

**Ruth:** Will you say more?

**Melissa:** I was lumped with my brothers. I've always been compared to my brothers.

**Ruth:** What was that like?

**Melissa:** I've always been one of them. I hate it. I don't know what I'd be if I weren't lumped with someone.

**Les:** Make a guess. What would it be like for you if you weren't lumped with somebody?

**Melissa:** I'm really scared to.

**Ruth** (*sitting beside Melissa*): If you weren't lumped with someone, would that mean that you'd have to be dead? In your family, in order to get out one needs either to run or to be dead. You're caught if you move in either direction. To be separate could mean to be dead; to stay lumped means you can't be yourself.

It is important that you learn about yourself and that you know you can still be alive. Does that make sense to you?

**Melissa:** Yes.

*While Melissa is talking with low emotion, Berenice is tearful with arms outstretched and trembling. Berenice participates in, even takes over, her daughter's emotions.*

**Ruth:** Good. Another thing, you said you were scared. Your Mom has been acting out what you said you were feeling. I bet that's something that happens often.

**Melissa** (*with wide eyes and animation*): You're right!

*Ruth is defining a lot for Melissa, rather than letting her come up with some observations herself.*

*When Ruth and I talk about this later we decide to continue to define things for Melissa and then to check out our definition. We want to control Berenice's intrusiveness and her defining, and to provide Melissa with an alternative. We take the risk of repeating what happens in the family. Melissa will be very difficult for us.*

**Les** (*responding to her agitation*): Berenice, what are you thinking?

**Berenice** *(filling the room with her high-pitched and loud voice, arms busy)*: Everything is my fault. Edgar says the only way he can get space from this family is to get out. Melissa says the same. Margaret Ann says she doesn't want to be like me.

This whole messed-up family is my fault. Everybody's laying it on me.

**Ruth:** Berenice, if you found out that was true—you were responsible for many of the problems in your family—what then?

**Berenice** *(in a gasping voice)*: They'd all be better off if I was dead.

**Ruth** *(calmly)*: And, after that flashes through your head, where do you go?

**Berenice:** I don't want to do that. My father hung himself. I don't want to do the same thing, but I might. There must be a better way to go, but I don't know what it is.

**Ruth:** Are you willing to find out this week?

**Berenice** *(still screeching)*: I think so. Yes, I want to.

**Ruth:** I think your family has been protecting you. It needs to be understood that nobody has to protect you here, and that you're not going to kill yourself because of something you find out. Are you willing to be clear about that?

**Berenice** *(whimpering)*: I need some more protection.

**Ruth:** You've got enough protection just being here.

**Berenice:** I think they're all going to hate me and leave me all alone.

**Ruth:** That could happen. Are you willing to be brave enough, to find out what's really going on with each person in your family, without threatening to hurt or kill yourself?

**Berenice:** Will you say it again?

**Ruth** *(calmly and clearly)*: Are you willing to be brave enough to listen and to find out what's going on with each person in your family and to find out how that relates to you? Will you be clear with them, and yourself, that you won't hurt or kill yourself?

**Berenice:** Yes.

*This was also a message to other family members. It is important to get this contract from Berenice. This will permit each family member to define him- or herself. We*

*need to confront her control over the family before*
*anyone else can move out of the fog. This confrontation*
*helps Berenice to accept responsibility for herself.*

**Ruth:** Super. Your family needs permission not to
protect you anymore. You are strong enough to learn about
them and what they have to say. Will you turn to each
person in your family and tell them what you mean?
**Berenice** *(to Melissa)*: You don't need to protect me
from anything during this week. It's okay for you to tell
me, what it is I do that you see as keeping you from being
yourself. It's also okay to tell me anything else you want
to.
**Ruth** *(questioningly)*: Even if it is different from your
idea of what is going on with her?
**Berenice:** Yes.
**Les:** And you will not hurt yourself, Berenice?
**Berenice:** I won't hurt myself. I won't kill myself
either, no matter what I hear from you, now or ever.

*People need to hear themselves say what they're just*
*beginning to think. It helps to integrate a new idea. The*
*danger is that someone will go along with us, without*
*actually meaning what they say. That Berenice changes*
*the words I give her indicates that she is making the*
*idea her own.*

**Berenice:** During this workshop, you can talk to me. I
won't kill myself or go crazy. It's okay for you to do what
you need to do. Tell me when I'm interfering with you.
**Melissa:** Yes.
*(Melissa's face softens: Usually, she glares at her mother.*
*Berenice says the same to Gerry.)*
**Berenice** *(turning to Edgar, in a high voice and sharp*
*tone)*: I don't want you to tell me what I'm doing that's
interfering with your life, except when we're with Ruth
and Les. I don't want you to do it at dinner, or in the
bedroom, or anyplace else.
**Edgar** *(blandly)*: I'll keep my comments for the therapy
sessions.

*In taking responsibility for controlling herself,*
*Berenice releases her family members to speak up for*
*themselves without fear of how she will retaliate. Her*

*warning to Edgar indicates that she is really thinking about what is important to her. She is not just adapting to our request. Her independent statement tells us that what we've been leading her to say makes sense to her.*

**Berenice:** I'm still scared.
**Ruth:** You're doing fine, even though you're scared.
**Berenice** *(looking pleased)*: I'm scared, but I'm tough.
**Ruth:** You're brave, and that's different from tough.
**Les:** I like you when you are being grown-up.
*(I collect the pieces of paper from the Barker family members. Les and I look at them later. Doing the assignment is more important than what they actually write.)*

# MONDAY AFTERNOON

# INDIVIDUAL FAMILIES—WITH LES

*The families are divided into two groups. I take Margaret Ann, Gerry, and Little Gerry along with the Dellapietras. Ruth has Melissa, Edgar, and Berenice along with the Quinns and the Sarnons. This division allows children of different ages to be grouped with their peers. Families with similar parenting issues are together. Also, we separate the Barker family.*

*Unknowingly, we had already made a big mistake with this family. From the time they signed up for the workshop, we have considered them as one family. We had assigned them to the same condominium. Berenice and Edgar were even sharing the same double bed.*

*As we begin, Little Gerry is playing with the toys and connecting with each person in the room. He and Marco move in and out with each other. Maria alternates between wanting to lead them, and wanting to sit with her father.*

**Margaret Ann:** Thank you for separating us from Gerry's parents. I breathed a sigh of relief when I found out.
**Les:** When you're home, is there any way in which you contribute to not having your family be separate?

*I wonder what part Margaret Ann plays in the family enmeshment. I have no indication of her contribution to this family mess.*

**Margaret Ann:** No, I don't think so. Only, that Berenice takes care of Little Gerry.

**Les:** You ask her to care for Little Gerry?

**Margaret Ann:** He goes to nursery school in the morning. Berenice picks him up and takes care of him in the afternoon, while I work.

Before I got here, I did a lot of thinking about that. I don't think we'll go on with it when we get home. That's what keeps some of us jumbled together.

I've also been aware that there has been a lot of competition. I compete with Berenice to be his mother. Gerry competes with Little Gerry for my time. Edgar competes with Little Gerry for Berenice's time. I think that's all very unhealthy.

**Les:** I like your awareness. I agree, it is unhealthy.

**Margaret Ann:** I don't like the state Berenice is in now. I don't want to become like that. I don't want Little Gerry to have the same problems that I've seen Gerry, Rusty, and Melissa have.

There's a part of Little Gerry's behavior I've been uncomfortable with. When you ask him a question, or make a statement to him, he always comes back with: "No, it's . . . something else. No, I don't want that." That happens when I talk to Berenice. Whenever I say anything, it's incorrect. It's as if she always has a better answer. I see the same thing in Little Gerry, and I don't think it's merely three-year-old stuff.

I see Gerry acting like a therapist to his Mom, Dad, and sister. I think that's unhealthy, too. It also takes a lot of his time and energy away from us.

**Les:** Will you tell Gerry right now what it's like for you as you watch him being the bridge, or the glue, for his family.

*I want to develop actual interactions, rather than to have Margaret Ann talk about things. I use the word "bridge," because Gerry was the physical bridge between the groups, in the morning exercise. Also, Little Gerry acts like a bridge between the family parts. In this room,*

*he has contact with everyone. In that way, he is a
bridge.*

**Margaret Ann:** Gerry, I see you sucked in to your
family's problems. It scares me. I see that taking time
away from us. I don't want our family to be an extension of
your Mom and Dad. I want us to be separate. I don't want
to feel like we're your parents' children. We're grown, and
we have our own child.

**Les:** Gerry, what are you hearing your wife say?

**Gerry:** Margaret Ann, I heard you say you want my
time and energy spent at home with my son. You feel the
drain of my getting pulled into my parents' problems.

**Les:** Will you share what you felt when you heard
Margaret Ann say that?

**Gerry:** I'm still scared for myself. It seems plain that
my parents can't take care of themselves without me. It's
hard for me to divorce myself from this feeling.

**Les:** When you think that and feel scared, what do you
do?

**Gerry:** When they get into a problem, I'm the one who
hears about it. I'll get a call at work. I'll get upset. The
next day, I'll hear the problem is getting worse, and I'll try
to do something. When I go over to do something about it, I
hear that they've tried all these solutions. I offer more
solutions. We never examine what's really wrong. Instead,
we ride the problem out till it settles down. Then we all
wait for the next one.

> *When someone talks, it is important to check out
> what was heard. I wondered if Gerry would misinterpret
> Margaret Ann's message. He didn't. He heard it
> accurately. In a situation like this, I ask, "Once you've
> heard that, what do you think?" or "When you think
> that, what do you feel?" or "When you feel that, how do
> you behave?"*
>
> *Gerry perceives the situation accurately, but he
> continues to behave as if it's his job to rescue his
> parents. He is vulnerable to his mother's neediness.*
>
> *I can go back and get some history from Gerry, or I
> can continue with his interaction with Margaret Ann. I
> decide to get more information about Gerry. So far, the
> couple's interaction seems straight and clear.*

**Les:** I need some more information. What really happens when you get drawn into the family problems?

**Gerry:** Someone calls.

**Les:** Your mother.

**Gerry:** Oh, Lord, always my mother.

**Les:** Always?

**Gerry:** Always.

**Les:** How long, how many years, have you been getting called in by your mother?

**Gerry:** It was when my brother got to the stage that he started fighting back at our parents. I remember getting in the middle to protect her. I remember many times pulling Rusty off her. I was about ten. Rusty was eleven.

**Les:** Where was your Dad when Rusty began to get physically violent?

**Gerry:** My Dad was not there at all. He was wishy-washy. The only time he would get involved was when Mom would force him into doing something. "Edgar," she would say, and he would have to go and punish Rusty. He would get home from work and be told how bad Rusty or I had been, and he'd punish us.

Most of the fights were between my mother and us. She was the energy, both positive and negative.

> *Gerry is describing a dilemma that many families get drawn into. The father, actively avoiding the family situation, is called in only as the punisher. If the only way Dad is brought back is through the bad behavior of the kids, the children can become the binding force for their parents. If Rusty was bad enough, Edgar could be drawn in.*
>
> *One thing really bothers me. Everything Gerry says is so smooth, precise, and clinically correct. He is a real artist. I haven't yet learned the purpose in the "con." Gerry and Dom Dellapietra are alike in their style and beliefs about themselves—caretakers and dramatic victims.*

**Gerry** *(continuing)*: I was afraid she'd get hurt. I felt like the guy on the bridge, with her below me in the river. No one was willing to jump in but me.

The only way I could get attention from my family was to be arrested, or hurt, or in the hospital. I didn't get attention or praise for being in the middle, for being the helper. I got attention from doing the kind of things Rusty would do.

Recently, I haven't let myself do that—to go out and get myself hurt. I have continued to have influence over my mother by being with her almost everyday.

It's my grandmother who gets the most attention from me. I'm with her everyday, because I work at her company. I've looked at other jobs, but I've never been able to move. As I think about it right now, I'm aware I can't do anything about it, until I have more of a feeling of self-worth. Everyone in the family has worked there. It's hard for me to work there, but that's what everyone has done.

**Les:** I appreciate how difficult it is for you to pull away. Your mother acts as if she really believes she won't survive without you.

**Gerry:** I can see another reason why it has been so hard to leave. It is my grandmother who always praised me. I think I stay in order to please her and get that from her.

**Les:** What are you feeling now?

**Gerry:** To be frank, just now there was a kind of strange rush inside me. Almost, like my blood started circulating for the first time. I'm picturing what might happen if I do leave. I'm going to have to make some decision.

**Les:** Gerry, you sound ready to put some new parts together in your contract. I hear that one part of your individual contract is to decide about your work situation and what you want as an occupational direction.

**Gerry:** Yeah, that's correct.

**Les** *(to Margaret Ann)*: This conversation started with you. Are you aware of anymore of your part in this?

**Margaret Ann:** What I remember from this morning is holding back and saying to myself, "If you can't say something nice, don't say anything at all." That's a lot of what I do.

**Les:** Where did you learn that?

**Margaret Ann:** My mother!

**Les:** Will you tell me about your mother?

**Margaret Ann:** My mother was the peacemaker between me and my father. She was always the peacemaker. Instead of confronting someone, she would sit back and take it.

I don't spend much time with her anymore, because I want her to get off her ass, and do something about the situation she's unhappy with. She's unhappy at work. She works in the same department of Gertrude's company that Gerry does. She's acting like an old lady who can't do anything about her life.

**Les:** So she's in the family business, too? What about the rest of your family's involvement there?

**Margaret Ann:** My family got into business early, with Berenice's parents. In fact, my father was one of the founders. He stayed on for 20 years as an employee, after Berenice's mother, Gertrude, bought him out. After 20 years, he went out and started his own business, and then, within two years, he died of a heart attack.

*This is an incredibly hard family to get out of. People seem to die as a way of leaving, or die soon after they leave.*

My mother and I continued to run his business for a year. We stopped when Gertrude called my mother and asked her to come back. She went immediately.

My dad was a workaholic during the day and an alcoholic in the evenings. He didn't know what to do outside that business.

**Les:** What was it like for you with your father?

**Margaret Ann:** He didn't know how to deal with a young girl. We spent a lot of time fighting. Mother would get in the middle, to stop the yelling.

**Les:** What are you feeling right now, as you remember?

**Margaret Ann:** Unconfident, scared.

**Les:** Scared of what?

**Margaret Ann:** I don't know.

**Les:** As I watch and hear you, I guess that you did a lot of growing up very early. Also, you learned, early on, to move away from what you are feeling. Are these true for you?

**Margaret Ann:** Yes, both are true. I know I did that. If anything went wrong, it was, "Look what you're doing to your mother."

**Les:** Who would say those words?

**Margaret Ann:** My Dad.

**Les:** Maybe that was happening for you now, as you were sort of talking against your mother.

**Margaret Ann** *(smiling, relieved)*: That's true, thanks.

**Les:** You got caught in the middle, like Gerry.

**Margaret Ann:** Yes, that has been my position. I don't like it. In this workshop, I want to get out of the middle:

the middle between Gerry and Little Gerry, between Berenice and Edgar, between our family and theirs.

*Margaret Ann has formulated a clear contract for herself and her family.*

**Angela:** This is an incredible drama. I feel sorry for you. How can anyone determine his or her own way? It's like you are all caught in Gertrude's claws.

**Margaret Ann:** The most powerful person in the drama certainly is Gertrude. Right now, Gerry is the prize, and I think he loves it.

*Margaret Ann has rounded off the story nicely. I move on, knowing that what has been accomplished is getting contracts and also getting some more information. I know that it is going to be a challenge to penetrate the intellectual, therapeutic armor of this family. Little Gerry is the most real one—everyone else seems programmed.*

# MONDAY AFTERNOON

# INDIVIDUAL FAMILIES—WITH RUTH

*I have Berenice, Edgar, and Melissa with me along with the Quinns and the Sarnons. Berenice is raring to go as I begin.*

**Berenice** *(speedily and breathless)*: On the paper I gave you, I had three answers. First, I want to unhook from my kids. Second, I have to decide what kind of relationship, if any, I can have with Edgar. The third is, I want to know if I can take care of myself without him.

**Ruth:** I read the paper, and I appreciate your clarity.

**Berenice** *(moving on, in the same breath)*: Taking care of myself is tied up with going outside the house to work. I feel competent about a lot of things, but I have a fear of working nine to five. Once I was working, and I got pregnant so I could stay home. The baby grew up, and I started taking care of other people's babies. I did that for 10 years. Then I got pregnant with Melissa. Then, I had a hysterectomy. Then, I went back to work for my mother. I couldn't get pregnant again, so I had to keep working. I had a so-called nervous breakdown and went into the hospital for 17 days. I guess I used that as an excuse not to work.

**Ruth:** Slow down, Berenice, I can't keep up with you.

**Berenice:** Okay. So I went to school and got my R.N. Then I went to work. I did well. When I got promoted though, I got fits of anxiety. Then, Margaret Ann got pregnant. I quit work to take care of Little Gerry. Something in me says its okay to stay home and take care of children, but it's not okay to stay home for nothing. And I'm damned sure it's not okay for me to work. My mother worked 100 hours a week. She's 70, and she still does. I decided I'd never do that. My grandmother stayed home and took care of me. Now I'm staying home and taking care of my grandson.

*In 2 minutes, Berenice has encapsulated the history of her adult life, blending three generations, from her mother to her grandson. She hardly breathes between sentences. Her style flattens everything out. She hides the facts and the important thoughts that she has.*

**Ruth** *(raising her voice)*: Stop! I cannot listen to any more. I have some questions. What do you think would be different if you allowed yourself to work?

**Berenice:** I wouldn't have any family. Everyone would go away. No one would need me anymore.

**Ruth:** That does not make sense to me.

**Berenice:** I believe that if I worked, Edgar wouldn't like it. He would leave. And, if I didn't have Little Gerry to take care of and to tie me in to my kids, they would leave me.

**Ruth:** If all this came true and everyone left, then what?

**Berenice** *(crying loudly)*: Then, I guess, I'd just die!

**Ruth:** Think about all this. Is that what you want for yourself—to pull on others and to keep them around so you won't die? I'm not surprised Melissa is angry with you. Think about whether you want to continue the same thing, generation after generation. It's amazing to me how things have been passed down through the women in your family.

*I want Berenice to think about what she is doing rather than just react.*

*(Later, I have finished working with the Sarnons and the Quinns. I notice that Berenice looks very sad: her face is*

*contorted and she is making very demonstrative, silent gestures.)*

**Ruth:** What are you thinking about, Berenice?

**Berenice** *(in a breathless and screeching voice, with flailing arms)*: Paula's talking made me think of how angry I am at Edgar. I don't care what he does.

**Ruth:** You're not making sense again. You're sounding and acting like a very little kid.

**Berenice** *(yelling and stomping)*: No, I'm not!

*(Edgar is moving more and more into the corner and bowing his head. Melissa has stiffened up. Her face is hardened, motionless. She is glaring at her mother.)*

**Ruth** *(firmly)*: Berenice, stop!

**Berenice** *(screaming)*: No, I won't.

**Ruth** *(to Edgar)*: What do you do when she has temper tantrums like this?

**Edgar** *(quietly)*: I can't do anything.

**Ruth:** Les and I were talking earlier. He wondered if you ever spank her?

**Edgar** *(dully)*: No.

*(Berenice does a double-take and begins to laugh. Others in the room join in the laughter. The tension eases. Even Melissa has a smile on her face.)*

**Ruth:** This seems like a good place to stop for the afternoon. There have been lots of important action for the day.

*(Everyone agrees. We move out of the room.)*

# TUESDAY MORNING

# PARENTS' GROUP—WITH RUTH

*While on our morning run before breakfast, Les and I assess the Barkers' situation. The general and primary issue, we both agreed, is their over-involvement with each other. Our goals for the next days are the following: to help each of the Barkers define themselves separately; to help Berenice control herself by thinking about what she's doing, so that she doesn't flood the family with her protestations of helplessness; and, to help further define the unit composed of Margaret Ann, Gerry, and their son. At this point, we have not dealt with Edgar's and Berenice's marriage. We have no agreed upon goal with Melissa. Our initial plan is to help Melissa know herself as different from her mother and grandmother. She has made no actual contract.*

*We divide parents from young people. In the parents' group, there is no activity with any of the Barkers. The four adults seem to have pulled back to let things settle. They did a lot the day before. Berenice is muffling her feelings. It's a relief for me to see Berenice waiting, rather than letting herself flow out without control.*

# YOUNG PEOPLE'S GROUP—WITH LES

*I have the older, verbal kids. Little Gerry is at the playground with Kitty, the play therapist. The group begins slowly. Melissa and Robin are sitting on the floor, playing cards. Robin appears to be teasing Melissa.*

**Les:** Melissa, what goes on inside you when Robin comes at you with his challenging remarks?

**Melissa** *(sullenly)*: Nothing, I guess I'm just used to it.

**Les:** What do you mean, "used to it"?

**Melissa:** My mother does those things all the time. I just don't pay any attention. If I let her know anything, she hits me.

**Les:** Your mother hits you?

**Melissa:** Yes. She does it alot.

**Les:** What does your Dad do then?

**Melissa:** He either doesn't know, or he doesn't do anything.

**Les:** Would you like some help to deal with your mother about this?

**Melissa:** Sure, but it won't do any good. Nothing does any good with her.

**Les:** Well, I'm willing to give it a go and see.

*Melissa has armored herself against the pain with her mother, because she gets no help from her father. She lets no one in. She has given up on anything helping. It will be very difficult for us to build some trust in her and to connect with her, this week. Hopefully, she will be open to Nicholas or one of the trainees.*

*(I ask everyone to draw a picture of their family. Melissa draws a picture of a family of turtles rather than of her own family. She is very hesitant about talking at all. It takes several attempts to get her to say anything about her picture.)*

**Melissa:** That's the way I'd like things to be. They're playing. They have flowers in their hair. They're a mock turtle family.

*I note her pain about her family situation. I decide not to draw her out anymore, at this point. At the very end of the session, I check back with her.*

**Les:** You have stayed very quiet with me and with the others.

**Melissa:** I'm not ready for saying anything or showing anything.

**Les:** I like your straightness, and I think I understand. When you are more ready, I am available to help, as I said earlier.

*Melissa looks relieved. I will need to watch carefully to keep her involved, and, also to be sure that I'm not letting myself get seduced into taking responsibility for what she does and doesn't do. This is what Berenice does.*

*(Kitty reports that Little Gerry played in a lively way and appropriately and shared well. He seems to be a well-adjusted three-year-old.)*

# TUESDAY AFTERNOON

# AFTER CHOCOLATE PUDDING—WITH LES

*The chocolate pudding group is over. Melissa participated and was primarily involved with Nicholas in appropriate interactions. All the families are now in the same room with both of us. Berenice is far across the room from me, kneeling on a mat. As soon as Ruth enters the room, Berenice suddenly yells out, in her high-pitched voice.*

**Berenice:** Les, you can go to hell for telling Ruth to tell Edgar to spank me. No man is ever going to touch me again, not ever. *(Her face is twisted, her hands form fists.)* No man is going to touch me. Edgar is never going to touch me again.

**Les:** Berenice, I don't understand. What do you want from me now?

**Berenice** *(crying)*: I don't know, but don't tell people to hit me.

**Les:** I didn't tell Edgar to hit you. I told Ruth that I thought you acted like you needed a spanking and that I wondered if Edgar had ever given you one.

**Berenice** *(screaming)*: He'd better not try.

**Les:** Stop it, Berenice.

**Ruth:** I'm curious, Berenice. I'm curious about your saying no man is ever going to touch you. You're yelling at Les now, and I notice that you don't let him connect with you. You just keep going on and on.

**Berenice:** My Dad knocked me and my mother around. Nobody's going to knock me around again.

**Les:** Berenice, you're going too far.

**Ruth:** Touching you, giving you a spanking, and knocking you around are all different things. How did your father spank you?

**Berenice:** With a belt.

**Ruth:** Have you ever taken a good look at how angry you are with your father?

**Berenice** *(sobbing)*: No.

**Ruth:** Are you ready to do some of that work now?

**Berenice:** Yes.

*(Ruth moves across the room and puts a pillow in front of Berenice who is still kneeling at the edge of the mat.)*

**Ruth:** See your father on the pillow. Tell him how angry you are that he hit you with a belt.

**Berenice** *(with a sob)*: There was no way I could please you, no way I could do anything right. Anything I did, you'd just blow up and come after me with a belt. I'm angry at you for that.

**Ruth:** Tell him again.

**Berenice** *(in a childlike way, with a choke in her voice):* I'm angry at you for that. I'm never going to let you hit me again.

**Ruth:** Tell him that clearly and solidly, again.

**Berenice** *(screaming):* I'm never going to let you hit me again.

**Ruth** *(with a commanding tone):* Berenice, sit up straight and take a deep breath. Okay, now take a couple more breaths so they go all the way down to your stomach.

*(Ruth puts her leg behind Berenice's back, as a brace, and her hands on Berenice's shoulders, so that she can't crumple.)* Look straight at your father and tell him again, without the screaming and without the choking.

**Berenice** *(with a snarled face and voice):* I'll kill you before I let you hit me again.

**Ruth:** I believe that's what you feel. You let your feeling get mixed up with your thinking. Sit up straight, and don't get so childish and out of control.

*(Berenice straightens herself.)*

**Ruth** *(continuing):* Now, tell him clearly.

**Berenice** *(slowly):* I'm never going to let you hit me again.

*Berenice contaminates her relationship with Edgar, myself, and other men, including her sons. She taints these current relationships with the past. Ruth works to help her tie the thoughts and feelings back into the past, where they belong. Berenice needs to learn to keep the past separate from the present. Also, she must keep thinking, at the same time that she is expressing feelings.*

**Ruth:** Say it again.

**Berenice:** I'm never going to let you hit me again.

**Ruth:** Again.

**Berenice:** I'm never going to let you hit me again.

*(With each repetition, Berenice becomes more centered and sounds more sure of herself.)*

**Ruth:** Now, I believe that, even if he were alive, you would never let him hit you again. Berenice, don't let that stuff with your father get mixed up with every man. You have to separate the past and the present.

**Berenice** *(screaming again)*: Well, I'm not going to let any man hit me.

**Ruth** *(loudly and very firmly)*: That's different. You shouldn't let any man, or woman, hit you. What you are doing now is letting your old business with your father run into your relations with Edgar, and your sons, and Les. That's a real problem. That's crazy stuff.

> *In her almost exaggerated calmness, Ruth is making a statement to Berenice—she's not going to be intimidated by her dramatic style. In addition, she is bold enough to label Bernice's behavior as crazy stuff. This gives the hard message that Berenice's behavior is her own responsibility. We're not going to treat her like a fragile person. She has many strengths.*

**Berenice:** But how else can I protect myself?

**Ruth:** By sitting up straight, and not contorting your body and your voice, by not getting your thinking confused with your feeling, and by keeping the now separate from the past. You don't protect yourself when you bring in the crazy stuff and act like an out-of-control little girl.

**Berenice** *(blowing her nose)*: Tell me again.

**Ruth:** You do protect yourself when you keep the past separate from the present and when you keep your thinking connected to your feelings. You do not protect yourself when you make a general issue out of something that is very specific and very old and when you get so dramatic about it.

Will you tell me what you just heard me say?

**Berenice:** That, when I'm acting like a child, giving way to those old feelings, then I'm not thinking. And I don't protect myself then. When I'm not messing up my thinking, I can protect myself.

Will you give me an example? How am I going to protect myself if someone's going to hit me?

**Ruth:** Unless you're thinking, you're not in touch with reality. Then you can't figure out what to do.

**Berenice:** Yes.

**Ruth:** The best protection for yourself is your thinking. Thinking about what you need to do, to keep yourself safe, in the here and now. When you don't use your judgment, you are unsafe.

**Berenice** (*looking squarely at me, and speaking seriously*)*:* Yes, I understand.

**Ruth:** And I know, when you're thinking, that you know the difference between your father and Les, between your father and Edgar, between your father and your sons. That is when you're protected. When you can tell who people really are, and what the situation really is.

> *I suspect Berenice took my comment to Ruth, about spanking, as a major insult. Her fragmented feelings today were generated by that insult. Her overreaction is an attempt to gain control over her fragmentation. Ruth has demonstrated another way she can gain control of herself.*

*(Ruth puts a hand on Berenice's knee. There is a silent agreement between them. They are finished. Ruth moves behind her, placing a hand on her shoulder.)*

**Les:** Berenice, do you feel finished with me?

**Berenice:** I still don't like you very much. I'm probably not finished.

**Les:** Will you go on now, or do you want to wait?

**Berenice** (*screaming again*)*:* Goddamnit, you wanted to see me get hit.

*(Straightening herself:)* I'm doing it again.

*(More calmly:)* Look, when we have been working so far, you told me a lot of things that are wrong with me. My Dad told me a lot of things that were wrong with me. I'd like you to tell me something that's all right with me.

**Les:** I hear you. It was *not* my perception that I was telling you what was wrong with you.

**Berenice** (*screeching*)*:* Yes, you were.

**Ruth:** Stay grown up, Berenice.

*(Berenice nods to Ruth and turns back to Les.)*

**Les:** Did you hear me say that I like you when you are being grown-up?

**Berenice:** I did hear that.

**Les:** I'm glad of that. Sometimes I think that no matter what I say, you won't hear me correctly.

**Berenice:** I am thinking right now. I heard you say, I was grown up. I didn't hear you say anything about liking it.

**Les:** Maybe, I didn't say that clearly, and I'm sorry. I like it when you deal with me in a grown-up way.

**Berenice:** Thank you.

**Les:** I also like you're calling me on it when I'm not clear.

**Berenice:** Yes. I feel finished. Thank you.

**Ruth:** What are you thinking?

**Berenice** *(with a smile)*: I'm thinking that maybe I'm not such a bad person after all.

**Ruth:** Anything else?

**Berenice:** I'm thinking that I asked for what I wanted. I didn't get it at first. But I hung in and got it straight. That's new for me. Usually I don't ask directly. I ask in a back-door way. If I do ask, and don't get something, I either drop back or I start screaming.

**Ruth:** What I like, is your clear thinking about what happened. You did hang in there, even though you were challenged.

*(Berenice looks warm and soft. Her face is not rigid.)*

**Les:** Edgar, what are you thinking?

**Edgar:** It's obvious to me that things are never going to change.

**Les:** Edgar, are you feeling frightened or angry at anyone?

**Edgar:** No, I just know things will never change.

**Les:** Edgar, I have several things for you to think about. Will you listen for a few moments?

**Edgar:** Yes.

*(Melissa and Gerry are also listening, and looking attentively.)*

**Les:** Number one, Edgar, is to remember that it is okay for you to leave, if that's what is best for you, even though Berenice changes. Second, your belief that things will never change sounds like it's something with significance from way back. Third, that belief does several things: it's exactly what Melissa believes, and that is really harmful for her; it acts as a curse for Berenice; and, finally, it isn't real. I think Berenice has already changed some. She did fine work this afternoon.

**Ruth** *(to Les)*: I think those are good things for everyone to think about. I also think it is time to stop for now.

**Les:** You're right.

# WEDNESDAY MORNING
# MEN'S GROUP—WITH LES

**Edgar** *(in a rehearsed, measured tone)*: I want to deal with anger.

**Gerry** *(jumping in, almost interrupting)*: I also want to deal with anger. What I see and hear are contradictions. I'm angry because you and Ruth use a different approach from the group back home. I don't like the way you are confronting me. I can tell you don't know how to approach me, so you're trying to push all my buttons to see how I react.

>    *By his high level of activity and his loud talking and brash manner, Gerry has been able to level almost any confrontation with him. We have been calling him, gently, on the fact that he's not working very much and that he is taking over everything, just as he did now, from his father.*

**Gerry:** Ruth is just trying to get at me.

>    *The message to me now seems to be "keep away." The fact is Ruth has done almost no work with Gerry. Gerry is responding either to Ruth's work with Berenice or to the lack of work with himself. Gerry is used to being the prize, the center of attention. For some reason, he has decided that Ruth and I are bad.*

**Les:** I don't understand any of this. It doesn't match with my reality.

**Gerry:** I'm shaking with anger. But, hell, anger is easy. Just don't put your therapy into action on me, unless you're very clear.

**Les:** Are you fragile?

**Gerry:** Possibly—yes.

**Les:** Do you really believe that?

**Gerry:** Now, all of a sudden you're handling me with kid gloves. Can't you be consistent about the way you deal with me?

**Les:** I think you're confusing the problems you brought with you, with your situation with me. You're saying that I've done something wrong, because you're in trouble.

**Gerry** *(reflective and quiet)*: That's probably true.

**Les:** I want to hear what you want to do. I've heard what Ruth and I aren't doing right, but I'm not sure about where you want to go.

**Gerry:** I'll have to think about that. *(He sits back, his trembling stops.)*

*(After a pause, he speaks again.)* On the first day, here, it became obvious to me that I had to get out of the family at home, stop being with my mother so much, stay away from the family business, and stay away from my grandmother. I'm happy with that. But when I find myself talking with you and Ruth about that, I feel concerned. I also now know that, if my mother kills herself, it's clearly not my fault. I know, also, that if I go back to Phoenix, and fit in with my grandmother again, it will be a defeat.

**Les:** You've come to some very important decisions, on your own. I'm really glad to hear about all that. Would you like to go ahead with your concern about the defeat if you don't follow through?

**Gerry:** I'm still mad at Ruth. But I feel good about sharing this anger. I'm not shaking. You know more about me than I've ever shown before.

**Les:** Again, you didn't answer my question. You shifted from it. I am concerned, because you've done an extremely quick turnaround. It's as if you're saying you've finished your therapy, to avoid actively doing anything.

**Gerry** *(stunned)*: Oh, ya.

**Les:** When you first began to talk this morning, I had a picture of you behind a fortress wall, with your guns pointing out. I think your quick changes are a way of trying to take the wind out of our sails. I bet you figured that if you make it seem as if everything's okay or that you're angry and we're no good, we will back off.

**Gerry:** Maybe you're right. I have moved quickly in how I feel. I know the most important thing in my father-in-law's life was leaving the family business. I've got to do that. That's all for now.

**Edgar** *(playing with Little Gerry, who has been kicking the wall)*: Little Gerry takes space for himself. It would be nice to be three and a half.

**Les:** Edgar, if you were three and a half, and getting what you wanted, what would you be doing right now?

**Edgar:** I'd be up on top of the mountain that's behind the condominiums.

**Les:** You don't seem to believe that you can get what you want where you are. You have to go someplace else to get it.

**Edgar** *(in a droning voice)*: I know that.

**Les:** What is that about?

**Edgar:** How can I put some more life into it, so you'll see? I believe that somebody else, that anybody else, is more important than me.

**Les:** When you were Little Gerry's age, who was more important than you?

**Edgar:** My cousins were more important than me. I was sad and lonely. I was always told to go to my room. "You'd better be a good boy when you come out," they'd say.

**Les:** I get a sense of how pissed off you are.

**Edgar:** When I get angry now, I still go to my room.

*Edgar's children have been trying everything to get him involved, and not to go to his room. Maybe Berenice was too, but whatever she did drove him further in.*

**Les:** If you were to come out of your room now, who would you tell about being angry?

**Edgar:** A crowd.

*(Together, we set up pillows representing his mother, his father, his brother, and his sister.)*

**Edgar** *(continues in his droning monotone)*: It is so difficult for me to get angry. You, father, never cared about anyone. I'm going to get even with you for not caring.

**Les** *(feeding lines, guiding him)*: Everything I've done, I've done for you—having kids, having a grandchild.

**Edgar:** Yes, I wanted to show him how good I could be.

*(To the pillow:)* I've stayed married. I didn't run around. I showed you I could be different from you.

*(To Les:)* I'm still chasing him, aren't I? I'm thinking I can reach him, but I can't. I can't go on now. *(He stops and moves back a little.)*

**Les:** Gerry?

**Gerry:** I'm feeling better, because I'm not holding back how I feel. I'm sad my father can't follow through.

*(Little Gerry picks up one of the foam encounter bats and whacks the pillows.)*

> *Little Gerry has a way of tuning into everyone in his family and charmingly acting things out for them. This could lead to large difficulties for him.*

**Les:** Tell your father, instead of letting your son act out for you.

*(Gerry, gently and appropriately, takes care of his son. Then, he turns to his father. One of the trainees takes over playing with Little Gerry.)*

**Gerry:** I'm sad for you that you never get angry.

**Edgar:** Sometimes I can let myself get angry. When the person I'm angry at isn't important to me.

**Gerry** *(picking up two of the encounter bats)*: Fight with me.

**Edgar** *(blandly)*: Yes.

*(Gerry hits Edgar. Edgar barely responds. Bill Sarnon, who has a passive stance similar to Edgar's and is about the same age, speaks.)*

**Bill:** You're running away. You're making the other person do all the work!

**Dom** *(piping in with bravado)*: Go on.

**Gerry:** I felt cheated, Dad, when you started to be angry and then stopped.

**Edgar:** I'm afraid of being angry. The only time I let myself be angry with Berenice, I tried to kill her. Luckily I didn't. I'll never get angry again.

**Les:** Before Berenice, who were you afraid of killing if you got angry?

**Edgar:** My father.

**Les:** Tell him.

**Edgar:** I wish I would have killed you. I'm glad I just told you. I don't know why I never told you before. I really wanted to hurt you then.

**Les:** Is that still true?

**Edgar:** No. I'm glad I finally told him.

**Les:** Tell your father that, no matter how angry you are at him or Berenice or anyone, you won't hurt or kill him, or anyone else.

**Edgar** *(with energy and conviction)*: No matter how angry I am at you, I won't hurt or kill you or anyone else.

**Les:** Bring Berenice in. Say the same thing to her.

**Edgar** *(flatly)*: I won't hurt or kill you, Berenice, no matter how angry I am.

**Les:** Edgar, your voice is flat again, what is going on?

**Edgar:** I feel empty.

**Les:** Go back then and tell your father about being empty.

**Edgar** *(very hesitantly, with progressive sadness)*: I wish you were here, I needed you. *(He sobs, quietly.)*

**Les** *(moving over to Edgar and putting an arm around him, holding him)*: Sometimes kids grow up thinking that keeping feelings away protects them from the loneliness.

*(Edgar, weeping quietly, acknowledges Les with a headshake.)*

**Gerry** *(after a moment)*: I'm glad you did that.

> When his father held back his anger, Little Gerry kicked the wall. When his grandfather hesitated to show anger, Little Gerry picked up the encounter bats and hit the pillows. When his grandfather was sad, Little Gerry cried and asked his father to hold him.
>
> Perhaps Rusty and Gerry have acted out their father's unexpressed feelings of anger and loneliness.
>
> Holding Edgar has been very important for some of the other men in the group, particularly David.

*(The group ends on a quiet, reflective note.)*

# WOMEN'S GROUP—WITH RUTH

**Berenice:** I have something to say to Margaret Ann. Something I've been thinking about since I stopped yesterday afternoon.

**Ruth:** It's okay to go ahead.

**Berenice** *(moving over to her daughter-in-law)*: It's something about Little Gerry that I want to say. I see you as a very capable person and a wonderful mother. I know you will take good care of your son.

*(Quiet and sad)* I know I don't have to hang on to him any longer.

**Margaret Ann** *(warmly)*: Thank you for saying that, Berenice. I know that the relationship Little Gerry has with you is a good one. But I am his mother and I have decided that I want to have more to do with him. I want to take over more of his care, and I am ready to do it.

**Ruth:** I respect both of you for what you're doing. Berenice, you are breaking a family tradition in which the grandmother is the primary caretaker. That's an important tradition to break.

**Berenice:** Thank you.

**Ruth:** Melissa, what is going on with you?

**Melissa** (*looking thoughtful*): I wonder if I'll do the same when I have a child.

(*Turning:*) Mom, do you see me as capable of raising my own child?

**Berenice:** Let's work on our relationship now, and not make promises for the future. When the future comes, I'm sure I'll be able to see my daughter as someone who knows what she can do.

**Melissa:** You mean, now I'm not capable? That's what you're saying. We've tried to work on our relationship millions of times, and we've never gotten anywhere.

(*She retreats into a sullen slouch.*)

**Ruth:** Berenice, you didn't respond to Melissa's request. Working on your relationship is what you want, not what Melissa seems to want. I think you need to respond directly to Melissa's straight question. Will you do that now?

**Berenice** (*to Melissa*): Right now, I don't see you as capable of doing that. You don't use good judgment about yourself, so I don't know how you could about a baby.

**Ruth** (*to Melissa, who is lounging on the floor*): Will you change positions? Sit up and respond to your mother.

**Melissa:** I'm going to have to get married to get away from my mother.

**Ruth:** I can understand you being angry with her right now. First, she disregarded your question, and then she said things you probably didn't want to hear. Am I right?

(*Melissa makes absolutely no response. She looks sullen and stoney.*)

**Berenice** (*beginning to get hyped up*): But I—

**Ruth:** Berenice, you need to stay quiet and out of it, for the moment.

*Melissa's dilemma is clearer. Her mother doesn't listen to her. Berenice takes over, based on her own internal responses rather than any knowledge of Melissa. Melissa's way of handling this is similar to her father's withdrawal and desire to kill.*

**Ruth:** I'd like to switch gears for awhile. Melissa, what I know is that it's hard to be a woman in your family. I'd like to look at that. Will you pick people from the group to represent the important women in your family dynasty?

**Melissa** (*brightening considerably, and beginning to choose women in the room*): My great-aunt was very religious; my grandmother, manipulative, nurturing, and rich.

**Ruth:** Good beginning, but—hold on, I forgot something. You didn't know your great-grandmother, so, Berenice, will you choose someone to be Melissa's great grandmother? Pick according to the myth about her.

**Berenice:** Rebecca was determined and rebellious. Her children, my mother and my uncle, were born 25 years apart. She rode horses astride in the 1860s.

(*Melissa sets up the family sculpture. The woman who is playing Rebecca sits in the middle, on a high stool, as if riding a horse. The religious great-aunt is placed next to Rebecca, but lower, sitting stiffly. Melissa's grandmother, Gertrude, holds on to Rebecca.*)

**Melissa:** Everyone is clutching, trying to hold on.

(*Next, Melissa places Berenice in the sculpture. She puts her mother with the older women. They are all trying to hold on to Berenice. Melissa chooses someone for herself. The Gertrude figure tries to clutch both Berenice and Melissa. Berenice is sitting on the floor looking up, worshipfully, at her grandmother. Melissa, sitting on the floor, but lower than her mother, is refusing to look at anyone.*)

**Melissa** (*continuing*): Everyone is hanging onto everyone. No one can get out. The thought of bringing a kid into this is horrible.

**Ruth:** The way you've put yourself in the picture, it is hard for you to look at anyone. If you turn around and look, you'll be caught.

**Melissa** (*with some agitation*): I want out. I don't want to be in this mess. I don't know how to get out, though. The people who aren't in the sculpture, who got out, are either dead or crazy.

**Ruth:** Is there anything you want to say to the people in the sculpture?

**Melissa** (*crying*): I wish you would let me out. I feel hopeless. I feel angry and stupid for being caught.

**Ruth:** Tell your mother what you think, as you watch her in this picture.

**Melissa** *(continuing to cry softly)*: I am sad that you got caught in this. I am sad that I am caught in this. I can't get out. I can't get out.

*This is the first caring contact that Melissa has had with her mother.*

**Ruth:** Berenice, I can really understand Melissa's difficulty. She needs help from you to get out. It's been a long morning. It's time for a break. Look at the video tape of this family sculpture. Figure out how you can get out and how you can help Melissa get out. Melissa has to have your help. I'm concerned that Melissa believes that the only way she has of getting out is to run, or hurt or kill herself.

*There is an irony in appealing to Berenice to help her child. To help Melissa, Berenice will have to let go of her.*

*(When we return from our break, I ask the women to form the sculpture again. Berenice speaks as soon as we begin.)*

**Berenice:** My shoulders still hurt from being hung onto.

**Ruth:** Okay. As you are back in the sculpture, how do you feel and what are you thinking?

**Berenice:** Trapped and pulled in all directions.

**Ruth:** When you looked at the videotape, what did you figure you needed to do?

**Berenice:** I need to break away.

**Ruth:** When?

**Berenice:** Now. I think I'm going to start by doing some separating. Until I saw the picture I didn't realize how close the ties were.

I realize now that Melissa can't accept the parts of me that are all right without getting more tied into the family. I understand more why she turns away and won't look at me. The way she was in the sculpture is her only way to survive this mess.

**Ruth:** I think that's true.

**Berenice:** I'm thinking about my aunt Rebecca.

**Ruth:** Turn to your aunt and tell her.

**Berenice:** You kept me alive when I was born. I wouldn't have lived if you hadn't kept me alive. My mother gave up on me. The doctor gave up on me. But it's not my responsibility to take care of you or of my mother. Even at 83, Rebecca, you have guts and determination I wish I had. You don't need me. You've done a hell of a good job taking care of yourself. I've got to take care of myself and follow that model you gave me.

*(Berenice pulls away the aunt's hand, which has been clutching at her shoulder. She is crying and at the same time, thinking clearly. Still crying, she turns to her mother in the sculpture.)*

**Berenice** *(continuing)*: There's nothing I can do, in this life, that will ever please you. No matter what I do, you still will never think well of me. I'm sorry you never learned how to care about me. I've let you clutch at me, hoping you would care. I know you're lonely and unhappy, but that's not my fault. You can't have me, Mom, or my kids. You're going to have to find some other way to get your needs met. You're going to have to leave me and my kids alone.

**Ruth:** Will you tell her that you're going to protect yourself and your children?

**Berenice:** I'm going to protect myself and my children. *(She pulls Gertrude's hand off Melissa.)* Leave my daughter alone. She is an okay kid. She's a neat kid, and you're not going to get her in your clutches. You're not going to destroy her like you tried to destroy me. I've had it.

*(She takes her mother's hands off her own shoulders, so that now both she and Melissa are free. Melissa turns to watch.)*

**Berenice** *(continuing)*: I'm done. I'm not going to let you destroy me. I'm really sorry for you, Mom. There isn't a damn thing I will do for you, if it means giving up myself.

*(Berenice turns and reaches, in a gentle way, to hold Melissa's shoulders from the front. They are looking directly at each other for the first time.)*

I don't know if I know how to love without clinging and clutching. I have a lot to learn.

**Ruth:** Melissa, will you tell your mother what you're thinking?

**Melissa:** I really don't think you're going to do anything. You're just going to go through the motions. I've seen you go through the motions before, hundreds of times.

**Berenice:** What do I have to do to prove to you that it's real?

*(Melissa lowers her head and looks at the floor. She holds her head casually to one side, as if nothing has been said.)*

**Ruth:** Melissa, look at your mother and answer her.

**Melissa:** I'm scared that when we get home, everything will be the same.

**Ruth:** Do you need to watch something?

**Melissa:** Yes.

**Ruth:** You need to watch and see if your Mom's going to carry through. That makes sense to me. I agree that you should watch and be careful.

I'd like to point out that there are many things you could do that would help your Mom to not follow through. You could be angry, for one thing. That would make things harder for her.

I also imagine that you know many things to do on your own to help support your mother.

As you go home and watch your Mom, one of the things you'll be needing is more support. I suspect that you can get this from Margaret Ann.

*(Margaret Ann smiles at Melissa.)*

**Melissa:** Okay.

**Berenice** *(to Ruth)*: Are you saying that when I get home, I need to deal directly with my mother, the way I did here?

**Ruth:** That's exactly what I'm saying.

**Berenice:** Melissa, I'll do it.

**Ruth:** Melissa, do you have anything else to say to your Mom?

**Melissa:** No.

**Ruth:** I think you have a good chance for yourself. You've done fine work this morning. Your mother has, too. You even helped each other. You built the family sculpture. Your mother used it to figure out some things she needed to do.

**Margaret Ann:** Berenice, I'm scared for you, because of Gertrude. I know you'll get separate from her, but it will be an incredible strain. I'm going to support you both,

Berenice and Melissa, because I love you and care about you.

**Berenice:** I love you, Margaret Ann. I want to share something with you. When I was looking at the videotape, I saw Gerry in Melissa's position. For twelve years, he was my mother's little granddaughter.

When I was pregannt for the second time, my mother had this idea that it had to be a girl. Right after Gerry was born, she dressed him in pink. When he was three, she used to dress Gerry in a tulle skirt and send him to ballet class. It was all right for Rusty to be a boy, because he was the first-born, but Gerry had to be what my mother demanded he be. I was really glad that Melissa was a girl; she saved Gerry.

**Ruth:** I am glad you have started to reclaim your children, Berenice. You and Edgar conceived them. You carried them and gave birth to them. Your mother didn't. Also, Berenice, I think you are a good mother.

**Berenice:** Really?

**Margaret Ann:** I think you are also, Berenice. I know, too, that Gertrude isn't capable of being rational. Something made her lose touch—her hard times in the Depression, or her husband's suicide.

*(Berenice, Margaret Ann, and Melissa talk for a few minutes. They talk about their difficulties with Gertrude and how they're going to help each other when they go back to Phoenix.)*

**Margaret Ann:** Before the session ends, I want to thank you Berenice. Thank you for doing what you did about Little Gerry. I have a specific plan now.

When we get home I want to arrange day care for Little Gerry all day. I'll take him and I'll pick him up. Grandma will be Grandma for him.

**Berenice** *(smiling)*: It's funny. I feel relieved.

**Margaret Ann:** Ruth, how do I tell Little Gerry about this?

**Ruth:** I think both you and Berenice might sit down together with Little Gerry and tell him.

*(Margaret Ann and Berenice nod to each other and share warm smiles.)*

*Many, many years ago Berenice allowed her son Gerry to be taken over and raised by his grandmother. He was raised as a girl and dressed in such as ballet skirts. What a profound impact this must have had on Gerry! His mother gave him away; his father didn't fight for him; and his basic maleness was assaulted. I understand much more about Gerry now.*

*Here, Berenice and Margaret Ann have decided that this won't happen to Little Gerry. An important family line has been broken.*

# WEDNESDAY AFTERNOON
# INDIVIDUAL FAMILIES—WITH LES

*This is the short afternoon. We all need a break. I have the Barkers and the Quinns with me.*

**Gerry** *(sarcastically)*: One of the things I learned this morning is that you can't hurt anyone with encounter bats.

**Edgar** *(almost aside to Les)*: I'm scared by Gerry. What is he angry about anyway?

**Gerry:** I'll tell you. I'm angry that you never fight back and that you don't address me directly, like even now.

*These two interact as Berenice interacts with Melissa: Edgar as if he is Melissa, and Gerry as if he is his mother.*

**Les:** The two of you are both having a hard time getting into anything. Edgar, one of the things I think Gerry needs to hear is that you won't hurt or kill him, no matter how angry you are.

**Edgar:** I won't hurt or kill you, no matter what you do or how angry I get.

*(Edgar picks up two encounter bats. He is still moving in his mechanical manner. Gerry moves vigorously to accept one of the bats. They struggle back and forth for a few minutes. Gerry hits his father hard and staggers, himself, in response.)*

**Gerry** *(dramatically)*: I think I'm going to faint.

*(He stumbles to a chair, breathless.)*

I was afraid I might kill my father.

**Les:** That's what your father said this morning—that he was afraid of killing his own father.

**Gerry:** I won't do that.

**Les:** Tell him.

**Gerry:** Dad, I won't hurt or kill you, for any reason.

**Les:** Gerry, is that true?

**Gerry:** Yes.

**Les:** Edgar, I like the way you stayed in there with your son.

*(Margaret Ann curls up in a chair and looks very scared. Berenice looks extremely frightened, too.)*

**Les:** Margaret Ann, what's going on?

**Margaret Ann:** I was afraid Gerry and Edgar would hurt each other. That has to do with me more than what was happening with them. Both my father and my grandfather had bad tempers. All my life, people told me I was the same way. My mother used to say that if I would only back off and leave my father alone, everything would be all right.

**Les:** That seems to still be powerful for you. Do you want to pursue that? Will you bring your mother out and talk to her?

*(Margaret Ann nods, yes. Les puts a pillow in front of her.)*

**Margaret Ann:** I'm angry you put that on me. That was always scary for me, Mom. I don't believe what you told me. That was your way of acting, not mine.

*(To Les:)* I feel relieved now. I never realized that or said it before.

**Les:** You're concerned about your own temper. Is it easier to see the anger in someone else than to see it in yourself?

**Margaret Ann:** I see what you're getting at. Yes, it's easier for me when Gerry acts on his rage. He has all the angry parts in the family.

**Les:** Edgar, the piece of work you did this morning fits in now. Will you turn to Berenice and tell her about it?

**Edgar** *(again, in his droning voice)*: No matter what I think or feel or do, I'll never do anything to hurt or kill you, or anyone.

**Berenice** *(straightening up from her little-girl slouch)*: Thank you.

*I move on to work with the Quinns. As I do, I am aware that Edgar will not give anything, or even any energy, to Berenice. He has withdrawn completely.*

# THURSDAY MORNING

# YOUNG PEOPLE'S GROUP—WITH LES

*Ruth has the parents and I have the older kids. This is the last time the families will be divided in this way. After the midmorning break, we will probably join the adults.*

*Everyone is using clay or drawing pictures. Melissa is sitting alone at the far corner of the room. She is moulding turtles and lotuslike flowers. After the work with Nick and David, I turn to Melissa.*

**Les:** Melissa, it still seems hard for you to allow me, or anyone else, in. You seem to really get dull and turn yourself off when I'm around.

**Bethany** (*a trainee, speaks after a long silence*): Melissa, I experience you as withdrawn and hard to talk to, except when you're talking about your boyfriend.

**Melissa** (*to Les*): My boyfriend is 24. I got rid of the one who was 33. My new boyfriend appreciates things about me that no one else notices or cares about. He gives me presents that matter—key rings and posters.

**Les:** So, you feel removed from most other people?

**Melissa:** In this family, I need to move out to make myself human. I haven't been human since Rusty's death.

**Les:** Will you say more about what you mean?

**Melissa:** When Rusty died, when he was killed, I mean—my mother thinks he killed himself. I think he was killed by somebody.

When Rusty was killed, I didn't even know he was dead. Mom sent me off to Girl Scout camp before I knew. I didn't go to the funeral. I didn't cry. I didn't see anyone else cry. I don't know now whether anyone else in the family was sad about his dying.

I never know how anyone in the family feels about me, except when they yell and scream—or when my mother hits me.

**Les:** Earlier when we met, I offered that Ruth and I help you talk with your family about some of these things. The stuff around Rusty's death is important, as is your mother hitting you. Shall we do that?

**Melissa** (*looking relieved, and softer*): Sure.

(*Bethany gives her a hug and makes a clay turtle, which she adds to Melissa's collection.*)

*One of the signs that the group is maturing is that the trainees aren't considered as being on our side any more. They are closer to the family members. At the evening meeting the night before, we talked about how Melissa has presented herself as hard and self-punishing. We planned for Bethany to connect with Melissa and to offer extra support. They already had spent considerable time together outside of the group.*

*Trainees are of tremendous value. They are able to do many things and facilitate many connections that we, as therapists, are not able to do.*

# PARENT'S GROUP—WITH RUTH

*Just before the morning groups began, Berenice came up to me, almost hysterical, and said that Gerry had driven a car off a cliff. Through her rantings, I finally learned that Gerry was only slightly bruised. The car was still stuck over the cliff. Gerry, at the beginning of group, was still out trying to rescue the car.*

*After the break, Gerry appeared, walking with a bounce, a small bump on his forehead. Melissa entered the big room, after him. She appears to have completely blocked this out. She doesn't even acknowledge Gerry's presence.*

*Little Gerry comes in with Kitty. Kitty speaks softly and tells me that Little Gerry has been jittery and upset all morning. I have to decide whether or not to have Little Gerry in the room when we talk about what has been going on with his father. He is carrying two puppets, one an alligator and one a rabbit. Quietly, he puts the alligator on his hand. When I sit down beside him and put the rabbit on my hand, he uses the alligator to bite me, over and over again, on the nose. He doesn't say anything. Afterwards, the alligator rebuffs the rabbit, who tries to talk to him. I back off. Little Gerry climbs onto his mother's lap.*

Gerry has managed to shift the focus back to himself. It seems as though we are back at the first morning of the workshop. Berenice is screeching. Edgar is sitting like a lump. Melissa is withdrawn. Margaret Ann is separate and quiet. We decide to begin directly with Gerry and not to allow things to get shifted back to the family.

**Les** *(commandingly)*: Gerry, begin.

**Gerry** *(lightly)*: Sometimes I feel crazy. Last night, I was driving back from town. I got to a place with a little detour for road building. There was a field and lots of equipment up there, off the road. I decided to drive the car off the road, over a little cliff, across a gully, and into the field. The car got stuck and hung across the gully.

If I had been able to start any of the heavy construction equipment, I would have stolen it and pulled the car out.

I was drinking. I was drunk. I started off feeling great—then I got drunker. I used to start off this kind of stuff feeling bad.

*(Suddenly, contrite and regretful, in a way that seems put on:)* I was taking a step backwards. I was looking to see whether my father would react.

**Ruth:** What is your fantasy about how you would have ended up, if the car hadn't gotten stuck?

**Gerry** *(brightly)*: I would have gotten away with it. The car would have been a little dented. As it was, I got up at six and got a tow truck to pull the car out. If the car hadn't gotten stuck, I wouldn't have to deal with the accident at all. I would have driven home, parked the car, and not talked to anyone about it.

**Ruth:** Were you afraid of getting hurt, or of getting in trouble?

**Gerry:** Definitely not of getting hurt. Definitely not of getting in trouble.

*Actually, Gerry could easily have gotten hurt or caught by the police. This is how he is a danger to himself and to others. How can we get to this with him?*

**Gerry** *(cockily)*: I was thinking of speeding on the way home, so I checked at the bar and found out the police went off duty at midnight.

**Les:** I think you set it up so that you would get caught by somebody.

**Gerry:** Maybe.

**Les:** Would you tell your father what you wanted out of this?

**Gerry:** I wanted to be punished. I wanted to be confronted. I'm always dodging back and forth, between giving you power and taking it myself.

*(They talk a little, Edgar with his flat tone, Gerry making up theories and explanations, with no specifics. The group gets edgy.)*

**Ruth:** Tell your father of a specific instance when you were little and you wished he would take more responsibility?

**Gerry** *(very hesitant)*: I don't know.

**Ruth:** Think of something.

**Gerry:** I skipped school, and my father found me and whipped me.

*(Les and I look at each other with surprise.)*

**Ruth:** It's interesting: the first thing you've come up with is something your father did act on. What you were talking about was being concerned with times your father didn't act.

**Les:** You want your father to do something, and, at the same time, you don't want him to do anything. You keep shifting responsibility, so you never have to take responsibility. You act out and never believe you will get caught.

It's amazing, considering the content of what we're saying, that Berenice looks bored, Little Gerry is agitated, Edgar looks tired, and Melissa isn't listening. Gerry has managed to defuse the confrontation.

It looks and sounds just like the opening session of the week, when Gerry threw up clouds of intellectualizing and vague theorizing, while the rest of the family sat back without affective involvement.

**Ruth:** Edgar, what's your responsibility, here?

**Edgar** *(turning and flatly)*: I know you can take the responsibility, Gerry.

*(Little Gerry moves off his mother's lap, and over to Bette Sarnon, who is sitting in between his grandparents. He directs Bette onto another chair, by pulling on her hand. He then stands on the chair between Edgar and Berenice, holding each of their hands. He is stretched out, arms wide.)*

**Ruth:** Something important is going on, Gerry. As you and your father talk about your separate responsibilities, Little Gerry goes over and stands between Berenice and Edgar.

*(Gerry looks nervous and doesn't respond. Little Gerry*

*gets down, goes across the room, and picks up the alligator puppet. He makes some snapping motions towards me and goes to stand between Gerry and Margaret Ann.)*

**Gerry:** What I really wanted to deal with here was my fathering.

**Ruth:** I've never seen you sit down and connect with your son. You have simply been agreeing to the changes other people suggest.

**Gerry** *(mechanically)*: I want to be a father figure. I don't want Little Gerry involved with so many parents.

**Les:** Gerry, look at your son's T-shirt.

*(It says "Super-Gerry" on the front and "Gotcha!" on the back.)*

**Gerry:** He went to the T-shirt shop and picked out the letters.

*(Gerry then goes on, with his robotlike voice and his irrelevant analysis. His parents might change, he suggests, or his grandmother might change, or Margaret Ann might do something different to change the situation for Little Gerry.)*

**Ruth** *(angrily)*: There's always somebody else, something that's going to make things get better. You're not taking responsibility for anything. It's all in the future. It's going to get better, you say.

Gerry, walk around, swing your arms, loosen up a little. You are like a computer: talking and saying the right things. Look around. People are bored. They're yawning. Your face is like stone. Your body is stiff.

And, as you're stiffening up, Little Gerry is getting louder and louder.

**Gerry** *(tightly)*: I can't even think about the possibility that I might not be doing an excellent job as a father.

**Ruth** *(quickly)*: That's the same thing that just happened earlier. You find a reason not to even look at something disturbing.

Gerry, do you know how to wiggle? Try a little wiggle with your whole body, just as Paula has been doing with her face.

*(Gerry smiles broadly. He wiggles his hips, then immediately goes back to a stiff posture. Little Gerry starts yelling, "Daddy, Daddy," then he wiggles, singing loudly.)*

**Little Gerry** *(over and over)*: Yummy, yummy, yummy, I've got dirt in my tummy.

**Ruth:** Gerry, will you say, "I'm keeping myself rigid, waiting for something to happen."

**Gerry:** I'm keeping myself rigid, waiting for something to happen. All the time I'm ready to react.

**Ruth:** All the time, you're in a rigid shell. You can't face anything, unless you've had a drink.

*I'm really pushing Gerry. Les looks over at me, with his eyebrows in a frown. Gerry looks worried and doesn't answer.*

**Little Gerry** *(handing his father the alligator puppet):* Here, Daddy, use it.

*(Little Gerry stands behind his father, pushing him toward me. As they get to the middle of the room, he grabs onto his father's legs, to pull him. He's laughing and rocking with him.)*

**Ruth:** Your three-year-old is getting set up to carry the burden of anger. The T-shirt with Gotcha on it, for instance. This is just like what happened with you and Rusty, acting out your Dad's anger.

**Gerry** *(his eyes down and shifting):* I guess I've been aware of that problem.

*(The minute Gerry speaks, Little Gerry jumps up and down, pulling on his hand.)*

**Little Gerry:** Daddy, I've got to go pee pee.

*(Little Gerry has tried to get his father off the hook. Margaret Ann calmly picks Little Gerry up and takes him off to the bathroom. Gerry stands like a statue. When Margaret Ann and Little Gerry come back into the room, Gerry is still in the middle.)*

**Ruth:** Gerry, will you scream as loud as you can?

*(Little Gerry looks at him, wide-eyed, covers up his ears and moves to cuddle up with his mother. Gerry sort of screams.)*

**Ruth:** Scream again. Imagine something is going on when you do that.

*(Gerry screams again, then he walks around with his back slightly bent. As he continues to walk around, his arms bend up and he lifts his hands as if he is holding up an enormous weight.)*

**Ruth** *(commandingly):* Stay in that position, accentuate it. Put words to how you feel and what you think.

**Gerry:** I'm Samson. I'm Atlas. I'm keeping the building up. I'm keeping the world up. I'm keeping the whole thing from falling down.

**Ruth** *(firmly)*: You're keeping the whole thing from falling down. Keep that posture. What else comes?

**Gerry:** It's all going to collapse. If I'm not there, everyone will be trapped. I think I can hold it up long enough for everyone to escape. I'll just hold it a little bit longer, and everybody will make it out.

*I believe that he means what he is saying: his voice has real emotion in it. This is the key that we've been waiting for. In the past, whenever there has been something with Gerry, he has either frozen up or acted out.*

*By accentuating his position, Gerry has revealed his grandiosity. Next, we will help him to confront his grandiose view of himself: that he is the strong man of the world.*

**Gerry:** I'm a martyr. I'd like to be a hero.

**Ruth:** Put yourself in to an actual physical position where things can be put on top of you.

**Gerry** *(getting solidly down on all fours)*: This is the position in which I can support the most weight.

**Ruth:** Don and Bob, put three or four pillows on top of Gerry.

*(The pillows are piled on. Gerry indicates that he feels nothing. More pillows go on. Gerry asks for even more and more. Finally, Don and Bob pile on, then Bill Sarnon, then Nicholas Sarnon and David Quinn, then Dom Dellapietra. Gerry is bearing about 1000 pounds. He finally sinks, with his head down.)*

**Ruth** *(sitting on the floor beside Gerry, calling to inside the pile)*: What's going on, Gerry?

**Gerry** *(with amazement and wonder)*: I'm still alive. But I couldn't do it. I didn't realize this. I didn't realize I would ever collapse. I thought I was invulnerable. I can't believe my invulnerability has a crack in it. It's true. I believe that if there's a plane crash, I'll survive no matter what. I've never thought I'd collapse. I can't believe this.

*Gerry has spent his life testing his invulnerability and proving his grandiosity. I imagine Rusty might have done the same thing. He ended up dead.*

*(The men have removed themselves. Gerry remains lying in the center of the floor, still piled with pillows.)*

**Ruth** *(still sitting with him)*: Gerry, you're not invulnerable. You're not going to live, no matter what you do.

**Gerry:** I don't want to believe there are things to be afraid of. I never have been afraid of anything.

**Ruth** *(firmly)*: There are things to be afraid of. There are many things to be afraid of. You're not going to live through everything.

**Gerry:** I've heard that before. I never realized that I could be dead.

**Ruth:** Yes, you could be dead. You could easily be dead.

**Gerry:** I don't believe that.

**Ruth:** You could very easily hurt or kill yourself.

**Gerry** *(astonished)*: But I thought I was invulnerable. How can I go on living? I don't like the idea of being afraid every time I turn around. How can I live, not be afraid, but know I'm not invulnerable?

**Ruth:** You can go on living and not be afraid. It's important for you to go on living, knowing that you're vulnerable and destructible, and also knowing that you don't have to be afraid all the time.

**Gerry:** It seems contradictory to me.

**Ruth:** I believe it seems contradictory to you. It's not really.

**Gerry:** Will you say that again?

> *This exchange illustrates one of the ways we use intensive, time-limited therapy. I'm willing to take on the role of parent and to actively make some clear statements about the reality of human frailty. Gerry clearly responds to that kind of parenting just as Berenice did earlier.*

**Ruth:** You can go on living and also know that you're destructible and that you're human, like everyone else. You don't have to go through life being afraid. You can learn how to take good care of yourself.

It's not okay that you set things up to carry 1000 pounds on your back or that you drive off the road or that you drink too much. You can die when you do these things.

*(As we talk, Gerry slowly gets himself up, shedding pillows. He sits cross-legged and faces me, with tears in his eyes.)*

**Ruth:** Edgar, join us. Face Gerry squarely.

*(Little Gerry begins to cry. Edgar moves to the center and sits with us.)*

I think he needs to know from you that he's not invulnerable.

**Edgar:** Gerry, you're not invulnerable. You're real, and you can't support the world. You can't solve all the problems. You can get hurt. You can get killed. I don't want that to happen to you. I want you to stay whole and alive.

**Gerry** *(in disbelief)*: You want me to stay alive?

**Edgar** *(crying)*: I want you to stay alive. Oh, how I want you to stay alive.

**Ruth:** Edgar, tell him how to keep himself alive.

**Edgar:** Don't do anything to hurt or kill yourself. Stay alive.

**Gerry:** I never believed I would ever die.

**Ruth:** Edgar, tell your son again that he can die, that he needs to take care of himself.

**Edgar:** It's important. You can die. You need to take care of yourself to stay alive.

**Ruth:** Edgar, Gerry needs to know something else. He needs to know that you're willing to carry your part of the burden of handling his mother and grandmother. That way, he doesn't have to do it all. That's the world he holds up. It's not his job.

*(Gerry nods agreement.)*

**Edgar:** I will take my part in dealing with your mother and Gertrude.

**Ruth:** Tell him it's not his job.

**Edgar:** It's not your job to take care of your mother or grandmother.

*(Gerry nods, breathing deeply, his eyes wide.)*

Your job is to keep yourself alive, to take care of yourself, and your wife, and your child, not to take care of your mother, or your grandmother.

**Ruth:** You've made it clear that Berenice and the dynasty are not Gerry's responsibility. The way he can get free is for you to give him permission to go.

**Edgar:** Gerry, you have my permission to go, to leave your mother, to leave Gertrude, and, to be responsible for yourself.

**Gerry:** Will the business keep going without me?

*Gerry is perfectly serious in asking this. It shows his sense of omnipotence—a whole company might stop, because he left.*

**Edgar:** The business will keep going without you. You can't keep it going. You're not expected to do it. The responsibility you have is to keep yourself alive, in one piece, and to take care of your own son.

**Gerry:** Okay, I'll do that. I'll make my place.

**Ruth:** Edgar, turn a moment to Berenice. Will you tell Berenice that her family and the business are not Gerry's responsibility?

*(Edgar moves and puts his arms around Gerry. He is holding him, like a child, from the back. Gerry looks sad and content.)*

**Edgar:** Berenice, Gerry does not have to deal with you, with Gertrude, or with the business. It's not his responsibility to do that.

**Ruth:** Will you support her, as she deals with Gertrude and the business? If so, also know that it doesn't mean you'll have to live together. That's a different thing.

**Edgar:** I'll support you. It's not up to Gerry to support you.

*(Turning:)* I don't think she believes me.

**Les:** Do you believe yourself?

**Edgar:** Yes.

**Les:** Then tell Berenice again.

**Edgar:** I will support you, as you deal with Gertrude and the business. Gerry doesn't have to do that.

**Berenice:** It isn't Gerry's responsibility to take care of me, or my mother, or the business. What I want him to do is to take care of himself and his family.

**Ruth:** Tell Gerry that.

**Berenice:** What I want is for you to take care of yourself and your own family. You don't need to take care of me. You don't need to take care of Grandma. You don't need to run the business.

*(In a clear and steady voice:)* Grandma is a very strong woman. She can take care of herself. I am a strong woman. I can take care of myself.

*Berenice uses her own words. This indicates that her clarity and steadiness are genuine.*

**Berenice** *(to Edgar)*: I don't believe you're going to help me.

**Ruth:** What I'm wondering about is whether you'll let him help you.

*(There is a long pause.)*

**Berenice** *(crying gently)*: I don't know.

*I'm reminded of her saying, "No man is ever going to touch me again." It's important for her to allow someone besides her son in to support her.*

**Ruth:** I think it's important to allow Edgar to help you. Your kids need to know that you'll take support from someone besides them. You need to know you don't have to stand alone.

**Margaret Ann:** No woman in this family has ever let a man help her. Gertrude has kept the company going, alone. Berenice will need to break another family tradition.

*(The group takes a short stretch. Les and I talk about how to finish with Berenice.)*

**Berenice** *(seating herself after the stretch)*: Sometimes, I want to tell Edgar to help me, and sometimes, I want to tell him to bug off. I think I need to finish up something with this.

**Les** *(speaking to the group)*: I have an experiment. All the men go on one side of the room. All the women go on the other side.

*(Everyone moves.)*

**Les** *(continuing)*: Berenice, get into the middle.

*(She does.)*

**Les** *(continuing)*: Now, everyone pull on Berenice's arms—men on one arm, women on the other.

*(Berenice is pulled on. She almost has to hold her breath to keep from saying anything. After several moments, she yells.)*

**Berenice** *(gasping for breath)*: Let me go, dammit! Let me go! I give up! I give up! I've been pulled apart all my life!

*(People stop pulling. They stand and listen.)*

**Berenice** *(continuing)*: Mom is pulling me. She says, "Come here, get away from men. They're terrible. You can't trust them."

Edgar's on the other side, with my father. Daddy says, "I love you, I'll take care of you. You're my little girl." And then he goes away. *(She hugs herself.)*

**Les:** Do you want to say anything to them?

**Berenice** *(loudly)*: Yes. All of you, I can take care of myself.

**Les:** And the other side of that?

**Berenice** *(getting softer, and more quiet)*: I'm hurt. I'm scared. I need someone to protect me. May God protect me from everybody—from you.

**Les:** When you're a little girl, and one parent is telling you one thing and the other parent says something else, it's really hard to choose. It's hard to know how to ask for help. I also know that you are smart.

**Berenice:** What do you mean?

**Les:** I mean that you can think. That you can figure out who the best person is to help you. Are you willing to do this exercise again and allow yourself to use your thinking? This is what you have been focusing on all week.

**Berenice:** And have them pull me? Okay.

**Les:** Berenice, look into people's faces this time. Decide who you want to have help you.

*(She is pulled. She turns to Terry, a male trainee.)*

**Berenice:** Help me.

**Terry:** What do you want me to do?

**Berenice:** Get them off me. Don't let them pull me.

*(Before Terry can act, Berenice turns to Bethany, a female trainee.)*

**Berenice:** Bethany, help me.

**Bethany:** What do you want me to do?

**Berenice:** Make him, and him, and her let go.

*(Together, Terry and Bethany set Berenice free.)*

**Berenice:** Bethany and Terry, hold me. *(She starts weeping, but quietly, without gasping.)*

**Les:** Berenice, how are you feeling?

**Berenice:** I feel fine. I told them what I wanted them to do. They did it, and I feel fine.

*(To Bethany and Terry:)* You can both go and sit down
if you want. Thank you.

**Les:** Are you now ready to talk to Edgar?

**Berenice:** Yes.

**Les:** Tell him exactly how you want him to help.

**Berenice** *(to Edgar):* There is something I have to do
that frightens me very much. Will you help me think about
it? I have to actually do it myself.

**Les:** That's not clear.

**Berenice** *(straightens herself up, and laughs a little):*
Part of me doesn't want help and isn't going to ask clearly
for anything.

*(Turning:)* I want you to be there, Edgar, physically.

**Les:** Berenice, we need to go back a little. Will you pick
someone to be your mother? Pick someone to be you.

**Berenice:** There isn't anybody in this room bitchy
enough to be my mother.

**Les:** Just pretend.

*Berenice is having a hard time telling Edgar how to
help her. Preparing to talk to her mother seems to
frighten her. Les wants someone else to play Berenice's
mother, rather than having her take the part. That way,
Berenice can tell Edgar how to help her. We're
rehearsing a scene to come, rather than exploring the
past.*

**Berenice:** Bethany, will you be my mother? Anna, will
you be me?

*(Bethany and Anna, another trainee, agree. They move
into the center of the room and stand. Berenice has them
face each other.)*

**Les:** Now, show Edgar where you want him in this
scene.

*(Berenice moves Edgar behind Anna and shows him how
to stand.)*

**Berenice:** Edgar, are you willing to be here through all
of this?

*(Edgar nods, yes. Berenice moves her stand-in, Anna, out
and moves herself in, with Edgar's hand on her shoulder.)*

**Berenice:** Mom, you've done a whole lot for me. You've
taken care of me when I was hurt. I really love you for
that. You have also interfered and tried to make a lot of

decisions in my life that weren't yours to make. You thought you could make decisions like who I should be married to, whether I should work, who my friends should be, and, even who my son should be married to.

*(Her voice suddenly becomes high-pitched.)*

I'm tired of hearing your opinion on my decisions.

**Les:** You seem to be having trouble holding onto things. Is there anything different you want from Edgar?

*(She turns to Edgar and puts both his hands on her shoulders, then turns back to Bethany, as her mother.)*

**Berenice:** I don't want to hear anymore about how great it is that Edgar has left. It's not the best thing that ever happened to me, no matter what you think.

I don't want to hear any more crap from you about Margaret Ann. Margaret Ann's a good woman. I don't know where you get your information, and I don't want to hear it.

I don't want to hear you put Gerry down. Gerry is working hard to change his life. What I'm saying is, I want you out of my life. All of us are grown up now. We don't need to be mothered anymore.

I'm not going to listen to you anymore. Anytime you call and give me that crap, I'm going to say goodbye and hang up. If I'm at your house and you start, I'm going to say goodbye and leave.

**Les:** That's really clear and straight. Now, also, look at the other side of things. Are there ways you can be with your mother?

**Berenice:** Of course, there's another side.

*(To Bethany, as her mother:)* I like you when you're fun. I like you when you're loving and caring. I don't like you when you're bitching.

**Les:** Turn to Edgar and let him know if there is anything else you'd like?

*(Berenice turns. Edgar gives her a hug.)*

**Berenice:** Thank you.

*(She leans into his hug and cries a little.)* It wasn't as bad as I thought it would be.

*(The group applauds.)*

**Edgar:** I want to tell you, Berenice, that I care very much for you, and I will help.

**Berenice** *(after a few quiet moments)*: Twice before I've been straight with my mother. The first time, she got terrible back trouble. When I made up with her, she recovered. The second time, she had a little heart attack. She got better when I came back.

**Les:** That is terrifying. It's amazing how powerful she makes you. She puts her life in your hands.

**Berenice:** I can't really give her a heart attack. I can't even give her back trouble. *(She laughs.)*

**Ruth:** Margaret Ann?

**Margaret Ann:** This has been good for me. I'm angry at Gertrude, too. I've been asking Gerry to express my anger. I'm not going to do that anymore.

*(Applause comes from the group. The morning session ends.)*

# THURSDAY AFTERNOON
# FAMILY GROUP—LES SPEAKING

*All the families begin together. After the Quinns have finished, Berenice speaks.*

**Berenice:** My kids and my grandchild have fulfilled my emotional needs. I've been a lot like Paula in that way.

A big part of my problem has been dependency and not thinking. I've changed the thinking part, and I'm going to let others help me.

I think there is still something I need to complete. If my kids are going to get away from me, they're going to have to see, and really know, that I can take care of myself.

**Ruth:** Good thinking. Remember back to the time before you met Edgar, to when you were a child. Who took care of you then?

**Berenice:** When I was little, I was taken care of by different people in the family: my mother, my aunt, and uncle—but never consistently by one person.

**Les:** It didn't matter who it was, as long as it was someone who was part of the family.

**Berenice** *(grimacing)*: That's the way it is with Little Gerry. I take care of him.

**Ruth:** I hear your voice and I see what your doing with your mouth. How old do you feel now, with that twisted kind of smile on your face?

*Berenice looks like a little kid. Asking her how old she feels can help catch her regression and use it therapeutically.*

**Berenice:** I feel three.

**Ruth:** Stay there. Be three, Little Gerry's age. There are lots of things going on. It isn't all right for you to get your needs met by anyone outside the family.

Be three for the rest of the session. Let yourself operate in the group, making contact with whomever you want. Focus on people who are not in your family.

**Berenice:** The first thing I want to do is run over and play with Little Gerry. I see this family thing.

*(Berenice begins to play with Dom Dellapietra, then Marco and Maria. In Dom she has made a good choice. He is a person who easily slips into child behavior. They begin to play in the corner. Dom quickly returns to the group and the "children" remain.)*

*Berenice kept herself three years old throughout this part of the session. When Ruth had angry encounters with two other workshop participants, Berenice sat by one of the trainees and let herself be comforted. When the angry encounter was over, she began again to play with stuffed animals. It's the end of this part of the afternoon. I check back in with Berenice.*

**Les:** Berenice, stay three for a moment more. What were you scared of?

**Berenice:** I was scared when people were fighting. When the Mommy and Daddy were fighting *(Angela and Dom Dellapietra)*, I was scared they would get hurt and both the Mommy and the Daddy would go to the hospital and the Daddy would never come back.

When the Mommy and the little girl were fighting *(Ruth and Bette Sarnon)*, and somebody called the Mommy nasty names, I was afraid the Mommy would go away.

I'm always afraid when people fight. I'm always afraid they'll go away or get hurt.

**Ruth:** Often, when people fight, they don't get hurt and they don't go away. It's okay to fight. Sometimes it's very good to fight. There are ways to fight so people don't get hurt.

*(Ruth stands up and turns around.)* I'm still alive. I'm still here. I can even sit on my own backside. *(Ruth sits on the floor. Berenice laughs.)*

Check with someone else who was fighting.

**Berenice** *(to Dom)*: How about you?

**Dom:** I'm more here than ever.

**Les:** Okay, Berenice, now you can make yourself big again. How did you see what went on?

*(Berenice puts down her stuffed bear, gets up off the floor, straightens herself, and sits on the chair.)*

**Berenice:** It all ties in with my mother. I'm afraid, if I talk back to her, she'll go away. That doesn't matter a lot now—to me as a grown woman, I mean. If my mother goes away, she goes away. I don't need her anymore.

My Dad beat my mother and put her in the hospital. My mother beat my father, too, and put him in the hospital.

In the past, I've had to be in control, one up on everybody. If anybody got beat up, it was going to be somebody else, not me.

**Les:** Are you certain that you won't hurt or kill yourself or anyone else?

**Berenice:** I am.

**Ruth:** Will you tell Edgar you won't hurt or kill yourself or him?

*(She does this with clarity and meaning.)*

**Berenice:** I know I can get support, and some fun, with people outside my family.

I know that I can really do the things I need to do with my mother. This was the unfinished piece: the terror and the anger.

**Les:** I admire your courage in looking at all these things.

**Berenice** *(turning)*: The last thing I want to say this afternoon is to you, Melissa. I will do what I need to do when we get home. I am glad you will watch to see.

# FRIDAY MORNING

# INDIVIDUAL FAMILIES—WITH RUTH

*The families are divided for this last morning. I've announced that this is the last day in which to finish work.*

*My plan (which was discussed in the training meeting)
is to work with Melissa and help her present, to the rest of
her family, the issues she brought up with Les in the young
people's group. We are particularly interested in those things
having to do with her hurting herself or someone else.
Unfortunately, as a result of the group division, Les, who
has done most of the work with Melissa, cannot be here.
The trainees, especially Bethany, will help me.*

**Ruth:** Melissa, are your ready to go ahead?

**Melissa:** Yes. Can you help me? I want to talk about
Rusty's death.

*(The Barkers are all sitting in the middle of the large
meeting room. I sit down on the floor beside Melissa and
put my hand across her back.)*

**Ruth:** Begin where you want. I'll come in and help
when I see a place.

**Melissa** *(in an angry, hurt voice)*: Mom, you sent me off
to camp. You have a way of making people make the
choices you want them to make. I felt pressured to go off to
camp. You pushed me away from the family.

**Berenice:** It was a decision both your father and I
made, to give you a choice. What do you mean, pressure?

**Melissa** *(loud and crying)*: You said Rusty would have
wanted me to remember him in a different way. He
wouldn't have wanted me there. My grandmother told me
to go. And she told me I shouldn't cry, that tears weren't
allowed. Then, when I came back from camp, it was as if
there was never a death. I never had a brother.

**Ruth:** Before, you seemed to want some information
about the death.

**Melissa:** I don't even know if he had an accident or
killed himself or was run off the road.

**Berenice:** I think he purposely ran himself off the road.

**Ruth:** Edgar?

**Edgar** *(looking glazed, shaking his head no)*: He just
went over. He just went over.

**Ruth:** Gerry?

**Gerry:** I guess. I never really accepted that it was an
accident. I think there was a lot more to the story.

**Edgar:** There were some things I never checked out.
There were a lot of things I didn't want to know. There
was a witness—he's never said anything, and we never
asked him.

**Berenice:** Rusty had a death wish. He had had so many accidents. But I think he had begun to change just before he died.

**Ruth:** Melissa, you've heard a lot of opinions. What is yours?

**Melissa:** I think it was an accident.

**Berenice:** Melissa was given the choice of staying or going to Girl Scout camp. She chose to go. After it was over, I knew we had made a big mistake. Melissa should have been there. And afterwards, we should have talked about it.

**Edgar:** I chose to have Melissa go away. I didn't want to have to bear her grief, too. I was having enough problems managing myself. I was wrong.

**Ruth:** What do you feel when you hear your parents?

**Melissa:** I think they're ready to let me feel something about Rusty's death. They're saying it wasn't right for me to go away. I don't think Mom gave me a choice or gave Dad a choice.

**Ruth:** It sounds like there are still many things with your mom.

**Edgar:** I was too close. Every time Rusty got hurt, I got hurt. Every time Rusty was joyful, I was joyful.

*(Looking at Melissa)* It's time we all knew where we are with this. I don't know of anything Rusty thought he couldn't do. He, too, thought he was invincible. He thought he could carry the world on his shoulders, like Gerry.

I know that no one is invincible. Melissa, I don't want you ever to try to prove that you are invincible. I want you also to know that I'm not invincible.

*Edgar has hit on the basic issue on his own. He addresses Melissa, the last in the line. She is the next problem.*

**Berenice** *(looking, with warmth, toward Edgar)*: Rusty was sunshine and joy and pain and sorrow. I've been through a lot of thinking about the loss of my son.

**Gerry:** It's hard for me. Rusty died at a time when he was out of prison and getting his life straight. Somehow it wouldn't have been so hard to take if he had been killed in prison.

Just before it happened, we had a fantastic evening. It

was the first time we had been together in a long time. Rusty and I decided we should go into business together.

**Melissa:** I'm surprised to find out any of you had any thoughts or sadness. I thought nobody cared at all.

**Ruth:** What about you, Melissa?

**Melissa:** It is important for me to hear that the others in my family cared about my brother. I didn't think they did.

*(The atmosphere is subdued. The Barkers are sharing with each other their feelings about Rusty, without being overly dramatic. Most people in the room are tearful. All are quiet.)*

**Bethany:** I've also heard you say, Melissa, that you didn't believe that people in your family cared about you. What do you think now?

**Melissa:** I don't know.

**Ruth:** There's something else we need to clear up that fits in here. The idea that you, Melissa, are not invincible. You are human. You need to take care of yourself. Never do anything to hurt or kill yourself, or anyone else.

**Edgar:** Yes, it's not all right to hurt yourself.

**Melissa:** I won't take chances to prove I'm invincible. I know now I'm not. When I saw Gerry yesterday—that could have been me. That's probably the most important thing that I've learned here.

*Her eyes are filled with tears. She has been sealed off from showing emotion for most of the week.*

I remember when I went to visit Rusty, he would let me ride around on his shoulders and he'd give me a candy bar.

I miss him. I never got to know my older brother.

**Ruth** *(after a long pause)*: Is there anything more you need or want to say.

**Melissa:** I'm still mad at Mom, because I wasn't there at the funeral.

*The most important thing to Melissa, right now, is to stay distant from her mother. She needs to prove she is different from Berenice. To do this, she identifies with her father and holds herself back in the same way he does. I suspect she harbors a wish to kill her mother, just like Edgar did with his father.*

**Berenice:** Melissa, I'm going to go on and do what I need to do, even though you stay mad at me.

**Ruth** *(to Bethany)*: For me, there are still two very important things. They have to do with killing and being hurt.

**Bethany:** I agree.

**Berenice** *(looking ready and available to go ahead)*: I can go on.

Melissa, I won't ever again hit you. I was wrong to do that. If you are angry with me and acting out, I will have to find some different way of handling it. I will not hurt you.

*(Melissa says nothing. She turns away from her mother, puts her head down, and covers it with her arms.)*

**Ruth:** Melissa, look up for a moment. Look at your mother.

*(Melissa moves around and looks up.)*

Tell your mother that you will not hurt or kill yourself, her, or anyone else, no matter how angry and upset you are.

**Melissa** *(with hesitation)*: Even when I'm angry, or anything else, I won't kill or hurt you or me.

**Ruth:** Say it again. Also tell your father that you won't hurt or kill yourself or your mother.

**Melissa** *(with more animation)*: Mom and Dad, I won't hurt or kill myself or you mom, for anything.

**Ruth:** Is that true?

**Melissa:** Yes.

*(The atmosphere in the room lightens up. There are smiles and some chatter. Berenice is looking softly at her daughter. Tears tumble down her face. Melissa gets involved with Little Gerry.*

*(Dom, Angela, and Maria have been particularly attentive to this work.*

*(It is later on in the morning. Margaret Ann begins:)*

**Margaret Ann:** We belong to a therapeutic community. This is something I need to talk about. I just don't know about it.

**Edgar:** I feel closer to you—but not locked in together—being in the community.

**Ruth:** Margaret Ann, you sound uncertain about whether you want to stay in the community. I think you, Gerry, and you, Margaret Ann, need to talk about what you need to do to keep yourselves separate. Will you figure that out and report this afternoon?

*(Gerry and Margaret Ann agree.)*

**Margaret Ann:** Gerry is therapist to his mother and father in that community. I don't see how that can ever contribute to our being separate.

**Ruth:** Talk to Gerry about what you need for yourselves and begin there this afternoon.

*(This is the end of Friday morning's session.)*

"I believe that this is the best birthday that David has ever had. He has gotten his life today."

—Robin Quinn

# 3

# The Quinns

*Robin Quinn arrived at Tahoe two days ahead of schedule. He had been out camping and claimed that he didn't know when the workshop was to begin. We arranged for him to bunk in the staff house for those beginning days. When we first met Robin, he moved and spoke deliberately and he didn't stop worrying about when his family would arrive. On their arrival day he put himself "on duty." Perched on the hood of a car in the parking lot, he began waiting many hours before he had to. Every few minutes, he would go inside and call the bus station to find out if the bus was on time. Finally, Robin decided to go to the station. There, he found his mother and brother looking for a taxi. They had taken an earlier bus and had already spent some time wandering around town.*

*When the taxi arrived at the condominiums, Paula stepped out looking very neat and proper. David popped out with a baseball hat on his head and a fishing pole in his hand. The first thing he said was, "I'm really glad you invited me here to go fishing." He acted as if he had no idea why he was present.*

*One of the advantages of the intensive multiple-family format is that we are able to observe people as they are in their daily lives rather than just as they are in our weekly, office sessions. Robin's early arrival, his anxious state, and his progressive agitation,*

*as he awaited his mother and brother's arrival, told us
a great deal about his strong attachment to his family.
Robin, although anxious, seemed ready to get down to
work, whereas David seemed to be here for fishing. We
wondered whether Paula had told David they were here
for therapy. Later, we learned that Paula had told him
that this was to be a vacation.*

# MONDAY MORNING
# FAMILY GROUP—LES SPEAKING

*The families are jostling around for who will work next.*

**Paula** *(cutting things off by standing up and saying
brusquely):* We'll go. We've got to go sometime anyway.

*(Paula, Robin, and David arrange themselves so that
they are sitting tightly together on the mats, in the center of
the room. Both Ruth and I move in with them.)*

**Les:** Continue to talk among yourselves about what you
would like to have different in your family when you leave
here at the end of the week.

**David** *(popping up, without hesitation):* I'd like to see
Robin listen more. Robin plays games, and I'm really angry
about that.

**Ruth:** David, tell Robin that directly.

**David** *(crisp and direct):* Robin, you never listen. And
besides that, you pretend that you get real serious, and yet,
you think it's real funny. That makes me think you're
making fun of me, and I don't like it.

**Robin** *(in a stilted, almost automatic way and shaking
his head from side to side, sending out a "no"):* I would like
to be more straightforward, and I'm working on it. When I
was young, I too wanted to be heard and noticed—I never
had a chance to come out and express myself.

*(Robin's breath is short, his movements are jerky, his
voice is intense. As he speaks, he turns and looks at his
mother. Paula looks back with a wide, adoring smile, but
her eyes have a piercing expression. The upper and lower
halves of her face don't match.)*

**Robin** *(continuing):* I spent a lot of time in my own
room.

*Robin's anxiety seemed to increase when his mother looked at him. His breath got shorter and he could barely talk. Ruth mentioned later, "If I were Robin, I'd be anxious. Paula's smile says, "Go on in whatever you're doing," but her eyes send out a glaring "Stop!"*

**Les:** Robin, you seem anxious. Will you share with your family what is happening with you?

**Robin** *(beginning to cry)*: If I stop and calm down, I think I'll be all right.

*(David and Paula are looking at Robin.)*

**Les** *(in a nuturing tone)*: Okay, then, stop and be with yourself for a moment.

*(Paula puts out a hand to Robin.)*

**Les (after a few moments):** Robin, will you continue?

**Robin** *(breathless)*: Not yet.

**Les:** I like your taking care of yourself.

**Ruth:** Paula, as Robin is getting ready, I'm interested in what you want to get out of being here?

**Paula** *(beginning to cry)*: I'm really glad that we're here. I see Robin as very different. I have missed him.

*(The minute that Paula moves to tears, Robin puts his head down and cries.)*

**Ruth** *(to Paula)*: Tell Robin and David what you mean.

**Paula** *(to Robin)*: I'm happy that you have taken the risk of being out on your own, traveling alone here. I think I couldn't have done that when I was your age. *(Turning to Ruth and Les:)* I pick up on Robin's hurt. I'm still carrying a lot of hurt with me. Robin did get intimidated by his older brother. When I was there, I tried to protect him.

**Les** *(having received a yes nod from Ruth)*: That information is important, and, the question is—What would you like to see different with the members of your family who are here now?

*(Paula then talks vaguely about leaving the workshop on Saturday, but she never says what she wants out of it. Even when we push her to be more clear, we get back only disjointed and incomplete thoughts.)*

**Ruth:** It sounds like your general goal for the time here, Paula, is for the three of you to get along better.

*Ruth states this general goal as a way of cutting off the unfocused talk. She then speaks to David, who has been excluded.*

**Ruth:** David, you want Robin to listen to you more and to take you seriously. Is there anything else that you want?

**David:** I want my mother to stop smoking, and I want to be able catch fish.

*David is wonderfully specific versus Robin and Paula, who are bonded together by overflowing emotion and unrelated thinking. David keeps himself separate by being very concrete.*

**Les:** David, I like your being specific and clear.

**David:** I also want to stop arguing with my mother. We argue a lot about what to watch on television.

**Paula:** I want more time for myself—I don't want to be interrupted every five minutes by David calling, "Mom, Mom!"

*I notice that when Paula is talking to David or about him, she becomes much clearer and more separate than when she talks to Robin.*

**David:** Okay to that.

*(There is a big smile on Robin's face as he watches his mother and brother, but again, when Paula looks at him, Robin turns sad.)*

**Les:** Robin, as soon as you catch your mother's eye, you look like you get anxious and sad. What is happening with you now?

**Paula:** I take a lot of responsibility for Robin's hurt. It has been hard for me to see Robin go through so many things. I hope that what Robin gets out of this workshop is that he feels comfortable with himself.

**Les:** Paula, what you want is important, and it was to Robin that I addressed the question. You need to let him answer for himself.

**Robin** *(volunteering)*: I want my mother to stop feeling sorry for me. I know I get keyed up, and I would like to learn to control some of that stuff.

**Ruth:** Robin, you sound clear now. That's neat. I like your idea about getting less keyed up and learning to control yourself.

**David** *(after a short pause in the conversation)*: My mother tells me to eat my meat, and Robin tells me not to. My mother tells me to be quiet and stay inside, and Robin tells me to go out and play basketball. They end up fighting with each other all the time.

**Les:** What is that like for you, David, when Robin and your mother seem to compete with each other?

**David:** It's like I have two parents instead of one, and they're each trying to be better than the other.

*(After David's remark, Robin begins to ramble in another direction. Paula, in turn, responds to Robin and goes off on her own tangent.)*

**Les** *(to Ruth)*: What is most apparent to me in this family is the number of incompletions. There have been many times, now, that David has been talking about one thing and then Paula or Robin bounce onto something else.

*(David looks relieved.)*

**Ruth:** Yes, and in they're bouncing around it seems that everything gets focused on Robin.

**Paula** *(quizzically)*: Yes?

**Ruth:** Robin, back away from your family. Move to the circle with the others.

*(Robin gets up and moves back into the main circle, leaving Paula and David sitting on two cushions, looking at each other.)*

> *Changes in the physical dimension symbolize and facilitate changes in the relationship.*

**Ruth** *(to Les)*: Perhaps, a good contract for this family would be to decide to finish things, rather than bouncing around. If they worked at completing thoughts and plans, David might be included in a way appropriate to his age, and Robin would be less anxious and could more easily give himself a clear direction. Paula would get the rest she said she wanted. I wonder what would go on if things were not centered on Robin?

**Les:** That is where I am, too.

**Paula:** I'm glad you asked Robin to move, Ruth, because essentially there are two families here.

**Ruth:** I agree. *(To Paula:)* Right now, what do you think about the family you have with David?

**Paula:** I am concerned about David because of his difficulty in school. This was one of my main purposes in coming here. Of all the numerous tests David has had, I am most happy with the recent testing. A psychologist advised me to step out of the role of being David's reading teacher.

*(To David:)* I feel that you lean on me. And that's heavy for me. You expect me to do everything, even many of the things that you can do yourself.

*Again, we notice how much clearer Paula is with her younger son than she is with her older son. She also seems to be very angry with David.*

**David** *(sitting impassively, grunts)*: Okay.
**Les:** David, will you say what some of your troubles in school are?

*Keeping in mind the absence of a father in this family, we decided that I should have the most contact with David. From now on, most of the work with David will be done by me.*

**David** *(breaking into tears, and covering his face)*: I don't know how to say it. I don't know how to say it.
**Les** *(gently)*: Say what you are thinking right now.
**David** *(through his tears)*: Last year at school, the kids used to bug me about my reading problems. Then I'd get mad, and then I'd just beat them up. *(Turning his head:)* I didn't like to do it, but, that was the only way I could tell them to stop it.
**Les:** Those reading problems have been really hard for you.
*(David nods yes.)*
**Les:** Your Mom says you really are capable of reading.
**David:** Yes, but it's not easy.
**Les:** I know that it's not easy, but what I mean is, there's nothing wrong with you, right?
**David** *(crying and breathless)*: I don't think so, but I don't know. It's just that I have to go all these places, and I have to have testing all the time, and I just wish I wasn't that way. I just wish I could be like everybody else.

*While David is talking, Paula's eyes are brimming. Robin has tears rolling down his face, but he is surprisingly quiet. Physically moving him away seems to have helped.*

**Les:** What has to happen so you can be like everyone else?

**David:** Read and practice.

**Les:** Maybe one of the most important things for you to figure out this week, then, is why you don't practice. Then decide to go home and do it differently.

**David:** Yes.

**Les:** I think so, too.

*We have helped David frame a contract not just to want to get better but also to figure out why he hasn't done the work necessary to getting better. The testing reports we looked at showed that David's specific learning disability did not account for all of his difficulty; his anxiety plays an important role.*

*(After outlining his goal, David is quiet for a long time, still crying. Paula sits with her hands pressed together, holding up her chin.)*

**Les** *(moving over to David and touching his shoulder)*: I like your willingness to share and be open with us.

**David:** I just want people to like me and not to make fun of me. And, for me, I'd like to learn to read. Also, I just wish I would know about it when my mother calls these places.

*(His voice becomes high-pitched and he turns to Paula.)*

I wish you'd tell me in the morning because then I'd be ready. I want to be told what's going on. I listen good. I don't like to be surprised by things like going to be tested for reading.

**Les** *(still with a hand on David's back)*: What goes on inside you, David, when your Mom tells you just a few minutes before you're going someplace?

**David:** I get real mad.

**Les:** What do you say to yourself when you get real mad?

**David:** Why does it have to be me?

**Les:** Do you also say to yourself that your Mom is treating you like a baby?

**David** *(in a very loud voice)*: Yes! That's true!

**Les:** Do you get mad about that too?

**David:** I get very mad. Like I want to play Little League next year and she doesn't want me to. She lets me do some things, but she just doesn't let me live my own life, like a kid like me should do it.

**Les:** What I'm hearing is that it's important for you that your Mom treat you like you're more grown up.

**David:** She thinks that in Little League they're going to throw the ball too hard, and it's going to hit me.

**Paula** *(defensively)*: From what the other mothers say, if David moves up into that next level, he won't get to play very much, because he's not old enough or big enough. This year he has gotten to play every game.

> *Paula has a perfectly logical reason for not permitting David to advance, but she discounts David's needs and his expression of what he wants.*

**Ruth** *(to Paula)*: I understand your real caring for both your children. I also see you get stuck acting as if you know more about the kids, and what's going on inside of them, than they do.

**Paula:** Yes.

**Ruth:** It seems to me that by the end of the week, if the kids know more about what's going on inside of themselves than you do, Paula, you will have accomplished a very good contract.

**Paula** *(turning to Ruth, with a huge smile)*: Yes.

*(David meanwhile has stopped crying.)*

**Les** *(to the whole family)*: This is a good place to stop. Robin, I like how you were able to keep yourself calm after you physically moved away.

> *Finally, we have a defined a contract that considers the entire family, and reflects our evaluation of their overinvolvement with each other.*

> *(As the Quinn family moves out of the center of the group, Bette Sarnon talks to David, with tears in her eyes.)*

**Bette:** I really understand, David. I'm a reading teacher. If I can help you while we're here, I'd like to.

**Melissa Barker:** David, I have trouble in school, too.

**Berenice Barker** *(patting Paula on the arm)*: I know how hard it is when you've got a child in trouble.

# MONDAY AFTERNOON

# INDIVIDUAL FAMILIES—WITH RUTH

*I am working with the Quinns, the Sarnon family, and one half of the Barkers: Berenice, Edgar, and Melissa. Les is with the Dellapietras and the other half of the Barker family.*

*Gathered in the small condominium for, the afternoon session we begin with the focus on Robin, who has remained anxious. To get a concrete idea of his view of the family, I suggest that he make a living sculpture of his family. I asked him to choose people in the room to represent himself, his mother, David, his father, and his brother, and then to set them up into a living picture, representing how he sees their relationships to each other.*

*Before I suggested the sculpture, Robin had been repeating, "I don't know what I want to do" and wringing his hands. The sculpture helps Robin contain his anxiety and focus his thinking.*

**Ruth:** Robin, this is to be your view of things, as they actually are now. Show us: Who is looking at whom; who is pointing at whom; who is standing next to whom.

*(Robin starts, very tentatively, to set this up by choosing Bill Sarnon to play his father. Both Paula and David attempt to tell him how to do it. They keep giving suggestions about who should be where.)*

**Paula** *(beginning to get up)*: No, it shouldn't be that way, Robin, it should be this way.

*I had made several comments as to how difficult it seemed to be for Robin to think on his own. I directly asked Paula and David to let Robin make decisions for himself. Despite this, they continued, and Robin continued to allow his family to criticize him and direct him. Finally, I decided to take a firmer approach.*

**Ruth:** Paula and David, stop talking and interfering. Robin, continue with your own ideas and thinking.

*At this point Paula and David reluctantly retreat and Robin shows that he actually does need some reminding. At times his anxiety is so high that he doesn't even remember who is in his family.*

*In the sculpture, Robin's father stands in the center. His brother Drake stands beside his father, but off to the side. "Robin," played by Nicholas, is standing directly in front of the father. Paula is at the father's side. David is a little bit behind Paula.*

*The sculpture that Robin sets up does not reflect reality. He seems to have placed people according to what he wishes were true.*

**Ruth:** Robin, now step back a minute and look. Is it as you know things really are now?

*(As Robin steps back, I move over to stand behind him, and supportively, put a hand on his back. He looks at the sculpture for a long time.)*

**Robin:** I want my mother to be in a different position. My mother should put herself where she feels comfortable.

*(Robin hesitates to act directly to change the sculpture. He seems to know something is wrong and is unwilling to change it or complete it for himself.)*

**Ruth:** Robin, this is your sculpture. These are your ideas. You need to put your mother, and anyone else, where you think they belong, and, where you want them.

**Robin** *(looking at Ruth, in a frightened way, and speaking in his loud tense voice)*: Okay, I'll do it.

*(Robin steps in to move his mother. Paula is playing herself in the sculpture and David pipes up to tell Robin where she ought to go.)*

**Robin** *(whirling to face David, his half-brother)*: You stay out!

**Ruth:** I like your drawing the boundary, Robin. This is an important beginning for you.

*(Robin now sets his father and brother on one side of the room, his mother and David on the other side of the room, and himself in the middle, going back and forth. He is agitated, hyperventilating, and looks flushed. His body looks tense.)*

**Ruth:** Robin, I can understand how you get anxious and have difficulty keeping your thoughts organized. It's hard to move back and forth all the time and never have your own place. Its like wringing your hands over and over. There is no resting spot.

*A defining statement like this serves an organizing function and usually results in a reduction of anxiety.*

**Robin** *(stopping and calming down)*: I'm finished. It's hard for me to do it. I probably haven't done it right.

**Ruth:** Okay. Now stand back from the sculpture. Look from a distance at the position you put yourself in. You had to move back and forth all the time. It's just like in here, when you take a step forward to complete something you quickly pull back and make your effort not okay.

*(Robin stands back, his eyes are shifting from one half-family grouping to the other, tracing the way he had been moving.)*

**Robin:** I didn't mean to set things up that way.

**Ruth:** But, you did, and it was your sculpture. It's all right the way you did it. It's all right to share what goes on inside you, even if it's not always organized in the way you might want it in the end.

**Ruth** *(switching gears)*: Paula, when did Robin become the family protector?

**Robin** *(with an anxious look, and in a very loud voice)*: Where did you come up with that?

**Ruth:** That's my guess from watching you be so hesitant and careful. Also, I watch you get real anxious each time there is even a hint of confrontation, especially from one of your family members. I think your anxiety diverts the issues and could be protective of others.

**Robin:** I don't know.

**Paula** *(in a slow and careful voice)*: Robin became the protector when he came to live with David and me and after David's father died.

**Ruth:** How come he came to live with you then, and what happened?

**Paula:** In a sense Robin was forced to come and live with me. I've always felt bad about that. When he turned 11, his father came downstairs one morning and said, "I've had enough of this rat race. I'm quitting and going off to live by myself. You will be going to live with your mother." Two weeks later, he arrived. I have always questioned Robin's feelings about this.

**Ruth:** As I hear you questioning Robin's feelings, I remember that Robin does this to himself also.

**Paula** *(after a long silence, with her characteristic stark, blank, frightening look)*: Yes, I understand it. You mean I question his feelings too.

*I am focusing on the separation that is needed, and confronting Paula's role in inhibiting that separation.*

**Ruth** *(to David)*: What are you thinking and feeling?

**David:** I don't know. I wish the family could be back together.

**Ruth:** What do you mean?

**David:** What I mean is that Robin's Dad would live with my mom, and me, and Robin.

*Neither Robin nor David has dealt effectively with loss. Neither of them has let go of their fantasy of what their family is, or of their idealization of their fathers. In contrast, I am aware that Paula has made such a stark separation from her family of origin that she neither remembered nor cared to remember much about anyone. She left most of her questionnaire blank, stating "I don't know and I don't care to know this information."*

**Ruth:** Paula, it is really hard for your children to deal with the reality of their fathers and their family.

**Paula:** It seems to be that way.

*(She turns and speaks definitively to David and Robin.)*

I'm not going to slip into a fantasy world just to be with you. There is no way, Robin and David, that these two families will be back together.

**Ruth:** Paula, I hear you making a clear statement and taking a clear position. It will be important for you to continue in this way.

**Paula:** Yes.

**Ruth** *(to Robin)*: Nice work this afternoon.

*Later in the afternoon, after the Sarnons had worked, Paula looks removed and iron-mouthed. I wonder if she is listening or if she is off in her own world.*

**Ruth:** What's going on with you right now, Paula?

**Paula** *(in an angry tone, her mouth moves like a marionette's)*: I don't know what is going on right now.

**Ruth:** You sound angry and I wonder if you are.

**Paula:** No, I'm not angry. I'm really just confused. I know that I have difficulty with my anger, and difficulty in expressing myself, but I don't think that's it right now.

**Ruth:** If you were angry or confused, would you be willing to say it?

**Paula:** Yes, maybe I would. Ruth, I think you're getting Robin confused.

*(Her face softens, her jaw is less tense, and she switches topics.)*

Right now, I'm wondering why we have come here. I am uncomfortable at this point, because I haven't yet established a real goal for myself. I really need to have a goal and a direction. What I'm concerned about, and what I want to find out about, is whether I'm doing anything to block David's or Robin's growth. I'm aware of some things I do that hurt them, and I want to know more.

**Ruth:** I have an idea about how you might proceed. Are you available for feedback from your children and other people in the workshop, regarding things they see you doing or not doing?

**Paula:** Yes, I would like that. I would like people to help me learn what it is I'm doing that might be putting Robin or David down, or interfering with them.

*(Turning to Robin and David:)* Will you tell me if I am putting you down or interfering with you?

*(Robin and David each nod their heads, yes.)*

**Ruth:** Paula, I think that is neat. You gave them permission to express themselves and to offer feedback directly to you.

Still, I don't understand if you are angry. You quickly moved away from that. It's me who is confused now.

**Paula:** I think I'm picking up anxiety or something from Robin.

**Ruth:** Paula, turn to Robin and tell him what you mean.

**Paula:** Robin, you talked with me earlier, at the break, about some things that were happening. I'm confused about what is actually going on.

**Robin** *(contritely)*: Yes, Mom. I did tell you some things earlier. I don't know why I'm here. I don't need to be here.

**Ruth:** Go on, Paula.

**Paula:** Robin, tell more.

**Robin** *(heated voice)*: Ruth keeps pushing me to talk.

**Ruth:** Robin, I get the sense that you are either very scared, or that you are the one who is angry.

**Paula:** I know that he is. Robin told me about how he hates you, Ruth, and how he hates being here. That's what he told me.

*During the break Robin complained to Paula about me. The complaint that I was pushing him to talk seems that he reacts to me just like he reacts to his mother. That complaint activated Paula, who then confused things by acting angry herself rather than letting Robin take care of himself. In this way, she repeated the family's pattern of mixing up issues whenever an attempt at clarification occurs.*

**Robin:** Yes. Yes.

**Ruth** *(to Paula)*: I'm concerned that you might be expressing Robin's feelings. Also, I think that you and I need to be careful to make sure Robin is not setting us up to fight. Robin could do this instead of dealing with his own fear or anger with either one of us. Robin probably has a lot of anger with you, plus he might have some anger with me.

*I am calling Paula in as an ally, by pointing out that one of the ways that she might get stuck is letting Robin use her as a shield. As my ally, Paula will not react to Robin's fear or anger so quickly, which in turn, will give Robin a chance to simmer down. It will also change their patterns significantly.*

**Paula:** I see.

**Ruth:** Robin, I think you need to be straight with me, and straight with your mother. If you're angry at me, you can tell me, and I'll solve the problems with you. If you are angry at your mother, I believe, she, too, would like to hear directly from you.

*This confrontation is meant to further define the boundaries and help separate people. Robin has tried to enmesh me in his circle of anger. I need to keep people separate, and issues clearly defined. If Robin is angry at me, that's all right, but it's not all right for Paula to be the one who expresses Robin's anger. I am getting clearer that Robins gets angry when anyone attempts to get too close to him. When the anger fails to keep people away, he gets anxious and symptomatic. Our approach will be to help him define his own boundaries.*

**Paula** *(with a laugh)*: I see how I might get caught being angry for Robin. I'm going to stick to my goal for myself.
*(To Robin:)* I'm going to stick to my goal and not get stuck in your thing.
**Robin** *(in an uncharacteristically calm voice)*: Me too, I'll stick to mine.
**Paula:** David, sometimes it is like you're putting all the heavies over onto me and to Robin. I want you to know the same thing. I'm going to deal with my things and I expect you to deal with your things.
*(There is movement in the room. Many people speak up to support Paula's decisiveness.)*
**Margaret Ann:** I'm glad you did that. You have some life in your voice, and some life in your cheeks. You look rosy and lighter.
**Ruth:** Paula, I, too, like your taking responsibility for yourself, and for feeling safe enough to bring things out.

*Meanwhile, David walks across the room and picks up one of the encounter bats. Looking at the floor he sits down and starts tapping one on the floor. I decide to note this to myself and not to comment out loud.*

# TUESDAY MORNING

# PARENTS' GROUP—WITH RUTH

*Paula has remained quiet all morning except for a few comments on the work others are doing. Paula, a recovered alcoholic, is excellent at confronting Dom's alcoholic style. Her comments are pertinent and well-put, and yet she pulls back as if she has said something wrong. When I urge her on, her expression softens, and she sits less rigidly.*
*It is now near the end of the three-hour morning session.*

**Ruth:** Is there anything you want to do for yourself this morning, Paula?

**Paula:** No, I feel good when I'm away from my children. I like myself when I'm here. This, I guess, is what you have been saying.

**Ruth:** Okay.

# YOUNG PEOPLE'S GROUP—WITH LES

*The session starts with David and Nicholas playing checkers as Maria watches. Melissa and Robin are sitting on the floor and playing cards.*

*Robin begins by making some seemingly inappropriate comments to Melissa about dinner the night before. "Why sure, Melissa," Robin says tauntingly, "We must have dinner again soon." I guess that the comment has to do with the challenge presented by Melissa who, even though she is many years younger than Robin, is attractive and seductive.*

*Robin is frightened by Melissa. He seems tense and switches topics. In a placating tone he says, "I have come here for my own good. I have to stop arranging my family." A little later, Robin goes on in a frightened voice, "My next step is to change me and not my family."*

*After several questions from me that attempt to ground Robin and find out about his agitation, or his taunting comment to Melissa, Robin finally bursts out with an angry explanation.*

**Robin:** My brother pushed me around and pushed me around, and then I left. He would get me to a point where I would yell and push and kick back. My father didn't do anything.

*I pick up on Robin's anger about having no one on his side.*

**Les:** Are you feeling like you are getting kicked here and that no one is doing anything?

**Robin:** No, I'm not feeling kicked.

**Les:** Will you say more about your brother and your father not helping? I'm interested in that.

**Robin:** I will not.

**Les:** Robin, do you need anything different, from me? You are really pushing me away. Also, I know that yesterday you were angry at Ruth.

**Robin:** I don't want to talk about it.

*Robin cut things off again. The group members are looking frightened. Robin's level of anxiety is frightening them, and I haven't been able to touch him. Sensing the need for more structure and safety in the group, I decide to have each person do a family drawing even though this move does not address Robin's anxiety. I will get back to Robin later.*

*(Robin draws a picture that portrays a divided family, as his sculpture had the day before.)*

**Robin:** I know my family is separate. My older brother has grown up and gotten married. I don't know what's going on.

*(He then connects very slightly with Melissa.)*

Melissa, I feel sad about your Mom and Dad's separation. What I need to do is bring my life up to date, and be with myself, David, and my Mom.

**Les:** Your face looks very sad, Robin. *(Robin is beginning to cry.)*

**Les:** You seem lonely to me, not knowing where you belong.

**Robin** *(crying softly)*: I have to accept that the family is not put together. The longing that it is still there is inside me—it's not longing for something that is real. I do have a place somewhere, and I don't know where.

I give myself credit for getting out of the house, for getting away from my Mom, and for going to school on my own. I need to find my place.

**Les:** You're doing a good job of setting your own goals now!

*This is the first real contact that Robin has allowed. He exposes his loneliness and isolation, without reverting to anger or anxiety.*

*(I talk to Maria and some of the others about their pictures before turning to David, who says he has drawn a picture of his family at Christmas. What he has drawn is a tiny picture of a Christmas tree and some*

*presents. He has drawn only in a small corner of the paper.)*

**Les:** Do you notice anything special about your picture, David?

**David:** No people.

**Les:** Where are the people?

**David:** Away, just not there.

**Les:** I like how observant you are. I also see that the picture is really little.

**David:** I like drawing small.

**Les:** What do you like about drawing small?

**David:** It looks neater.

**Les:** I have a hunch that I want to check out with you. You don't take a lot of space on the paper, and it seems to me, that you don't take a lot of space in your family either.

*(David is quiet, so I continue in the same calm tone.)*

If you were to use up a large spot, what would happen in your family?

**David:** It would be hard if I took up more space; there isn't any more for me. Anyway, if I took up too much space, it would mean I want too much.

I get to do my own thing, and that is okay, except when someone messes it up—like my Mom sometimes, like on the Little League thing. But you know, we do a whole lot of things together.

**Barbara** *(one of the trainees, to David)*: I wonder who takes care of you when you're feeling little. I bet there is no one around.

**David:** That's right. My Mom works a lot and doesn't have a lot of time to spend with me. Sometimes we sit down and talk about my reading, and that feels good.

*Here is more evidence of David's unreal view of things. Paula hasn't worked for a long time. Six weeks before the workshop she began her first job in several years.*

**Les** *(to Barbara)*: One of the things that I have a hunch about, Barbara, is that when David's father died, David decided he wasn't going to let anyone else in. He doesn't bring any people into his picture. He keeps things and himself real little, and he doesn't let anyone take care of him.

**David** *(after listening carefully)*: Yeah, that's right.

**Les:** Would you be interested this week, in learning to feel okay with getting bigger yourself, and taking more space for you?

**David:** Ya, I guess.

**Les:** I look forward to that time.

*Because of David's quietness and slightly sullen tone, I decide not to move on at this point. The question of taking space is one I'll come back to, soon.*

## TUESDAY AFTERNOON

## CHOCOLATE PUDDING—WITH RUTH

*Paula begins the chocolate pudding group by telling everyone that she does not want to get messed up and that she is particularly worried about her hair. There is some laughter in her voice, but the laughter isn't expressed in her body, which is stiff and tense. Robin, who is also in the group, continues to act in his same anxious way with lots of quick, loud chatter.*

*In the beginning both Paula and Robin handle the pudding very cautiously—putting it on the unclothed parts of themselves, and then, fingerful by fingerful, cautiously experiment with putting it on each other. This is the picture of their relationship—one fingerful from Robin on Paula's arm, and one fingerful from Paula onto Robin's arm. They each put the exact same amount of pudding on the exact same place on each other's body.*

*After a few minutes, Paula gets more involved. Her gestures and expression loosen up to match the occasion. She relaxes her face, and her voice sounds less gravelly and strained than I've ever heard it. Robin, in contrast, is becoming more and more nervous, as he gets messier. Neither Robin nor Paula initiate any involvement with other people, even though others try to touch them. Robin will not face me or interact with anyone else.*

*By the end of the pudding group, Paula successfully keeps her hair free of pudding. She expresses surprise that she let herself do something like this. She even lets out several good belly-laughs. At one time Paula, laughing, said, "I'm real, I'm real." She then turned her face to*

Bill Sarnon and let him rub the pudding around on her cheeks.

When the session ends, Robin is covered with chocolate pudding from head to toe. However, he maintains his nervous, stand-offish aura. He let people put pudding on him, but he wouldn't touch anyone except Paula. He touched her only in the most cautious manner.

## AFTER CHOCOLATE PUDDING—WITH LES

We have all been back in the main room for awhile. Bill Sarnon has just finished his work.

**Ruth** (standing up, and offering one of the red encounter bats): Robin, will you do these with me?

**Robin** (caustically): I'm not mad at you, really I'm not.

**Les:** Robin, it could be that you're not really angry with Ruth, but one of the things I know is that Ruth is angry with you. Is that right, Ruth?

**Ruth:** Yes, I am angry at you, Robin, and I would like to do these with you. Will you do these with me?

This is an example of how we use ourselves and each other. Ruth is actually angry at Robin. She exposes her own feelings as a model of how things can be settled. We want Robin to have a direct confrontation with another person rather than continuing the confused, secret skirmishes he is used to.

(Ruth takes several full baseball swings at Robin, and he responds with half-hearted pokes. Paula looks very serious. She draws back into a corner, her chin in her hand. David begins to weep loudly. Paula moves over to comfort him.)

**Ruth** (swinging the bat): I'm angry at you because you talk about me behind my back. I don't like it when you won't tell me straight what's going on.

(As Ruth goes on, Robin pokes with the bat and yells back at her. Several times it is clear that Robin has Ruth confused with someone in his past.)

**Robin:** You hit me before, you hit me a lot of times.

**Ruth:** That's not true Robin, I haven't hit you before.
*(Robin and Ruth circle each other several more times in the middle of the room. Finally, Ruth calls, "Stop." Both Robin and Ruth take a moment to catch their breaths.)*

*We are still trying to engage Robin. Unexpressed feelings keep him anxious and worried. We use present experience, when possible.*
*A fight like this includes not only the combatants but also other people in the room. I noticed that David, Paula, and other group members were reacting. Some seem frightened.*

**Ruth** *(to Robin)*: I just dealt with you directly, and I feel better. I still don't know if you have finished with me. It is okay with me that you and I fight fair and square.
**Robin:** Okay.
*(David, in tears, is standing as if he wants to comfort Robin. Paula stands up beside David and puts an arm around him.)*
**Les:** David, what are you thinking and feeling?
**David:** It's scary for me. I don't like to see Robin acting in that way. I don't know why Robin would do what he was doing, or why he won't just tell Ruth right out, and, why he won't just do it straight. I think it comes easier doing it straight. Then you don't have to go all through this hiding and nervous stuff.
**Les:** That's smart of you, David, and I agree with you. It is easier to be straight.
**Ruth:** I'm wondering why the fighting was scary for you, David.
**David** *(beginning to cry again)*: I've been around it all my life. *(He covers his eyes with his fists.)* Robin used to care for me and stuff. I thought he was the kind of person who would just come out and tell things.
**Ruth:** David, I'm not exactly understanding all of this. You sound disappointed with Robin.
**David:** When I was growing up, sometimes when Robin came to visit he would get real mad at my Mom. That's what I was scared about. Like when you guys started fighting out there, all these things came back.

*David has intuitively gotten to the heart of Robin's anger at Ruth. It's redirected anger at his mother.*

**Ruth:** You have memories of Robin and your Mom fighting and there not being any reason for it?

**David:** Yes, stupid things. Like I'm not eating the right kind of food and stuff. And then, Robin would get real mad and they would get into fights. And I didn't like that. It scared me a whole lot.

**Les:** So some of the fighting was about you.

**David:** I didn't know what I was doing to make him angry. I really didn't do anything, I don't think.

**Les:** It sounds like you were right in the middle, between your Mom and your brother, and that you wondered what was your fault.

**David** (nodding and taking his hands away from his eyes): If I didn't do something right, then Robin would ask Mom why I didn't do it, and then they'd start fighting.

**Les:** I can understand your being scared. They were in a battle about who knows better about you.

**David:** Yes.

**Ruth:** They were in a battle about who is your better parent.

**David:** Yes. That's what I meant. Because Robin says, "David, you shouldn't eat meat," and Mom says, "You have to eat your meat, David."

**Ruth** (to Les): When that goes on, it must be hard for David to think for himself and to find his own way.

**Ruth** (to David): Is there anything you would like to say to Robin?

**David** (to Robin): I wish you wouldn't tell me what to eat and what not to eat. I know how to lead my own life. I can do my own thinking about what I want to eat. I know what's good for me.

**Les** (nudging a little): David, its okay to even say more if you want.

**David** (to Robin): You are my brother, Robin, not my father. I don't want you for a father, Robin. I already have a mother. I had a father. I don't like having two parents when I really don't. It isn't right. Mom has to raise me up, not you. At least, that's the way I want it.

**Robin** (relieved and relaxed): Okay then, I'm not going to tell you anymore. I think maybe that's good for me too. I don't think I really can handle it.

(Paula looks toward Robin with that look that could kill. Her mouth is tight, her eyes are stony, her whole face is rigid.)

*Paula with her look seems to be resisting any change
in the family's relationship.*

**Les:** Paula, just wiggle your face a little, and let them
finish.
*(Paula does this. Both Robin and David look relieved.)*
**David** *(to Robin)*: When I don't do something right, you
always come in and tell me. That's what I don't want.
**Les:** David, I like how straight and persistent you are.
Will you tell Robin what he could do differently?
**David:** Robin, if I want some help with my homework,
I'll ask. I want Mom to do the rest, like telling me how to
set the table, and stuff like that. I want my mother to be
my mother and you to be my brother. You can help me in
sports, but only when I ask.
**Les:** So you want Robin to be your brother and not
your father.
**David:** Yes.
**Les:** I really like how you're talking straight to Robin.
Talking straight, in this family, is one of the most
important things.
*(To Robin:)* Will you respond?
**Robin** *(without the tension)*: David, it makes me feel
good that I can have a better relationship with you. I can
stand back and be your brother. I've always wanted it to be
that way.

*This defining of roles and relationships between
David and Robin is most useful for both of them. Robin
must not only separate from his mother but also from
the burden he decided to take on with David. David will
be freer to know and learn about himself now.*

**Ruth:** Paula, wiggle your face and tell Robin that
you're going to help him to be David's brother and not
David's father.
**Paula** *(to Robin)*: I'm going to keep you out of being
David's father. *(Her eyes are sharp, Robin cringes.)*
**Ruth** *(to Paula)*: I notice how uncomfortable this is
right now, and I'm not sure what's going on.
**Paula:** This is a place where a lot of the friction has
come. Robin has tried to override my decisions and it
hasn't mattered what I say or do.
*(Paula then looks directly at Robin.)*

It is my house and I am the provider, and if I feel something is right for David, I'll go with it. I am your mother, too, and if I feel something is right for you at a given time, I'll go with that. I can make my own decisions, and now in the future if you guys can't stick to this I won't take two little kids telling me what to do. I'll be in charge.
*(She turns to Ruth and Les.)*
Right now I feel really neat. I really feel like I'm me.

*Paula's strong stance reflects an important restructuring. She needs to maintain this position, and also incorporate more tenderness into her relationship with her children.*

**Paula** *(to Robin)*: I am concerned, because when you get mad at me, you hit me. You strike out at me. That is real hard for me. When that happens, I get very angry. I don't want you to hurt me and I don't want to hurt you, Robin.

**Les:** Will you tell Robin that its not okay for him to hit you, and that, you won't hit him?

**Paula:** Yes. Robin, don't hit me. I won't hit you. We can now begin to solve problems in another way. Also, David is not your concern. *(Turning and softly smiling:)* I feel good.

**Ruth:** I like your clarity.

**Les:** One more thing, Paula. Do you think that the frozen glare you get on your face is sometimes your way of trying to stop or to control Robin and yourself?

**Paula** *(thoughtfully)*: Yes, maybe so. In fact, I think that's right. I can feel me stiffen.

**Les:** Will you be responsible for wiggling your face, instead of glaring, from now on? I think that would be very important in continuing to change your position in this family.

**Paula:** Sure. I can do that. It will be fun.

*(Paula moves up in her chair, and her face softens. Many of the group members clap for her as she takes this different position.)*

**Robin:** I don't feel anxious at all and I haven't let my hands touch each other. I like that.

**Paula:** One last thing for you, David. You are going to have to accept someone else helping you with your reading. I'm not going to do it. I'm not going to let that interfere with my life, or let myself interfere with your life anymore in that way.

*This will be an essential change for the family.*
*Paula and David maintain their overinvolvement with*
*each other through David's school problems.*

**Les** *(to Paula)*: What are you feeling, right now?

**Paula** *(wiggling her mouth)*: I'm feeling good now. I can take care of my own business, and I am going to help the kids take care of theirs.

*(At the very end of the afternoon Robin speaks up, in his boisterous voice.)*

**Robin:** There's one more thing I want to say to you, Ruth. It's about my indirect thing. Today, at the pool, I just wanted attention when I was pacing back & forth in front of you. What I need to do differently is to say, "Ruth, I need attention from you, and it's hard for me to ask you."

**Ruth:** That would be good, Robin. I could respond to that.

**Robin:** I think that sometimes you look down on me. Like, today, at the pool, I think it's your own thing, but I was hurt.

**Ruth:** Wait a minute, Robin. I like your being aware of what you need to do differently, and I really like your talking straight now. You are following through well with what we have been saying.

It's important, also, for you to know that I wasn't looking down on you, but that the pacing and hand-wringing make it difficult to be comfortable around you.

**Robin:** Yes, but you're real hard on me.

**Ruth:** When you act in those ways, yes, I'm hard on you. I won't respond to your indirectness. I will tell you to stop and expect that you respond to me appropriately.

**Bette** *(to Robin)*: Ruth is right. I wasn't direct with you either about how you seemed. I think you owe Ruth some thanks.

**Robin:** Thank you, Ruth. Thank you, Bette.

**Paula:** I know Robin does this. What should I do? How can I approach him?

**Robin:** Just tell me to knock it off, Mom. Just remind me that I'm being inappropriate.

**Bette** *(to Paula)*: When Robin acts inappropriately, all you usually do is laugh. This supports him.

*These comments, from Bette to Robin and Paula, are excellent examples of the group processes and interaction, which is so valuable when working with families. Bette has helped Robin think of his inappropriate behavior out of the context of his conflict with Ruth or his mother. Bette also helps and supports Paula, so that she (Paula) gets the message from a friend, as well as from Ruth.*

**Les:** Bette is correct, Paula. It's most important that you not laugh. Robin is correct, too. You need to tell him to stop.
*(To Paula:)* What I sometimes experience is that when I confront Robin, he ends up fighting with me. The fight then takes precedence: I end up defending myself, and Robin doesn't have to take responsibility for his behavior. I think you might get caught in that same way. *(Paula nods, yes.)*
At those times it's important that you don't get into a fight with him, and that you not let Robin make the issue, anger, rather than his scare and anxiety.
**Paula:** Okay. I think you're right, Ruth. *(Turning to Bette:)* Thank you Bette, you helped me.

# WEDNESDAY MORNING

# WOMEN'S GROUP—WITH RUTH

**Ruth:** Where are you this morning, Paula?
**Paula:** I'm more my own person. I'm able to look at my children as people in their own right, and not just look at them as things I'm responsible for. I see that most of my problems come when I get tangled up with them. When I stay out, things are much better for me. I've gotten into these traps not only with the kids, but also, with other people. I manage to get myself in the middle.

*This is the same problem Robin portrayed in his family sculpture. The middle is also one of the dangerous zones David tries to stay out of by keeping himself small and alone.*

**Ruth:** Were you in the middle when you were a child?

**Paula:** I was in the middle with my sisters. I always feared that, whichever way I went, I would get trapped, forgotten. It is part of my nature to do this. That's part of how I get set up—because I sense someone is going to really listen, then I move in, and then these people lay a trip on me. They get me too involved.

**Ruth:** Paula, will you be more specific about what you mean by getting yourself too involved and feeling trapped and forgotten, in the middle, with both your sisters?

*(Paula responds by pulling back as if she has already revealed too much.)*

**Paula:** I really can't remember much.

**Ruth:** I hear that there have been difficulties for you, and that you feel that you can't trust people.

**Paula:** That's true. What I need to do now is just be who I am now.

**Ruth:** I support you knowing what you need and saying it. I also suspect that right now you might be feeling afraid, and thinking that you will get in the middle, trapped and forgotten. Is this so?

**Paula** *(with an astonished expression)*: Yes, I guess you are right.

**Ruth:** I suggest that we investigate that, now. Are you up for it?

**Paula** *(pulling back)*: No, I don't want to go back there. I understand what you are saying though. I think, maybe I pull away from people, and into David and Robin, because of this. Then the boys prove, Robin, I mean mostly, proves I'm trapped.

*Paula does not want to get involved in any regressive work which contacts her family of origin. She has remained consistent in avoiding this and getting trapped again. I don't push her.*

**Ruth** *(with warmth and a big smile)*: You are really insightful. At a more comfortable time for you, will you think about your past and come up with a specific scene, where you were feeling caught in the middle, trapped, and forgotten?

**Paula** *(looking relieved and alive again)*: Yes, that would be better for me.

*Paula's ability to make connections and to draw her own conclusions is really important here. I hope she will trust us enough to go further for herself before the week is over.*

## MEN'S GROUP—WITH LES

*As I walk to the men's group, I think about David's unobtrusiveness. David's tiny picture was an illustration of it. In our Tuesday session, I suggested that this represents the box that David keeps himself in to keep himself safe. At the end of the kid's group, David implied that he would like to get out of his box, and even let someone else in close to him.*

*The major work of the morning is done by Edgar Barker. He talks about feeling empty, without emotion, in his family. He thinks this is related to the absence of his father. I help Edgar construct a scene in which Edgar tells the image of his dead father about the things that had been missing in his life as a child. Edgar concludes that keeping the same things out of his adult life may be a kind of homage to his father's memory.*

*Domenic Dellapietra picks up this theme and talks about what it means to him that his father was an alchololic, that his mother and father were divorced when he was 12, and that his stepfathers were all alcoholic men, with whom he never could make a connection.*

*While Domenic is talking, I sit holding Edgar. Edgar had never before let himself be held by a man.*

*Robin is quiet throughout. I don't know whether he is calm because his mother is not present, because he is relieved by yesterday's work, or because Paula had taken command. Maybe he has simply gone underground. Robin also had refused, on several occasions, to acknowledge any difficulties or feelings that he might have with his father or brothers.*

*Throughout the morning, I am quite aware of Robin's attentiveness to the group's work and invite his participation. Robin stays out and watches. He is calm, relaxed and present throughout. I decide it is okay to leave him as an observer.*

*Of all the members in the workshop, the missing-father theme is most important to David.*

*David is sitting alone. As Domenic talks about his alcoholic father and stepfathers, David begins to slump down in his chair and look littler and littler. After Domenic stops talking, I comment on David's position.*

**Les:** David, you've been sitting in the background this morning, and yet it looks as if what you've heard has been important to you.

*(David becomes tearful.)*

Edgar and Domenic have been talking about what they've missed from not having fathers. I know that has been important to you, and that you have been concerned about your father.

*(David begins to sob, still saying nothing.)*

Does it sometimes seem hopeless to you? Like you will never be able to get for yourself what a father can give?

*(There is a small nod from David. Robin remains quiet.)*

When you saw me holding Edgar, did you think that kind of holding was something you would like?

**David:** Yes.

*(I move over, with Edgar's assent, and put my arm around David. He collapses into tears.)*

**Les:** It is okay for you to stay here as long as you want, David. I like that you've let me into your box.

*I imagine what it is like to be in a particular child's shoes, and then I say it out loud. Putting myself in his place and expressing my perception often helps members get past their reluctance to make contact.*

# WEDNESDAY AFTERNOON

# INDIVIDUAL FAMILIES—WITH LES

*Wednesday is the short afternoon of the week, with time after 3:00 P.M. for the families to go off by themselves. I take one group of families, the Quinns and the Barkers; Ruth takes the other.*

**Les:** David, you seem to be sitting apart from the group again.

**David:** I'm feeling okay. I'm just listening.

**Les:** Where are you today, Paula?

**Paula:** I feel freer. I feel more myself. I feel more independent. I'm also feeling more comfortable with David and Robin, because I don't feel smothered by them.

**Les:** And you, Robin?

**Robin:** I feel more comfortable, too.

*(Robin and Paula are sitting back to back, literally supporting each other.)*

**Les:** Paula, will you sit up and take a different position?

**Robin** *(anxiously protesting as his mother moves)*: But my mother wasn't bugging me. Why did you ask her to move?

**Les:** You seem anxious about my asking your mother to move away a little. I wonder what you are thinking as you are sitting separate.

**Robin:** I'm thinking that I need her for support or I can't do it. Sometimes I can't talk to other people and then I pace and even my jokes come off the wall.

**Les:** I like your responding to me directly, and I like your awareness. What do you want to work on regarding that?

**Robin** *(anxiously)*: Nothing right now. I think I'd like to go with Melissa and Nick and some of the others this afternoon but I could never do that.

**Les:** Will you at least ask the others and then you will have some options for yourself.

**Robin:** Yes, I could do that.

**Les:** Will you ask Melissa now?

**Robin:** Melissa, what are you going to do?

**Melissa:** I don't know, but our family will be together.

**Robin** *(to Les)*: I'm glad I did it.

**Les:** What are you thinking and feeling, David?

**David:** I'm happy. I'm feeling good about what I did this morning. I'm glad I let you in my little box.

**Les:** What are you going to do this afternoon, on your time off?

**David:** I don't know. They want to do other things and I want to go to the rodeo. *(To Paula)* I want to go to the rodeo, Mom.

**Paula:** I would be glad to talk about that.

*(As it turns out, Paula, David, and Robin decide that they will do two things in the afternoon. Going to the rodeo will be one of them.)*

*(By the end of the session, Robin has managed his anxiety, and reports he is looking forward to the afternoon off. He will also ask Nick.)*

# THURSDAY MORNING
# PARENTS' GROUP—WITH RUTH

*For most of the morning Paula has been very quiet about herself, only participating a little in the work Bette and Bill Sarnon do. With the session more than half over, Paula speaks up.*

**Paula** *(beginning to cry)*: I've done a lot of thinking about what it will be like when David and I go home, and I'm afraid for him.

*The mid-week break, signaling the limited time remaining in the workshop, frequently results in anxiety about going home.*

**Paula** *(crying loudly)*: I don't know what I'm going to do. David is a fine boy, and I want him to get the best out of life.

**Ruth:** What are you afraid of?

*(Paula's next phrases are halting and disconnected. She talks about raising David for ten years. The number ten focuses her thoughts.)*

**Paula:** Ten years ago . . . I've got a lot of guilt back there.

**Ruth** *(placing a pillow in front of Paula)*: Paula, put David out in front of you now. Tell him about ten years ago and your guilt and fears.

**Paula** *(sitting forward, with sadness in her voice)*: David, I'm afraid that, when you grow up, you're going to find out about your father, and what I did to your father. And when you find this out, I think, you're going to look at me and say, "Oh, you bitch." I hope, David, you never find out.

**Ruth:** It sounds as if you think you have to be really, really careful around David.

**Paula:** I do. David, your Dad really hurt me. And in turn, I hurt him. In your mind, David, he's the best Dad that ever was. And that's why I can't say very much about him to you. I think there are times you wonder why I don't show that I miss him.

**Ruth:** You sound scared that David is going to find out all about this. What I know is that David doesn't let himself find out anything. He doesn't even let himself learn in school. He doesn't let himself grow. Maybe he holds himself back to protect you, because you are scared of him finding out things.

My opinion is that David really needs to know the facts from you. This will help him to live in reality and to learn about the real world.

> *In school, David is failing: he doesn't let himself "know." In the family, Paula has many important secrets: she limits his knowing. Paula keeps herself central to all of the family, or trapped in the middle, by keeping the secrets. Holding back the facts also contributes to the uncertainty about what is real to Robin. It's likely that Robin, who is older than David and was around when the events occurred, knows the secrets, and that knowing is very difficult for him.*

**Paula** *(looking horrified)*: What are you saying?

**Ruth:** One of the things I know about kids, and that I know about David in particular, is that he can handle facts much better than he can handle secrets. What's important in helping him grow up is to let him know that you believe he can handle the information and that you can handle it, too. Talking about the truth with David shows respect for his ability to grow. It will also do alot to relieve your stress and scare. It may even help Robin, also.

**Paula** *(protesting)*: But, it will hurt David.

**Ruth:** It may be very difficult for him.

**Paula:** David fantasizes all the time. He thinks his father was a hero.

**Ruth:** That's exactly what I meant. You need to let him see reality. It would also be helpful for David to watch you, Paula, face reality. Robin has trouble with reality, too. I think that you need to help David and Robin deal with what's real.

**Paula:** All right, I'll do it.

*(She strongly nods her head, yes, and looks relieved. I move over next to Paula and give her a hug.)*

**Ruth:** You really look different now.

**Paula:** I feel different. I'm still scared.

**Ruth:** Now that you have expressed your willingness to talk about the secrets, will you tell us the facts? We will be prepared to help you then.

**Paula** *(nodding)*: I never should have married David's father. I was two months pregnant. I wanted to give David a legal name.

Larry hurt me, physically. He was an alcoholic, too. He didn't drink until late in my pregnancy. I hoped it might work out. He beat me several times, even when Robin was there. This was before I had David. The whole time I was in the hospital delivering David, Larry was home drunk. When I got home with David, he went on drinking. He became violent. He almost hurt David many times. He would be very rough with him, sometimes even throwing him down. I could barely stop him. I had to protect David constantly. Finally, we separated for a while. When I thought things were better, we got back together.

Larry always went back to his Korean war experiences when he drank. Once he got me in a corner of the kitchen and started to choke me. This time I thought I wasn't going to be able to get out of it. I picked up a knife from the table behind me. Before I could get it up between us, Larry hit me so hard I went from the kitchen into the living room.

*(Everyone in the room is on the edge of their chairs. Some have tears in their eyes.)*

I knew I couldn't do anything to protect myself. Thank God Larry was so drunk that he passed out. A friend took me to the hospital and cared for David. I was in the hospital for three days with a broken jaw. After that, David and I hid from Larry for six months. We stayed with different friends in other towns.

*(Paula begins to sob.)* I feel so guilty that hiding all of this has hurt David. But I had to protect him. *(Paula sighs and rests her chin on her hands.)*

Finally, Larry did stop drinking, and David had to have a minor operation. So, I went back together with Larry. We moved to a new house. When Robin came to visit, Larry once started to get violent with Robin. I think if I hadn't been there, he would have killed him.

Larry didn't drink again, but he got very suspicious of me. He worked nights and I was alone days, while he slept. If I even went to the grocery store he would question me about who I saw.

I couldn't live that way. I really did do something then, but I'm not going to say here what I did. David and I had to go back into hiding again. I knew I had to stay away, or

Larry would kill me. Two months later, I found out that Larry was in the hospital with cancer of the liver. He wasn't expected to live. He wanted to see David.

I took David, who was three then, to see his father. They said their goodbyes. Larry died five days later.

**Ruth:** I need to know about the time you did something you can't talk about.

**Paula** (*shaking*): I can talk about it, I guess. I almost killed him again. I really wanted to and I had it all planned out. I was waiting. He found out. I knew he would kill me if he only got the chance.

**Ruth:** Paula, you needed to defend yourself. I'm glad you did, and I'm glad that you didn't kill him or let yourself get killed. It must have been difficult for you. It sounds like Larry was disturbed.

**Paula** (*looking relieved and sad*): Thank you.

*As I hear and watch Paula, I see how she has lived her life: setting it up over and over again so that she is frightened, trapped, and then forgotten. She continually proves to herself that she can't trust people.*

*I understand how Robin became the protector. He literally stopped the abuse to the point of being abused himself.*

**Ruth:** Paula, in the past, you have really put yourself into harmful situations. You got yourself hurt very badly and could have even been killed. Would you ever do that again?

**Paula** (*emphatically*): No.

**Ruth:** Imagine that your mother, father, and sisters are in front of you. Talk to them about this.

**Paula** (*hesitantly and quietly, at first*): All of you, listen. I am worth living. (*Stopping, then much louder:*) I am alive and I will stay this way for a long, long time. I'm not drinking, and I'm never going to endanger myself again.

**Paula** (*sitting back, with tears in her eyes, and a softness in her face*): That's enough.

**Ruth** (*with a quiet smile*): I agree.

(*Berenice Barker moves over and holds Paula from behind. Paula turns around and begins to cry in her arms. Paula is still for a few minutes, as other members of the group comment.*)

**Ruth:** I can see that there are things you still wouldn't want David to know. Les and I will be willing to help you with what we think he can handle.

This silence has been a burden for Robin, because he saw the violence between you and his stepfather. He protects David and you by hiding what he knows. This contributes to his anxiety and his not being comfortable in leaving. David protects you, by not letting himself know or learn.

**Paula:** When I woke up this morning, I had a feeling something would happen. I'm glad that I trusted my feeling and that I trusted you. I understand it. I don't need the protection.

*It's not unusual for parents to be uncertain about what their children can understand—particularly children who are already troubled. How much David can manage, is a question that we, as therapists, take the responsibility to help answer. The benefits of David's knowing reality, without all the gruesome facts, are enormous. It will give him permission to ask many questions, to find many answers, and to grow up. The potential risks in telling David are small. He has many ego strengths.*

# YOUNG PEOPLE'S GROUP—WITH LES

*Robin is sitting on a hard bench. His feet are tensely braced against the stone ledge under the fireplace. He's beginning to breathe quickly. Before I can say anything, he begins to talk.*

**Robin:** I have something I want to tell you, David. I am your brother and I want to be your brother. I don't want to come on like a parent anymore. Tomorrow is your birthday. I want to take you out and have you pick out your present—whatever you want.

*(David is delighted and is bouncing around. Robin then moves on to tell Nicholas that he, like Nicholas, spent 10 years playing tennis as his main sport.)*

**Robin:** My mother gave me the choice of what I wanted to do. I chose tennis.

**Nicholas:** That is the exact opposite of what my mother did. She told me exactly what to do. I had no choice.

*(Robin, David, and Nick spend some time comparing their mothers. They discuss what things they can decide on, and what they are forced to do by their mothers.)*

**Les** *(to David)*: How did you feel, when Robin and your mother argued about what you should do?

**David:** Robin used to get me to go out and play tennis. He used to push me to play and to get involved in tournaments—almost the way Nick's mother does.

*(Turning to Robin:)* I didn't like it when you pushed me. But I sure wanted to make you happy by doing it.

*(David goes on to tell how Robin used to jump out and scare him a lot, or sit on him and torture him with tickling.)*

**Robin:** That's exactly what my brother used to do: scare me and tease me. That's what I did to David. I stopped when David began to get me back. I'm learning here how to be separate and how to be in charge of my own anxieties. I can stop myself now.

**David:** Now, I have more faith in Robin. I'm also bigger. I can stand up for myself, and get him if I need to.

*I decide to bring up something that illustrates the opposite.*

**Les:** David, I noticed something this morning. When you spilled the milk at breakfast, one of the trainees asked you to clean it up. You said you would, but you didn't. David, what was going on then?

*(David looks blank.)*

**Les:** I wonder, David, if you sometimes have trouble being bigger because part of growing up is following through on things.

**David:** I was going to get back to it.

**Nicholas:** David, that's a bunch of bullshit! I asked if you had done it and you said yes, you had.

*(David continues to hem and haw.)*

**Les:** Say what is going on with you, David.

**David:** I used to do the same thing, when I was really little. I would always end up in trouble then, too.

**Les:** What do you think about all that?

**David:** Right now, I think that's really stupid. I'm going to be 11 tomorrow, but sometimes it seems like I act like a three-year-old. That is not very smart. Right now I feel like a three-year-old.

**Les:** From what you say, it seems you do a lot of things that make you end up feeling stupid and young, like a three-year-old.

David, you were three when your Dad died. It's as if there is a part of you that keeps wanting to stay back there.

**David** (*very sad and quiet and then smiling*): Yeah.

**Les:** What is your smile for?

**David:** I did some pretty stupid things when I was three.

**Les:** I have a fantasy that there is part of you that believes if you grow up past three, you're going to have to forget your Dad.

**David** (*in a cracked voice, and sinking into his chair*): Yeah. I just always think of what my Mom told me about what my Dad said. That was, that she should help me do my things, because he wasn't going to be there. I guess that's just why I'm not starting to grow up, like still throwing acorns at girls, or always needing help with my reading.

**Les:** You really seem sad right now, David. Will you talk about your sad?

**David** (*after a long pause, in a slow, heavy voice*): I don't know.

**Les:** Make believe that your Dad is here right now. Remember how some of the other people have done that?

**David** (*beginning to cry*): I just can't do that.

**Les:** What do you think would happen if you did?

**David:** I would feel so sad. I wouldn't want to do that. (*In a halting, tearful voice:*) I don't want to think about him.

**Les** (*moving toward David*): David, do you think about your Dad a lot now?

**David:** Yeah. Like when I see carpenters' tools like a hammer, or screws to fix something. I ask, "What would my Dad be doing with that?" I guess I'm hooked on thinking about him.

I always think about that war, too. My Dad was in that war. I guess I'm hooked on thinking about that, too. I like war.

**Les:** My guess is that, whenever you get back to thinking about your Dad, you end up feeling like you are 3.

**David:** I remember going to Disneyland with him and working on the rototiller in the garden and stuff like that.

**Les:** You don't want to forget any of those pieces, do you David?

**David:** I see all of the other guys with their Dads and it makes me feel like a piece of junk.

**Les:** Because you don't have a Dad?

**David:** That's why I wish Mom and Robin's Dad were back together. Then I would have a Dad. I wouldn't be junk.

**Les:** I really hear that.

**David:** Sometimes I wonder if I should call Robin's father my Dad, but I'm not used to doing that. If they were married, I would.

**Les:** I'm aware that part of you says, "If I grow up, I'm going to lose my Dad, and then I'm junk."

*(David bursts into tears.)*

What I want you to know, David, is that it is really important that you don't forget about your Dad. I know how important he was to you. It's okay not to forget about those things.

> *Permission to not forget about his Dad ends the resistance of the three-year-old part of David and allows his sense of reality to work.*

**David:** But, I should grow up, too. Is that what you're saying?

**Les:** I wonder what your Dad would think about that, if he were here. If he were here in this room, what do you think he would say to you about that? What do you think he would want for you?

**David:** For me to grow up and not to think I'm junk. I would, if he wanted me to.

*(David's eyes light up. He straightens his body.)*

I think I'll start acting more grown up right now. I don't need to be a three-year-old, who just likes to cause trouble and stuff.

**Les:** You're sure that's what he'd want? For you to grow up?

**David:** Yes.

**Les:** If he were sitting here in this room right now and giving you some advice about how to do that, what do you think he'd be saying to you?

**David** *(in a more grown-up voice and sitting tall)*: "David," he'd say, "I wish I were here to help you. I wish you would grow up and ask me advice and stuff." *(David smiles broadly.)*

**Les:** Since your Dad knows that he's dead, what do you think he would give you as advice, since he's not around?

**David:** He'd say, "Don't be with kids who like to break windows and do bad stuff. Be with the right kids."

**Les:** That's surely a piece of important advice. You really know the advice he'd give you.

**David:** Yup. I just don't listen to it. If he were around right now, I would listen to it. Because he'd get real mad if I didn't. He'd always want me to listen and not backtalk. I'd listen to him, because he was my father.

**Les:** Pretend he's here right now. Tell him that one of the things that you're going to do, as part of growing up, is to listen to good advice.

*(David grunts doubtfully.)*

**Les:** Stand up and see him in front of you.

**David** *(standing)*: Yes, I see him.

**Les:** Now, I'll give you some words. Tell your dad, "One of the things I'm going to do now, as I grow up, is to listen to good advice."

**David** *(breaking into tears)*: It's hard for me to do that, because I never really talked to him before or asked him questions like that.

**Les:** I know it's hard for you. That's why I'm here, willing to help you.

Part of growing up is beginning to figure out which things you can learn yourself and which to ask help for. To know you can ask, to learn that you can do it, and also to learn that you don't have to do it all by yourself are all important. So, will you see your Dad in front of you and let me give you the words again?

*(David nods, yes.)*

Tell him that, as you grow up, it is important for you to learn about things, to ask questions, and to ask for help when you need it.

**David** *(in a clear strong voice)*: Dad, if you were alive right now, I'd ask for advice. I'd listen to it, and I wouldn't do stupid things, like I do now.

Since you're not alive, I guess I'll have to listen to myself. I will listen to the right things, not the wrong things. I will grow up to be an eleven-year-old, like I'm gonna be tomorrow.

**Les:** Tell your Dad that you are smart and that one of the things you will do, because you're smart, is to ask other grownups to help you.

**David:** I know how to pick other grownups to help me, Dad. I'll do that, too.

**Les:** Is that right for you, David? Is that what you're going to do?

**David:** Yes.

**Les:** David, I want you to know now how much I respect you and how much courage I think you have. You've done some very difficult things.

There might be other important things you want to say to your Dad. Will you think about them? Let me know if I can help you with that?

**David:** Yes.

*This is an example of redecision work with young people. An essential element in David's grieving process, and his attachment to the fantasy memory of his father, is that he decides to keep himself small and isolated. Part of his isolation is in insisting that he can do things by himself, even when he can't. He pushes away any grownups who want to help him. He stops any learning from himself and others.*

*We take a break from the session.*
*(During the break, Robin approaches David. He is holding a cup of juice in his hand.)*

**Robin:** David, that was beautiful work. It took a lot of courage.

**David:** It wasn't easy, Robin. You can work, too.

*(David spends the rest of the break playing checkers with Nick.*

*(When the group restarts, Robin and David listen to Melissa Barker. Finally Robin speaks.)*

**Robin:** I was noticing the work that Melissa and David did. She does it differently than I do. I'm uncertain and I'm wishy-washy about it. Even though I'm not pacing or wringing my hands, it seems like it's really hard for me to change.

**Les:** What is it you want to make different for yourself?

**Robin:** I want to be on my own. I don't want to be taking care of my mother and brother!

**Les:** Imagine your mother is sitting in front of you in that chair *(I put an empty chair about three feet in front of him)* and tell her that.

**Robin:** I want to be on my own . . . *(His voice trails off and he looks scared.)*

**Les:** Put some words to what you are feeling.

**Robin** *(still talking to the mother-chair, seemingly oblivious to the rest of the room)*: I'm scared. You're always drunk—you're not around—you're all I've got—if anything happens to you . . .

**Les** *(softly)*: Go on, Robin.

**Robin** *(sitting up as if a sudden awareness hit him)*: I've been taking care of you ever since then but I'm not a little kid anymore—I don't need to take care of you—I need to take care of me!

**Les:** Tell her you will take care of yourself.

**Robin:** That's right! I will take care of myself. You are old enough to take care of yourself. *(He says this with obvious joy.)*

**Les:** Nice work, Robin. One more piece—will you put your dad out there and see if there's anything you want to say to him?

**Robin** *(thoughtfully)*: I'm angry at you. You didn't take care of me, either—and you were supposed to. I'm not doing your job with mom any more, either. I'll take care of myself even though you wouldn't take care of me. *(Turning to David)* I'm your brother—not your father or your mother. I won't take—that's not right—I'll take care of you like a brother, not like a father. *(Turning to me and looking satisfied:)* I'm done!

**Les:** You sure are. Nice work!

# THURSDAY AFTERNOON

# FAMILY GROUP—LES SPEAKING

*Everyone is together in the large meeting room. Later, we'll divide into men's and women's groups. All of the adults have been involved in Paula's morning revelations. It's important for them to see how she goes ahead.*

**Ruth** *(to Paula)*: Are you ready?
**Paula:** Okay.

*(Paula invites David and Robin to move to the center of the room. The three of them sit facing each other. Les moves next to David. Robin brings the Kleenex out into the middle.)*

**Les:** Do you need some help, Paula?

**Paula:** Yes, just get me started.

*(Ruth changes position. She moves between Robin and Paula.)*

**Les** *(to David)*: This has to do with some work your mother did this morning, while you and I were in the other group. It has to do with you, and it has to do with Robin.

David, I know your mother needs to talk to you about some very important things. This may be very hard for her, and it might even be hard for you.

*(David looks at me with wide-open eyes; his mouth is dropped open.)*

What I want you to know, David, is that there are a lot of people here, myself included, who are available to you, if you want some help.

*(David nods.)*

**Paula** *(cautiously)*: There are lots of things, David, that I've never told you about. I think it's important that you know them, because I think you'll understand more then. I want to do this while we're here.

*(David looks scared. He looks at Robin. Robin is breathing faster but he is not agitated.)*

I know you loved your Daddy very much. It has been hard for me to talk about him, because there were a lot of things that happened between us, a lot of things that I got hurt by. Some of it was arguments and some of it was hitting. All of the time it was drinking.

**Les** *(reacting to Paula's condescending tone, and the term Daddy)*: Paula, stop for a moment. I want to give you some of the help you asked for. What I want you to know is that David is eleven years old.

**Paula** *(with a big sigh and a smile)*: Yes, I know he is.

**Les:** David did a lot of important work for himself this morning. It was related to being more grown up. It is important that you give him credit for being grown up. Tell him things in a grown-up way.

**Paula** *(with a quick smile)*: Yes.

*(Turning:)* David, I took you away when you were small. You didn't live with your father for the last eight months of his life. We moved away from your father several times

and lived, just you and I, together. We did that, because I was afraid your father would hurt me or you. He was drinking a lot, and sometimes he was violent.

*(David bows his head and begins to cry.)*

**Les** *(to Paula, and at the same time stroking David's back)*: You're doing fine. What else do you think David needs to know about how rough things were for Robin and you, or about how you, Paula, have been protecting him and yourself?

*(To David:)* Now that Robin and your mother know that you're grown up, and that you can handle some of these facts, things don't have to be unreal, even though they're painful.

*(To Paula:)* Go on.

**Paula:** No, there's not any more facts, not really. Just that, I have always been afraid you would hate me, David, if you ever found out that I left him and that I sometimes fought him back. *(She shifts her sitting position so that she's further from her children.)*

**Ruth:** Paula, does David know about the last few days before his father died? And how his father said goodbye to him?

**Paula:** No.

**Ruth:** Tell him that part, too. It is important that David have closure on his father's death.

**Paula** *(to David)*: There were arguments and hitting. Some of it came because your Dad drank too much. We left and stopped living with him. He became ill. He went to the army hospital and found out he had cancer. The doctors couldn't do anything to help him. And so, through his friend, Al, he sent word that he wanted to see us. We went.

**David** *(wide-eyed)*: I remember.

**Paula:** You sat on his bed. He talked to you and said goodbye. He knew he wouldn't see you again.

Remember I told you, a long time ago, that one of the last things he said to me was "Don't baby, David. Let him grow up to be a man."

**Les:** I like that you're beginning, just now, to let David grow up. Part of growing up to be a man is to knowing what's real.

**David:** I understand all this, and I feel better now.

**Les:** What do you understand?

**David** *(hesitantly)*: I thought he didn't do that.

**Les:** What do you mean?

**David:** I thought he didn't drink or hurt anyone or anything. I guess I didn't know him.

*(Paula is looking intently at David. Robin is much more relaxed than ever before. He has managed well to keep himself separate.)*

**Les:** So you're learning something new today. What do you think, and what do you feel, as you learn this new stuff?

**David:** I guess my father was different.

**Les:** Will you say more?

**David:** I thought he was nice and didn't drink and never smoked either.

**Les:** If you thought he was nice and didn't drink, it must have seemed strange that your Mom and Dad split up. Will you say what's going on inside of you?

**David:** I'm just different.

**Ruth:** Will you explain "different"? I'll bet your mother, in particular, would like to know.

**David** *(to Paula)*: Now I know why you never would talk about him: because it made you feel bad. I wondered a lot why you never wanted to talk about him. That part made me feel bad. Now I know. I'm glad you told me.

**Paula:** Are you saying you understand why I didn't talk about it?

*(David nods, yes.)*

*For David, the basic reality needed to be talked about. The specific, horrible details are unimportant. They may even be harmful.*

**Paula:** I felt bad, David, because I have always tried to be honest with you.

**Les** *(to David)*: I wonder, David, if you might have some other questions that you have held back, knowing that your mother didn't want to talk about things.

**David:** No.

**Les:** You had a lot of ideas in your head. Now you are finding out that many of them are not real.

**David:** I thought they were real, because she always said how nice he was.

**Paula:** But he was nice.

**David:** I know, but he wasn't when he was drinking or hurting us.

**Paula:** That's right. Something else I tried to explain to you, David, is that the war does things to people that they never get over. That was part of your father's problem. He had seen too much and been through too much in the war. When he drank, that all came out.

**Les** *(to Paula)*: Are there any questions you have right now?

**Paula:** No.

**Ruth:** I have one. I wonder if you're saying anything bad about yourself, David, or about your Mom right now.

**David:** No, I'm just sad, and I love my Mom. I'm glad I know it.

**Les:** I can understand that. Is there anything you want from your Mom, or from anyone else in the room, to help you with your sadness?

**David:** No.

*(David begins to cry loudly. I touch him. Paula is also crying. Robin is sitting forward and taking a deep breath.)*

**Ruth** *(with her hand on Robin's shoulder)*: Will you share what you're thinking, Robin?

**Robin:** It may be sad, but, in the long run, it is joyous. This has been something real and awful in my life. I've never been able to talk about it. Right now, I feel like I'm caught up, that everything is real, that I can face David. I can know that everything's straight with you, David, and that makes me feel really good.

*(To Paula:)* This really took guts, Mom.

**Paula:** Thank you, Robin. This has been hard for you, too, and unfair for you.

**Robin:** Yes, and mostly it has been unfair to David. Now that this is straight, he has a chance.

*(Robin is laughing and crying at once. He reaches out and touches David.)*

I believe that this is the best birthday that David has ever had. He has gotten his life today.

*(I continue to hold David. People in the room are beginning to show some relief from the tension that grew as the story was being told.)*

**David** *(sitting up)*: It's all over.

**Ruth:** What do you mean, "It's all over?"

**David:** I've always known something was wrong, because Mom never liked talking about Dad. Now it won't be so hard for me, and it won't be so hard for Robin and Mom. They won't have to hold everything in and be so worried and fake about it anymore.

**Les:** That's true. I guess right now you're feeling a lot more grown-up.

**David:** And letting a lot more people come in.

*(At this point, Ruth and I look at each other and move back. We ask the family if there's anything they want to do to finish up. Robin says that the only thing he wants to do is give David a hug. They embrace and move out of the center. David moves over and falls into his mother's arms, crying. Paula stiffens.)*

**David:** Mom, I really love you.

**Ruth:** Paula, David is hugging you and saying that he loves you, and you seem to be pushing him away. Let him hug you. Let him be finished with you.

**Paula** *(smiling broadly, and being hugged by David):* Okay.

# FRIDAY MORNING

# INDIVIDUAL FAMILIES—WITH LES

*I am with the Sarnons and the Quinns. I begin, as I usually do, reminding people that it is Friday.*

**Les:** As we start this morning, remember that this is the last working day. Reflect on how you were when you came into the workshop. Think about what you've done so far and what you still want to change. I'll check in with everybody before beginning.

**Paula:** I feel good about what I've done so far with my family.

**Robin:** I'm still anxious some even though I'm hardly doing those round and round things. There's something unfinished.

**David:** I'm quiet and good today.

*(We begin the actual work with the Quinn family later, after the break. The young people have been out playing and are reluctant to come in. When Robin comes in, his mother has already begun.)*

**Paula:** Right now, I feel more detached from Robin than I did a year ago. I think it's good. I'm also concerned about Robin.

*(To Robin, wiggling her face:)* How has being here helped you?

**Robin:** One of my goals was to get away from home, away from you. My worry about the workshop was that I would get too close to you. This week I feel different from you. I like the new relationship between you and me.

(*Turning to me:*) I don't feel any bad feelings about my mother, or that I have to make anything up to her.

**Paula:** That's what I wanted to know from you.

**Robin** (*holds and taking deep breaths*): Sometimes my mother speaks for me, rather than to me. What I've liked this week is that my mother has spoken directly to me.

**Les:** Paula, what I've noticed all week is how different things between you and Robin are, compared to the way things are between you and David. What I just noticed is that when you finished things up, Robin got more tense. I think you two are having a hard time saying goodbye and knowing you will live okay alone. You've been taking care of one another for so many years. (*Robin is crying now and I respond.*)

**Robin:** Yes.

**Les:** You started reacting, even more when I talked, about you and your mother taking care of each other for a long time.

**Robin:** Well, we have been taking care of each other.

**Les:** I think Paula is having a hard time letting you take care of yourself. You are having a hard time believing she can take care of herself.

**Robin:** I know I can, though. I know I can get apart from my mother, and take care of me.

**Les:** Robin, are you clear that you will not ever do anything to hurt or kill yourself no matter how far apart you are from your families?

**Robin** (*questioningly, and less anxious*): I am positive about that. Yes, I am sure.

**Les:** Would you tell your mother and brother that?

**Robin** (*turning, beginning to wring his hands and then stopping*): Mom, David, I won't kill or hurt myself ever—that's the truth.

**Les:** Good. I believe you. Now imagine your dad is in front of you and tell him the same thing.

**Robin** (*to Les*): That's harder. I think I'll sit on my hands as I do it. (*Everyone cheers and supports Robin as he now goes ahead.*) Dad and Drake. I won't harm myself in anyway no matter what.

**Les:** Robin, is that true?

**Robin:** Yes.

**Les:** Good. I also believe you on this one. (*The whole room cheers and Robin beams.*)

148

**Les:** Robin, now let's shift back. Do you also believe that your mother can take care of herself, without you?

**Robin:** Yes.

**Paula** *(without feeling)*: I could go away, without feeling any discomfort about leaving you, Robin. I have plenty of problems of my own, but I can take care of them without your help.

**Robin** *(with relief)*: Yes.

**Barbara** *(one of the trainees)*: Paula, the way I see you getting stuck is with your absolutes. You say you will feel no discomfort about leaving. But I think it's natural for you to have some pain and discomfort about leaving your son. When you speak in absolutes, I think, you must sound unbelievable to Robin. He gets anxious because what you're saying can't be true.

**Paula:** That's a good point. In the last couple years I've felt that, to get my point across to Robin, I had to be very definite.

**Les:** Paula, Robin probably doesn't understand everything. That's not your responsibility. Nor are you able to make him understand.

**Paula:** But I'm concerned about it.

**Les:** You're still trying make him understand things the way you do. It is his responsibility to understand, and it is his separate right to understand some things differently than you do. Also, you're underestimating him, if you keep trying to help him understand by overstating things.

It is going to be hard for you when you leave here. David will ask questions he's never asked before, and Robin might be angry with you. There are all sorts of possibilities. You can't make them go away.

**Paula** *(soft and tearful now)*: I know.

**Les:** I think one of the things Robin should hear from you is that you have resources on your own, and that when you get back, you will take care of yourself.

*(Turning:)* Am I right Robin?

**Robin:** Yes.

**Paula** *(to Robin)*: Through the things that I've experienced in my life, I've picked up some knowledge that I can use every day and rely on. I can really take good care of myself.

**Robin:** I believe that. Now I have to act on that.

**Les:** What do you mean, Robin?

**Robin:** I believe what my Mom told me. But it's one thing to believe it, and another to act on it.

**Les:** What do you mean, "act on it"?

**Robin:** Knowing that my Mom can take care of herself, and then not calling her up every two seconds and things like that. I feel finished now with all this.

**Les:** Will you tell your Mom that?

**Robin** *(to Paula)*: I feel finished now, Mom.

**Les:** David?

**David:** I'm beginning to wonder about my birthday tonight.

*Even though Robin is now quiet and finished, we don't believe that his problems are solved. But if Paula can maintain her separateness, she will be able to parent Robin more consistently and with more nuturing, support and encouragement.*

"Before this week, I would have died rather than talk about what I did. Now I know I'm okay—that I can talk."

—Bill Sarnon

# 4

# The Sarnons

## MONDAY MORNING

## FAMILY GROUP—LES SPEAKING

*The Sarnons arrived last night, after dinner, and remained nearly invisible until the this morning's session. Ruth and I are in the main living room with all four families. Instead of eating breakfast, Bette went running. Her face is taut and clean. Bill is obviously having a lot of trouble with his injured leg. As he lowers himself onto a pillow in the center of the room, he holds his leg out stiffly. Nick gives him an arm to lean on. Bette cries when David Quinn talks about his trouble in school. She tells David that she feels sad for him, that she is a reading teacher, and would like to help him. David cries softly in response.*

*I asked each family to talk together about what they wanted to get out of the week—to identify what their problems were and what they wanted to change. This task structures the session and reduces the anxiety of starting.*

**Bill** *(In a low monotonous voice, with his head down)*: From my standpoint, what we're here for is . . . *(He drifts off and talks about the background of his marriage, about his stepson, telling that Bette's divorce occurred when Nick was twelve. We can barely hear him.)*

*When Bill talks, no one in the room pays much attention. Bill wanders on, but we refrain from intervening.*

**Bill** *(continues getting back to our question)*: Since the time of our—Bette's and my—marriage, Nick and I haven't gotten along as well as we should. We both tried for six months. Then Nick didn't try. When Nick didn't try I backed off. Then Nick suddenly started to try harder. One of the things I want to get out of this week is a closer relationship with Nick.

*Bill begins to make a contract. It is only beginning, because we don't yet know anything about the family's way of interacting or whether this is something Bill wants or thinks he should want.*

**Ruth:** I think we need some more information. Will you talk among yourselves about this?

**Nick:** Bill has a daughter who just got married. And my real Dad just got married and has a new son. (He stops and looks at his mother before going on.) I was an only child. My real father lives near us, in Milwaukee, and I see him in the summer.

**Bill:** Can I say more about Nick? He's had problems in school. I see these problems as the result of his not very close relationship with his father. Nick has a very close relationship with his mother. I'm not filling the spot as his father. I think that some of Nick's problems have to do with something missing.

**Les:** Bill, stop! You're flowing over with information. It's getting hard to keep track. So far we haven't heard your family talking together about why you're here.

**Bill** *(putting his head down and lowering his voice even further)*: I'm sorry.

*Bill obviously cares about his family. His anxious but tentative approach invites people to ignore or rebuff him. His head-down response and apology make it hard to confront him.*

**Ruth:** What do you mean exactly by school problems, will you talk together about that?

*Bill and Bette respond separately but simultaneously.
Their answers are a little surprising. Though Nick is
having trouble with math, he's doing extremely well in
his other subjects and is a star basketball player. He
also gets along well with friends. He's only in the ninth
grade, but he looks like a high school senior.*

**Ruth:** Nick, are you a little behind yourself in school?
**Bette:** No, he's not. He just looks big for his age.

*Bette jumps in instantly to speak for her son. Her
defensive response indicates the closeness between mother
and son. We see that they form a twosome and keep Bill
on the outside. We are also being kept on the outside.
They repeatedly ignore our direction for them to talk
together.*

**Bette:** Nick's trouble with math doesn't have to do with
his study habits. He got 99 in math at summer school. I
think things are too easy for him and he gets bored. He
liked math at the beginning, when he was 7.
**Ruth:** Bette, I'm aware that you think you know a lot
about what goes on inside Nick. How did things get to be
this way?
**Bette** *(abruptly switching topics)*: I admire Bill's candid
way of putting things.

*Bette enthusiastically tells her version of Bill's and
Nick's relationship. She seems to delight in talking
about the other people in her family. She blocked out
Ruth's question about Nick and herself.*

**Bette:** I always saw myself as trying to get the two of
them together. During the last year they've both been
trying, and things have gotten better. But there's
something else. Nick has also gotten himself into some
trouble—horrible things!
**Ruth:** What do you mean?

*Ruth decides to move ahead rather than to confront
Bette on the switch.*

**Bette:** I won't tell them in order, but there are so many
things. He stole a bicycle once, and took the bike apart and

sold the parts. When Bill and I went out in the evenings, we had Nick agree not to have friends over or go out. He broke the agreement. He would climb up on the roof and throw eggs at cars. Then came the worst thing ever. (Bette gestures dramatically with her thin arms. Nick sits back, arms across his chest, looking bored and angry.) He started drinking. He was a star player on the basketball team and several times he came home drunk.

*We don't share her apparent panic about the "horrible things" she describes.*

**Bette:** All the kids who signed Nick's year book made comments about him as "The Drinker."
**Ruth:** You're very involved in Nick's life.

*Again, Ruth tries to make contact. This time, Bette is more responsive. Ruth and I are beginning to see how slowly we will need to go with Bette. We wonder why.*

**Bette** *(leaning forward with hands in praying gesture):* He's really important to me. (She begins to cry. So far, she only expresses emotion when she talks about the connection between Nicholas and herself.) I feel guilty. I spent too much time doing things for myself during Nick's life. He has needed more of me than I was able to give him. I took up running when he was a baby. When he was six I'd take him to the lake and leave him with some toys—asking another kid to take care of him. I'd say, "I'll be gone for a short time," and then I'd run maybe 10 miles, sometimes 20. Up to two or sometimes three hours later I'd come back and he'd be there all alone. I was selfish. I should have been there all the time.
**Ruth:** Bette, am I hearing this as what you want to do for yourself and your family here this week?
**Bette:** Yes, I need to rid myself of guilt, and relieve myself of being responsible for Nick. We talked about this guilt a little. We've come a long way. But we have farther to go.
**Ruth:** In this week we are available to help you finish that involvement with your son and move on.

*Bette's connection with Nick is intensified by her guilt from the past. When Ruth attempts contact and contract formation, Bette responds verbally, but moves away by folding her arms around her knees, up in front of her. We don't pursue the guilt issue further, because this is the first session.*

**Ruth:** But there's still a missing piece. Bette what about your relationship with Bill?
*(Bill moves over and pats Bette's knee. Bette unfolds and nuzzles him.)*
**Bill** *(responding for Bette and again trying to represent the family)*: We have a very good marriage.
There is basically only one thing I'd like to do here. I want to plan for the future. My disability will make our style of life different in the years ahead. I want to have some plans for that. I'll probably have to have an artificial knee. That means I'll have to sit a lot. In my current job, as head of a pathology lab, I need to stand much of the time.
**Bette:** No, you won't have to change that much.
**Bill:** No. One leg would be shorter. Walking and standing for any length of time will be difficult. I'll have to change my job.
**Ruth:** Bill, I like the way that you directly clarified your thinking with Bette even though you took over her answer. Am I hearing that another one of your goals for the week is for you and Bette to make a family plan?

*We will take every opportunity to support Bill or anyone in this family who defines him- or herself. Bill is the protector and burden carrier; Bette is very much the champion of the victim. That championship presents problems: Both Nick and Bill are well comforted and taken care of, but both are treated as though they can't think or feel for themselves.*

**Bill:** Not to exclude Nick, of course.
**Ruth** *(with an exagerrated astonished look on her face)*: I think it will be okay to exclude Nick. Ten years from now, he'll be 25. I can't imagine you'll want to be hanging around much, Nick. *(There is some laughter. Nick looks with a smile from Bill to Bette.)*
**Ruth** *(getting back to her original question)*: What's on your mind for you and Bill, Bette?

**Bette:** I'm afraid he won't deal with his feelings around the accident and—

*Bette treats Bill's anger at his accident as the family's major problem. So many people have blamed her family's troubles on Bill's anger that Betty believes it and uses it to explain away her family's current discomfort. She maintains that comfortable explanation by not listening to, or accepting, any other explanation. Bill's anger is her frame of reference. One of our goals will be to help this family change its frame of reference. We will proceed to do the individual work that will relieve Bette's need to hold on to an oversimplified explanation of the distress.*

**Bill** *(quietly interrupting)*: There's more that we have to plan about, Bette.

**Les** *(putting a hand out)*: Again, I like you clarifying things and challenging Bette, but it's also important that we hear from Bette, without her being interrupted before she is finished.

*This transaction exemplifies our dilemma. Bill's interruption and his apparent irritation might have led to the reference we were looking for. He challenged Bette's plan to help him with his anger. His interruption also illustrates how this family comments on each other's thoughts. This leads to overinvolvement and unclear boundaries. We react to the Sarnons' nonverbal relationship. Throughout this past sequence, Bill lovingly touched Bette's knee, modulating any disagreement. Nick's response confirms our current hypothesis: This family shares the myth that a good relationship has little room for disagreement.*

**Nick:** I really like Bill a lot.

# MONDAY AFTERNOON
# INDIVIDUAL FAMILIES—WITH RUTH

*The morning was long and tedious. People have not had enough individual attention so we decide to divide the group. I take the Sarnons, Quinns, and the older Barkers. Les takes the younger Barkers and the Dellapietras.*

*I meet my group in the living room of one of the condominiums. Two sofas flank a small fireplace, with cushions between them. I sit on a pillow, to one side of the hearth.*

**Ruth:** Who wants to begin?

**Bill** *(sunk in the corner of the sofa, still speaking in his monotone)*: I'm the one that brought this family. I don't believe they really understand the importance of why they've come to the workshop.

*He returns to the theme of the morning. Bill seems clearly determined to make some changes for himself and his family.*

**Bill:** I had no family the first time around—with my parents—and no family the second time around—with my first wife. I believe this is my last go. I came from a large family, but I was isolated in it. When I got married the first time, I knew it was a mistake after one week. I wasn't very smart in that marriage; I stayed married for twenty years.

*This says a lot about Bill. He knew that something is wrong, but he didn't do anything about it for 20 years.*

**Bill:** What I realize now is there just aren't any twenty-year periods left for me. I am forty-six. My knee is a problem. I can't let any more years go by without making plans.

**Ruth:** What will happen if things don't come together for you here, this week?

*Wherever we hear themes of death and desperation, we pursue them. If someone has decided to die either intentionally, through suicide, or indirectly, through accident or illness, we move to close the escape hatches.*

**Bill:** I will have to do something myself.

**Ruth:** What do you mean?

**Bill:** I'll try again on my own.

**Ruth:** Does that mean you'll leave your family?
**Bill:** It could mean . . . I could . . .

*He trails off. I go back to pick up on the urgency of his words. I especially remember his response, in the questionnaire, that the cause of his death might be suicide.*

**Ruth:** Are you suicidal?
**Bill:** I don't think so. The idea of killing myself has crossed my mind, but I've never considered it seriously. I have a family history of depression, alcoholism, and serious mental disorders. My sister is a schizophrenic. I've been depressed off and on for a long time.
**Bette:** I'm worried about Bill. He's probably not going to get over his depression because, I think, his depression is related to his accident.
**Ruth:** Are you worried about Bill's depression, Nick?
**Nick:** Yes, I'm worried that it's my fault, because I haven't been a real son to him.

*Again, Bette and Nick are defining Bill's depression. Bill can't even have his own depression. I move to see if I can encourage some separation.*

**Ruth:** Bill, you say that you come from a family of unhappy people. (Ruth turning to Nick and Bette). It's my hunch that Bill's depression is not related to you, Nick, or to the accident, Bette. It may not be related to anything that you, Bette, and you, Nick, even know anything about.
**Nick:** No matter what, I would still try to be as good a son as possible to Bill.
**Bill:** Thanks, Nick. It's good for me to know that, because I didn't have a good relationship with my daughter.

*Bill speaks in a grave tone. This isn't a casual remark.*

**Ruth:** The important time in your relationship with your daughter occurred many years before the accident. *(I look directly at Bette.)* Bill, were you depressed before the accident?
**Bill:** Yes. Sure, I was depressed before the accident, but I could use physical activity as a way to get out of my

depression. Since the accident, I can't do that. I don't have
that way of getting out of myself.

Right now I feel more relaxed because I'm finally
getting started. This is something that I've never done
before. I need to do something.

**Bette:** Yes, Bill does need to do something. You need to
get angry, Bill. *(Bill responds so quietly that no one can
hear him.)*

> *Bette needs to control the direction and object of
> Bill's anger. She keeps herself hidden by continuing to
> define his task and direction.*

**Ruth:** Bill, I can't hear you. I want you to talk so
loudly that the pictures on the back wall shake. *(As soon as
I say this, Bette leans over and touches Bill, as if to quiet
him.)*

**Ruth:** Bill, it seems to be really familiar that people try
to guide you and make you behave in certain ways.

**Bill:** You're right. It dates from my childhood when
people were always trying to make me be different. My
mother was a domineering person, and at 86, she still is.
She always wanted me to be good, be perfect in fact, and to
be the best. I had to be the best. I had to be the best . . .

> *I particularly note his repetition of "the best."*

**Bill:** . . . my father was passive. He wasn't there very
much. When he was there, he kept his distance.

> *Bill's description of his mother and father concur
> with my sense of what's going on in his present family.
> Bette wants her son and her husband to be perfect, the
> best. Bill is generally passive and lets himself be
> defined, but here he is determined to get his story out in
> his own way and in his own time, family rules
> notwithstanding. I decide to follow and support Bill's
> lead to speak up for himself both in his original family
> and here.*

**Ruth:** Will you give me an example of how your mother
wanted you to be?

**Bill:** She never wanted me to cause any trouble. She
always expected me to have my own money, to be on my

own, never to ask her for anything. I had to excel at school, because she wanted me to be all the things that she couldn't be.

*This is similar to the way Bette acts with Nick. Bette's father was disappointed she wasn't a boy.*

**Bill:** My younger sister and I were the only ones in the family who followed Mother's line.
**Ruth:** What did the others do?
**Bill:** My brother became a C.P.A., but he's depressed, alcoholic, and now on his fourth marriage. My sister is a schizophrenic. She has been hospitalized for years.
**Ruth:** Bill, I imagine that as you sit and look at things now, it still looks best that you followed your mother's line and didn't become alcoholic or schizophrenic. Will you now sit back and think a minute about whether you see similarities between your old family and this current one.

*I want to see if I can gain entry to the family system via Bill's lead. I also support his definition of things.*

**Bill:** One similarity I see is that I'm continually attracted to domineering women. I mean strong women. Bette is strong, but not domineering at all. (He says this with emphasis, reaching over to her again.) I may have followed my father's role, in being quiet and often absent. The thing between Bette and Nick is similar, too, I guess, to the way my mother acted toward my brother.

*The Sarnons have gained some understanding of the problems and the family members have more than enough information. Right now I am wondering if Bette heard Bill's comparison of her relationship with Nick to his own brother's relationship with his mother.*

**Ruth:** Bill, I'd like you to know, as it seems that you perceive many women as trying to change you, that I'm not going to fall into that trap. I can't make you be perfect or different, and I don't want to. I like you as you are, and what's most important is that you define what you want, and what you will change here.
**Nick:** I believe Bill could do anything that he really wanted to.

*The myth of perfection has been challenged, and
again Nick is smoothing things over. We have been
working for a long time, but Nick's statement takes us
back to "go." I call a short break. When we return, I
change the emphasis.*

**Ruth:** Bette, what was your first husband like?
**Bette:** He was a good person—nice, hard-working—but
he was not at all supportive of me. Nick puts him on a
pedestal. My first husband talked a good line, but didn't
live it. Bill talks very little, but he acts and lives his life.

*Bette is eager to cooperate, but it is hard to have any
flow in the communication with her. She answers
succinctly, and then things just stop. I try to make
contact in another area.*

**Ruth:** I'd like to go on Bette. Will you pick an age
when you were a girl, and describe what things were like
for you in your family then?

*This is an active approach to getting historical data.
It can make the work lively and real, and involving for
others as well.*

**Bette** *(in a flat voice)*: I am 10. I have a brother who is
four—the most wonderful gift a ten-year-old girl could
have. I have a twin sister, Barbara. She and I are not at all
alike. I am dull, tall, skinny, ugly, and I wear thick glasses.
My sister is shorter, curvier, with beautiful blonde hair and
blue eyes. (Bette laughs dryly at this description.) I solved
all the issues about the differences between me and my
sister by not feeling I had to be as pretty as she was. I
decided to enjoy my brothers instead, and was close to
them.

*Bette tells this with a noticeable flatness and
uninvolvement. She doesn't get things going. I am
frustrated and impatient. I wonder if some physical
movement will help.*

**Ruth** *(picking up two pieces of rope, each about three
feet long)*: Bette, that's important information that you

have just shared. Will you experiment now and tie one of these to Nick's wrist and hold on to the other end of it? Tie the other one to Bill's wrist and hold on to the end of it, too.

*Bette always connects herself to the two men in her current family. In addition, she has just told us about getting away from her twin and attaching herself to her brothers as a child. Bette looks uncomfortable as she ties on the ropes.*

**Ruth:** You are in control of them for the rest of the afternoon. You can give them as much rope as you want to, and you can bring them in as close as you want to. (Bette looks frightened) What are you feeling right now, Bette?
**Bette:** I don't know what you're trying to get from this. What do you expect?
**Ruth:** I have nothing particular in my mind. I want you to see what you experience or feel as you have them on the other end of the rope. I will be interested in what it is like for Bill and Nick.

*One of the major ways we move people, in the early days of the workshop, is to bring their dilemma to life. I simply hoped Bette might make an emotional connection. Her response ("I don't know what you're trying to get from this") reflects her defensiveness against showing herself in an unstructured situation.*

**Ruth:** Bill, what are you thinking, tied to Bette?
**Bill** *(flatly)*: I don't know what's going on.
**Bette** *(instantly)*: I think what Bill is trying to say is—
**Ruth** *(interrupting)*: Bette, you need to pull the rope a little bit when you're thinking for Bill. (Bette laughs.) You need to pull the rope everytime you're interpreting for either your husband or your son. (Nick smiles broadly.)
**Ruth:** What is your smile about, Nick?
**Nick:** Actually, I've got *her*. *(He has wound the rope up so that he has about three times as much rope as Bette does and can jerk her around.)* Mom, you can try to control me as much as you want. But I've got all the slack. You may have the end of the rope to pull me with, but I have enough of the middle so that I can do exactly what I want.

*The rope trick reflected a familiar response in Nick. He allows himself to put up with only so much control. His not doing his math, drinking, and sneaking out are ways of taking up some of the slack. He gives himself the advantage in the connection between himself and his mother.*

**Nick:** You should have watched what I was doing, Mom. Next time you should be more careful about how much slack you're giving me.
**Bette:** I purposely gave you slack so that you could feel freedom and become more trusting.

*Nick and Bette compete for control of their relationship. Being close is not so important; not being separate is.*

**Nick:** I don't want you pulling me around. I want you to trust me enough to let go.
**Ruth:** Nick, will you say to your mother: 'I don't know if you'll ever let me go.'
**Nick:** I hope, Mother, you'll let me go when I'm old enough. *(To me)* I do feel as if she'll never let me go. I know she'll let me have some slack, but I feel she'll always try to have a piece of me—for whatever suits her needs. I do feel manipulated and hung onto by Mom. Sometimes. But sometimes I don't.

*Sometimes we stimulate action by suggesting words. We note responses, carefully. Sometimes people may accept our view, as Nick did, or reject our view when we're not right. Either way we get information that is important.*

**Ruth:** We'll stop right there. We won't go any further at the moment. Nick, I like your clarity and courage to say what you think.

*I decide to leave them with this experience, before they begin rationalizing and over-explaining. When proceeding might undermine what has been done, we stop.*

**Bill:** I think we've had a good start.

**Ruth:** *(Turning to the other families)* Is there anyone else who has something to do?

**Bette:** Ruth, why didn't you suggest to Bill that he has unfinished business with his mother?

*Bill pulls on the rope quickly and hard. There's some laughter and awareness in the room. I refuse to answer Bette's question and the afternoon session ends for the Sarnons.*

# TUESDAY MORNING

# YOUNG PEOPLE'S GROUP—WITH LES

*The parents are with Ruth. The young people are with me—Nick, David, Robin, Melissa, and Maria. Gerry, Jr., and Marco, the youngest children, are with Kitty, the play therapist.*

*By the time I arrive, the kids are already connectioning nicely. I take a few minutes to let them finish their games, Checkers and Sorry, as I watch what's going on. What sticks out is Nick's quietness. When the games end, I start with him.*

**Les:** What is most important in your mind now, Nick?

**Nick:** I'm trying to get my family together—my mother, my stepfather, and me.

*He sees himself as a helper. He changes the subject, from himself to the other members of the family. This is exactly what the rest of his family does.*

**Nick** *(continuing)*: Bill would try to be nice to me, and I couldn't respond, and he couldn't respond to me. Lately things have been going better. There's a lot of tension in the house, still. I try now, though, to treat Bill like I treat my real Dad—to kid around a lot. In a sense, I lost my dad. That's made it more difficult to accept Bill.

**Les:** What has to happen to change things for you Nick?

**Nick:** I'm going to help Bill get out of his depression, and then I'm going to start treating him like I do my real Dad.

*Nick is sliding over the surface of things again. Taking care of Bill, helping him get out of his depression, is a way of avoiding his own sadness about losing his real father and not being good enough for his mother.*

**Les:** Everyone in your family puts a lot of energy into making sure things are nice. This must be hard, because you must have some feelings about losing your Dad. Will you share more about that?

*Nick rambles on. He speaks very slowly and essentially shares nothing. The other kids are getting restless. I stop and ask Nick and the rest of the group to draw pictures showing the worst day in their lives with their families. The purpose of this drawing assignment is to change the group energy from restlessness to productive working to see if Nick will reveal any more of himself. After we go through some of the pictures, Nick is eager to talk about his.*

**Nick:** I've done two pictures, and neither is quite right. The first is a picture of Bill's and Bette's wedding. I wanted things to be just right. I'm not satisfied with the picture. The other is of the time when I set up a play in a basketball game, and the other team broke it up. It's not as good as I wanted it to be.

*I'm finding it a struggle to work with Nick. Unless I find exactly the right word, unless I, too, am perfect, he doesn't respond. My comments slide off his back. I have two specific goals for him—loosening up with people, and easing the strict standards he sets for himself. I want him to decide he is worthwhile even if he is not perfect, hopefully while he is here.*

**Les** *(putting an empty chair in front of Nick)*: Imagine your mother is there, sitting in the chair. Describe what she looks like. Begin talking to her. Tell her what it is like for you when everything has to be perfect for her.

**Nick:** She looks thin and straight and hard. I'm angry with you, Bette. I can never do anything right for you. You're never going to like anything.

**Les:** Will you switch chairs, Nick, and answer as your mother?

**Nick** *(as Bette)*: Nick, you don't have to be perfect. I know you work hard to please me. You work so hard in basketball that you nearly kill yourself.

**Nick** *(switching chairs)*: You cut me down, Mom. I did the best I could, and you cut me down. You are condescending.

*(He switches back to the Bette chair. I talk to Nick, as Bette, to explore Nick's perception of how his mother thinks and feels.)*

**Les:** Bette, who in your background wanted you to be perfect?

**Nick** *(Mimicking Bette, he assumes a stiff posture and parent-like voice)*: When I was a kid I trained eight hours a day for swimming and running. My father said, "Bring back better," when I came in second in a race or brought home 99s in arithmetic.

**Les:** Then, when you were a kid, Bette, you were perfect.

**Nick** *(as Bette)*: Almost perfect. *(He switches to the Nick chair and, as Nick, sits strongly forward and speaks with force.)*

**Nick:** I'm not even almost perfect, Mom, and you don't even see me. You're doing the same thing to me that your Dad did to you.

**Les:** Do you get into battles with your mother about what's right for you? My hunch is that math could be one of those battles, or even some of the other things you do.

**Nick:** Yes. I've got to bring my Mom around to my point of view. Maybe I'll calm down and not be bitter toward her, then.

*The separation issue becomes clearer—in Nick's view, Bette is attempting to live through him and is acting like her father did. Nick gets angry. Then he feels bad for being angry and for not living up to her expectations. This is another example of the competition between Nick and Bette as they struggle to determine who knows best about Nick.*

**Nick:** Here's what I would like to do. I'd like not to be bitter towards my mother. That would be enough. I wouldn't be fighting with her. I wouldn't keep trying to get back at her.
**Les:** That's a clear statement for yourself, Nick. That's really fine. We will help you do that.

*Nick has not only made a clear contract about what he wants to get out of the workshop, he has also allowed himself a small connection with me. The structure we provide, dividing kids from parents, makes it easier for Nick to separate a little from his mother.*

# PARENTS' GROUP—WITH RUTH

*Bill and Bette are sitting in chairs in a semicircle with the other parents. Bill is leaning forward with his arms propped on the arms of the chair. Bette sits next to Bill and is leaning in toward him. As he speaks, she moves her chair with a grating sound toward his.*

**Bill:** I need some help in learning how to make decisions.
**Ruth:** Okay. Bette, will you move to another chair, next to someone else so that you can watch as Bill works?

*I ask Bette to move, because every time Bill talks about himself, Bette has literally put her hands on him. Many times this stops him. Changing their physical relationship is a metaphor for the potential changes in their relationship.*

**Bill:** There have been many times in my life when I've let other people make decisions for me. As things turned out, those decisions were wrong. If I'd made the choice myself, I think I would have been right.

*Bill's statement about himself and his tentativeness are important. I ask him to move back through his life, and to stop and experience some of the times he has had difficulty making decisions. This is progressive regression. I've moved Bette away to stop her interference. I hope she will see that what's going on with Bill now is not the result of the accident, or of the fact that Nick hasn't been a good son.*

**Ruth:** Bill, will you remember a time, in the recent past, when you had difficulties making a decision?

**Bill:** The most obvious one was deciding about my residency after being an intern. I had to make a decision about two job possibilities. I let someone else decide which job I should take. A year into that residency, I became aware that I should have taken the other job. I felt terrible and helpless to do anything then—it was too late.

**Ruth:** Will you share an incident from an earlier time in your life when similar thinking and feeling went on?

**Bill:** It was my first year in medical school. I was doing fine. But I had never intended to go to medical school. My advisor told me I should stay in medical school—that eventually I would find something I liked. My advisor was wrong.

**Ruth:** And any time earlier?

**Bill:** When I first entered college I let my advisor put me into a premedical program.

**Ruth:** There certainly were lots of times, is there anything even earlier?

**Bill** *(haltingly)*: When I was 10, I was on deck in a baseball game. The bases were loaded and there were two outs. My older brother said we needed a run so badly that I should stick my head out and let my head get hit. That way I'd get on base automatically. When I got to bat, of course I did this. I got hit in the eye and had a lot of trouble for months with blurred vision. *(He laughs.)*

**Ruth:** It's not funny. When you don't use your own judgement, you get yourself into situations that end up with you being hurt. Its not okay to get hurt or to laugh at hurting yourself.

*Bill's laugh is gallows humor, something that we consistently confront. The laugh confirms his negative view of himself.*

**Ruth** *(continues)*: Stay in that place and time, when you were 10 and your eye was hurt. It seems that now you may ask people to make decisions for you so you won't have to take responsibility for your own thinking and your own actions. That way you can maintain that predictable old spot.

**Bill:** Yes, that makes sense to me. The strongest influences in my life were my mother and the church—they were always right and always responsible. I guess I am used to making others responsible.

**Ruth:** Be 10 right now. Where is your father?

**Bill:** He was passive, but always supportive. *(Bill's face tightens up. He begins to cry.)*

> *In regressive work, we look for the point at which information and feeling meet. This is the first sign of genuine emotion in our work with Bill. Up until now, everything has been delivered flatly.*

**Ruth:** Move into this other chair and be your father.

**Bill** *(as his father, Bob)*: I never knew that you needed my help. You were always so self-sufficient. Also, I had my own problems, Bill. I didn't see what was going on with you, and you didn't show me. I'm sorry.

> *"Self-sufficient" can be replaced with the words "not a bother"—Bill's description of what his mother wanted him to be.*

**Ruth:** As you say, Bob, you missed a lot because your son, Bill, wouldn't let you give him help, and you had your own problems too. Do you know where all this came from?

**Bill** *(as Bob)*: From the relationship with my wife. If I challenged her, there was a major battle. To expect that Bill wanted any help would have been a challenge to my wife's idea of what a son should be, so I stayed away from that. I hadn't challenged my wife on anything, since before the children were born.

**Ruth:** So, Bob, in some ways Bill's silence helped you out.

**Bill** *(as Bob)*: Yes.

**Ruth:** Change chairs now and reply to your father. *(Bill returns to his chair.)*

**Bill:** I understand, Dad.

**Ruth:** Stay with what you're feeling and continue.

**Bill:** I'm sorry, Dad. (Holding back tears) I love you.

**Ruth:** Tell him what you are sad about.

**Bill:** I'm sad I didn't show you. I understand it was my fault now.

**Ruth:** Do you believe it was all your fault?

**Bill:** Yes, I think I always have. I'm finished with my father here. I want to talk to him in person.

> *There are two parts in Bill's impasse. First, he is shielding his father. Second, he is taking all of the blame and responsibility upon himself. We see both of these characteristics in his current behavior. We will continue to follow these issues.*
>
> *Bill's close-out response is also important. He leaves no opening to proceed so we stop.*

**Ruth:** That sounds important, Bill.

> *I've done enough pushing. I'm aware that Bill is holding his father and me off, as if it were somehow very important.*
>
> *I shift to Bette to find out her response. When that response reveals little feeling about herself or her relationship to Bill, I ask Bette to give some information about her childhood.*
>
> *I constantly seek information about why Bette seems so sealed off and protective. Is it something from her past? Is it something current that we don't know about? Is it me or us? If it is me, what do I need to change?*

**Bette** (*smiling widely but tightly*)**:** My twin was smart and popular and pretty. I was fairly smart, and I had some friends, but I was not pretty.

**Ruth:** Bette, I don't understand your smile right now. What you are saying sounds sad to me, not funny. When you smile it's hard to get in touch with you. It seems that, when you get close to something, you flash that smile. It blocks your own feelings, and me, or others, out.

**Bette:** I don't think I do that. Can I go on? My twin and I dressed alike, before the day she drew a line down the center of our bedroom. We used to fight a lot, but that stopped with the separation. My twin built a wall, with a rope marking the middle of the room. The dressing alike stopped one day, around the same time a boy in the school yard asked me why Barbara and I wore the same clothes. I said, "Because we're twins." And he said, "How can that be? She's pretty and you're ugly." At this point, I said I'd never again dress the same.

**Ruth:** That must have been a very important and difficult day for you. How old were you then?

**Bette:** I was 10, and it wasn't difficult.

**Ruth:** I feel closed out again. All this important information comes in a flat tone and with a lot of verbal nudging on my part. Bette, you volunteer some things and then dam yourself up, as if I were poison or something. Are you frightened of me or angry with me?

**Bette:** No!

*Bette acts as if she has to do everything just right, as if others, if they ever get the chance, will be as cruel to her as that boy was. I can try to push into the deep hurt or anger. However, every place I go, I seem to get stopped. Finally, I decide not to pursue the point. The relationship between Bette and myself is strikingly shaky and sterile. I also suspect (based on this session) that Bette links me to her twin sister. My third hunch is that she really sees me as harmful. Whatever she feels, I can get nowhere.*

*Berenice Barker, who comments now, had talked with Bette at dinner Monday night. They seemed to be getting along well.*

**Berenice:** Bette, how did you feel, this morning, when I said I was upset that you always make things nice and neat and that you have no emotional involvement with me?

**Bette:** I admired you for saying it.

**Berenice:** That's nice, but it's another stopper. No matter what I say, you remain polite and removed.

*(Other women in the group tell Bette that it is hard for them to make contact with her. Finally, at Paula Quinn's suggestion, Bette asks Bill if he also feels she blocks him.)*

*This illustrates how the group acts as a confrontation instrument. Members use experiences and information that the therapist doesn't have. I have to be careful that a scapegoating process does not occur.*

**Bill:** Yes, I do. That's why we're here.

*Bill defines the contract for the couple. The group support has been, and will continue to be, essential for Bill.*

**Bill** *(to Bette):* We talk about things. We make decisions together. But I get the feeling that you never mean what you say. If I go along with your words, I often think I'm doing something you don't really want to do. If I point this out to you—that what you say and what you want are different—we get no place. I'm upset about it. I wish this could be different.

*Bill's clearly confronting Bette is essentially the first shift in the family's pattern of interaction we have seen. It seems to have occurred through group support. Perhaps Bill needed the group to confront Bette's armor and to take a firm stance.*

**Ruth:** Bette, will you respond to Bill?
**Bette:** I don't understand what you are saying.
*(Bill shrivels and slouches at this response. I turn to Bill.)*
**Ruth:** It could be that Bette is not going to be able to change during this week. In fact it is very likely so. What would that mean to you, Bill? What would you do if Bette were to continue doing just what you have described?
**Bill:** I can't think about that.
**Ruth:** Will you think about that?

*This is a poignant statement. I hear it time and again. Bill's underlying belief is, "If I do think about it I will have to act. That action is terrifying to me. Learning that he can express himself without destroying others or being destroyed, is the cornerstone of much of the work Bill will do.*
*The meeting ends with Bette and Bill getting more feedback from the group.*

# TUESDAY AFTERNOON

# CHOCOLATE PUDDING—WITH RUTH

*All three of the Sarnons are in the chocolate pudding group with me. They sit next to each other on the lawn in bathing suits, bowls in their laps. Bette, sitting stiffly, speaks first.*

**Bette:** Of course this doesn't really count as part of the therapy. It doesn't make sense for me to be here anyway.

> *Bette discounts the significance of the entire group and her participation in it. I decide not to confront her at this time.*
>
> *Bill begins the group. He is wearing his usual sulk and his nice-boy position of being willing to do or try anything. He is devoted to doing what he's supposed to do. Nick's eyes gleam as he sits down across from his mother. As soon as the rules for the chocolate pudding game are announced, Nick dives into his pudding bowl and throws two handfuls at his mother. He is aggressive with her, and he clearly delights in getting at her. Bette looks astonished. She regresses to about the age of 15. Bette and Nick spend the next several minutes of the session playing teen-agers: running around, laughing, smearing pudding on each other, and being almost oblivious to anything else that is going on in the group. Their play has many stimulating, but not necessarily seductive, elements. It is important to watch how Bette comes alive with Nick, as she does with no one else. Bill, sulking and serious sits back and watches what goes on. He dabs one fingerful of pudding at a time on himself, but on no one else.*
>
> *Some of the other kids in the group move in to play with Nick. When Melissa moves in, Bette sits down abruptly, wearing a long face. She tries to look prim. It isn't easy, because she has pudding all over her body.*
>
> *I decide to test the limits of Bill's quietness. I smear some chocolate pudding on his shoulders. No response. I put a dab on his nose. He sits there with a stone face. I put some on his chest and draw a heart over his heart. Bill neither protests or responds. Only once he puts a scant teaspoonful of pudding on my hand. After a few minutes he throws a tiny bit. It misses me. He speaks.*

**Bill** *(in a small, low voice)*: Someday you will know why I don't give anything back. I'll tell you something about why I don't give anything back. I'll tell you when I'm ready, but I'll tell you.

*(Bette has a scared look on her face and steps in.)*
**Bette:** Ruth, I'll tell you why Bill is the way he is. Bill, what you ought to do is—*(I gently shush her.)*

*The pudding group, frequently has unexpected outcomes, because it bypasses common defense positions. We must use effectively whatever develops for the final outcome to be useful to the client and or to us. (I think it was the unusual nature of the chocolate pudding session and the oddness of my physical confrontation with Bill that allowed him to share his secret on the following day.)*

*People leave to shower, before continuing the afternoon session. Nick is still excited about having had the chance to get at people, particularly his mother. Bette has reinstalled herself in her rigid, be-nice manner and still sees no reason for the exercise. Bill limps slowly after the others, still covered with pudding.*

# AFTER CHOCOLATE PUDDING
# (LES SPEAKING)

*After cleaning up, the chocolate pudding group members rejoin the large group. We are curious if Bill is ready to work. He begins his opening statement is in his old style—apologetic. As it turns out, he is fearful, not apologetic as we first thought.*

**Bill:** I hope very much that I'm not messing things up.
**Les:** What are you concerned about?
**Bill:** I feel a threat to my marriage, and a threat to my position, if I talk here. I'm concerned that I'm letting out something that should be secret and that I'm messing things up. Saying this in public could threaten my wife, my work, and my suit against the man who was careless. I'm afraid of what I'm contemplating. I'm scared of committing murder. I'm scared of committing suicide.

*The difference between Bill's bland, matter-of-fact tone and the horrifying nature of his words attracts our attention.*

**Bill** *(continuing)*: Even suing the man who crippled me won't take away my bitterness.

**Ruth:** You talked a little while ago, outside, about being angry at several people. Here are two pillows. Pretend those are the people you're mad at and talk to them.

**Bill:** To be perfectly honest, there were three people. *(Ruth puts out a third pillow).*

*The noise and distracted confusion in the room reflects the blandness of Bill's delivery. People aren't listening even though what he is saying is dramatic. Ruth hands Bill an encounter bat made of foam. She gives him no instructions. I stand up beside him. Bill begins to hit the first pillow, putting words to his actions.*

**Bill** *(his voice is weirdly quiet)*: You tried to kill me. I'm going to hit you. You swung the jeep around knowing I was the one who would get hurt. It was a game to you.

*No amount of encouragement from Ruth or me has helped Bill to change his robot-tight stance.*

**Les:** What's going on with you, Bill?

**Bill:** There's nothing there.

**Ruth:** Stay with that idea, that there's nothing there, and speak to them.

**Bill:** I'm worried that there is no one there and I will just have to lie here.

**Les:** Continue.

**Bill** *(standing in the middle of the room with his head forward and his shoulders slumped.)*: I never wanted to kill you. I want this to be over with. *(Talking to the pillows:)* I just want to be finished with this. I won't kill you or anyone or myself.

**Les:** Now also tell Bette and Nick that you won't hurt those men, or anyone else, including yourself.

*Bette's face has opened up a tiny bit. She shows some pain, as Bill makes his reassuring statement to Nick and her.*

*Bill shifts the focus again and then stops. This is significant. Nick and Bette have been frightened of Bill's determined anger. His statement clarifying that he won't hurt or kill anyone is relieving.*

**Les:** Ruth, do you have any place to go now? Bill seems stopped.

**Ruth:** Yes. What happened when the car turned over?

**Bill:** The driver was showing off, going back and forth from one side of the road to the other. He drove up onto a hill on the right side of the road, and the jeep flipped over. I was right behind the driver, and I was the only one who flew down the side of the mountain. I ended up far away from the jeep with my leg crushed. Bette organized everyone to search and to bring me back.

**Ruth:** Bill, as you talk now I notice your mouth is tightly closed, your body is hunched, and you hesitate. You don't let any sounds out freely. Will you put yourself into the physical position that you were when you were thrown and landed? Close your eyes and, beginning deep in your stomach, let all the sounds out from that time. *(Bill gets into that position: lying on his side with his leg twisted under him. He remains silent.)*

**Ruth:** You need to make noise. *(Bill begins to breathe deeply but still isn't making any noise. Bette looks particularly stressed and sad.)*

**Ruth:** Bill you need to scream. You can't depend on Bette or anyone else guessing where you are and what's going on. You need to speak up for yourself. *(Bill becomes more and more agitated. His hand goes up to his head. He falls back on the pillows that are in the middle of the room.)*

**Ruth** *(continuing)*: You can't wait for somebody to guess what's going on. *(Bill begins to get up, then kneels forward, and covers his head with a pillow. Ruth and I move over to touch him.)*

**Ruth:** Put some sounds to what's going on, Bill. Nobody can even hear you.

**Bill:** I don't want people to hear me. I just want to stay here in silence.

*This comment sums up Bill's life position: "I just want to stay here in silence." I can imagine that he has said it many times, in many ways, to himself.*

**Ruth:** Don't keep waiting, and suffering in silence. Don't set it up so that other people never know what's

176

going on with you or have to guess. *(Ruth puts her hand on Bill's stomach.)* The sounds can come from all the way down here.

**Bill** *(looking very pained)*: This is not the issue.

**Ruth:** Yes, it is. Right now the issue is your being quiet and not saying what's going on with you. It won't work here for us to play it like Bette does. We can't guess what's going on and lead you off on our guesses. It's safe now to do something different.

*Bill is being pushed up against his original decision.*

**Les** *(to Ruth)*: I don't think that suffering in silence is new for Bill.

**Bill:** You're right. I can't go on right now. This isn't the time for me to continue. I've been quiet for a long time. I'm just not ready to let out the sounds.

**Ruth:** Okay.

**Les:** Bill, I respect your firmness. *(Bill goes back and sits down. Bette moves over to touch him. Several other group members speak up, including Edgar Barker, who is about Bill's age.)*

**Edgar:** It seems so obvious, but it's not to men like you and me, Bill. We have to learn that sometimes it's necessary to call for help. *(Bette is leaning over Bill solicitiously. Again she's losing herself in tending someone.)*

**Les:** Bette?

**Bette:** It's important to me that Bill work out his anger about the accident. You didn't know it, but he's angry toward me about it. I didn't know until this year that Bill thought I was negligent, too. I should have been the third pillow out there. He thinks the way he was pulled up permanently damaged his knee—that I helped to cripple him. We talked it out, but I still think Bill blames me for getting him up on the mountain in that jeep and for pulling him up wrong. I'm scared he won't be honest with himself.

**Ruth** *(softly and warmly)*: I think you should stay away from Bill for a while. Don't take a part in helping him seal things over now. This way you can see what is really going on with him and, if you're frightened, also keep yourself safe. *(Bette begins to cry. Nick gives her a box of Kleenex and a pat on the arm.)*

**Les:** Nick?

**Nick:** Bill scares me.

**Ruth** *(to Les)*: I don't want the issue to get shifted to Bill's anger. What I think is most important is how Bill has decided to suffer in silence and never call for help.

*Sometimes, people shift topics to avoid painful experiences for themselves and to protect other family members. Often the shift seems reasonable, logical, or friendly. Our job is to stay on track. Ruth reframes the being silent slightly to suffer in silence, which will become our key phrase for Bill. When Bill decides not to suffer in silence, he will become an active member of his family, rather than an outsider. Consequently, Bette's relationship with Nick will necessarily be different and perhaps we can get to her fear.*

# WEDNESDAY MORNING
# MEN'S GROUP—WITH LES

*We are in one of the smaller meeting rooms in the main lodge. As I look around the room I notice Nick. He looks listless. He is hardly moving.*

**Les:** Nick, what are you thinking?

**Nick** *(very slowly)*: I don't want to get into anything, because I don't want to hurt anyone's feelings.

**Les:** What do you mean?

**Nick:** I have been thinking about my father, about how he might be missing me. I wish I were with him more. I want to see my Dad very much, but I've got to be careful that I'm not a burden. I feel sorry for my Dad, because he never puts himself first.

*Nick continues to look at the difficulties he is having, apart from Bill and Bette. It is interesting that this comes on the heels of Bill's move toward changing the way he acts in the family unit.*

**Nick:** Things don't work for my father. He's in debt. It's hard for me to visit my father, because I can't stand to see him doing so badly. It doesn't seem right, because he works all the time. I don't see how he screws it up.

**Les:** What does that mean to you?

**Nick:** Every once in a while, when I slack off, I'm afraid I'm going to grow up to be just like my father. I want to be like my dad, who's a nice guy, but I've also got to be what my mother wants. I think I can be gentle like my dad, but I'm not going to screw up like he did. *(Nick suddenly gets sad.)*

**Les:** I am aware of your sadness right now.

**Nick:** I'm getting sad because I feel sorry for my dad. I figured he would learn from his mistakes—screw up once, but not again.

**Les** *(pulling a chair out in front of Nick)*: Put your father in that chair and tell him.

**Nick:** I'm sad because you don't learn from your mistakes.

**Les:** And experiment with these words: I'm scared that maybe I'm like you, and I try hard not to be scared. *(Nick repeats these words and is shaking his head, yes, as he does so.)*

**Les:** Now tell your father: I'm me. I'm not you, and I'll be my way.

**Nick** *(with great animation)*: That's right, I'm me, and I'm my way. I don't have to be scared I'm like you, and I'll tell Mom that too.

> *Nick's enthusiastic response shows that he is making his own sense of things and "aha-ing," as the light bulbs go on and he lets go of an old decision. It is particularly good to hear him take the initiative to tell his mother.*

**Les:** Its okay for you to make mistakes, and it doesn't mean you're going to screw up all the time.

**Nick** *(with a gleam in his eye)*: It doesn't!

**Les:** Is there anything else you want now?

**Nick:** I wish I could be an adult and tell my Dad what I think he should do.

**Bill** *(moving over to Nick)*: It is all right for you not to be grown up right now. *(Bill puts his arm around Nick. Nick begins to cry. Bill's reaching out to Nick has an impact on the group, particularly on David and Robin. We take a break. After the break I check in with Bill. He says only one thing.)*

**Bill:** I'm waiting. I'm waiting, because I have a major piece of work to do.

# WOMEN'S GROUP—WITH RUTH

*Bette waits until the end of the morning to speak.*
**Bette:** It's funny. I've taken courses in the past and always talked a lot, but I don't want to talk much here.
**Ruth:** Bette, are you angry or scared about something here or something with me?
**Bette:** No, what makes you ask that?
**Ruth:** From your last comment, Bette. It also seems as if, for you, everything has to be just right, and I thought maybe it hasn't been right for you here.
**Bette:** I don't see myself that way. But I've heard myself use the word "perfect" quite a lot.

*Bette is being cautious again. My next option, "Will you pretend," is both soft and confrontive. Pretending allows an escape hatch for someone admitting something that is true. Very few people feel a need to defend against this.*

**Ruth:** Will you pretend for a minute that what I'm saying is true, and look into where the perfect-stuff comes from?
**Bette:** When I was a kid, I would bring home a report card with four A's and one A-minus. My father would say, "You've got to do better." My mother didn't go to college until her kids did. In fact, she graduated the same year, and from the same college, I did. She graduated summa cum laude, and I graduated cum laude. She started working on her Ph.D. right after graduation, and kept working on it until her first heart attack. My mother spoke five languages. She had a passion for studying. She was different from other mothers. After I was married for a year, a high school friend of mine called my mother to find out my address. My mother didn't know it. (*She laughs.*)

*I feel a rush of sympathy for Bette. I understand the awfulness of growing up in a family with such competition among the women and such rejection from her mother, even when Bette was grown.*

**Ruth:** It must have been hard for you to make it in a woman's world, Bette. You saw your twin as the pretty one. You defined yourself as the ugly one. You couldn't be the smart one, because your mother made herself the smart and accomplished one. There wasn't much room for you. Later your mother didn't even know where you lived. I wonder if you decided very early to survive by joining the boys?

**Bette:** It's true. I prefer men to women.

**Ruth:** Stay with what you feel now.

**Bette** *(crisply)*: Well, it was just awful, naturally.

*Bette let me side with her for only a brief time. Bette shies away from contact with a woman—in this case me. In the past it was her twin and her mother. Does Bette believe that in contact with women she will end up the loser? I am puzzled about how to proceed—the only one she really lets in is Nick.*

**Ruth:** It was hard to be a girl, and a young woman in that family. Am I right to hear that your only contact was with the boys? That contact with your sister or your mother wasn't allowed or, when it was, you were the loser? And, you had to be perfect for your father.

**Bette** *(stand-offishly)*: What's wrong with that?

**Ruth:** There's nothing wrong with it. I feel heavy and sad, because it doesn't seem to me that there was a real place for you, Bette.

*(Other members of the group have a try at getting in touch with Bette, bringing up examples of feeling left out as children; she continues to turn everyone down.)*

**Ruth:** Were you the first or second twin?

*I'm grasping at straws and still looking for some way to get in. I think I am stuck. I need to talk this over with Les and the trainees.*

**Bette:** I was the second. My parents knew all along that twins were coming. They thought we would be boys. I like boys best. All the emphasis in the family was on the boys.

**Ruth:** There doesn't seem to have been room for girls, except perhaps for your mother who was necessary and your pretty sister, who slipped in just ahead of you. *(Bette laughs and purses her lips.)*

>    *At least I know where I stand with Bette, how she views me. I am a competitor and unavailable for nurturing. Only men count with her. The question is, how can I use this information to help Bette?*

# WEDNESDAY AFTERNOON
# INDIVIDUAL FAMILIES—WITH RUTH

*I have half the group: the Sarnons and the Dellapietras. We meet for a two-hour session before free time in the afternoon. We are in the living room of one of the condominium apartments. The Dellapietras have finished talking and Bill is sitting on the bottom two steps of the carpeted stairs to the second floor. He leans forward.*

**Ruth** *(to the Sarnons)*: Is there anything you would do for yourselves, before we break for the afternoon?

**Bill** *(in an unprecedently firm voice)*: I have something that I need to do.

**Ruth:** What do you want from me as you proceed? (I'm excited, but I keep my voice calm. I'm also tired and looking forward to some time off.)

**Bill:** Listening, understanding, and helping. This is something I haven't talked about here before. In fact I have never talked about this. It's something that is very difficult, particularly in a mixed group. *(Bill's voice is clear and strong. The rest of the room settles down to listen, even the children are listening and playing quietly.)*

**Bill:** When I was a boy, I grew up in a family that was very strict. No movies, no cards, no drinking, no nothing. We just went to school and went to church. We went to evening prayer meetings every Wednesday, and Bible school every Saturday, and church every Sunday. Because of these things, I see that I didn't get a lot of the things that I should have gotten, and some things did go wrong. And so, at the age of 14, I remember that I was playing checkers with my sister on my bed. One of the checkers fell off the bed onto the floor, and I jumped over the bed to pick it up. My sister jumped on top of me. I can remember having an erection and an ejaculation. That was the first time that I had ever had that. My sister noticed it. She didn't know what it meant, and I didn't know what it meant either. After that my sister and I had close physical relationships—no intercourse—but touching. This went on until I was seventeen and she was thirteen. I went away to college. That ended it. She went to college, and in her last year she had a nervous breakdown. She has been in an institution ever since. *(With this Bill breaks into loud weeping, but he continues speaking.)* I know that she is schizophrenic—that's partly genetic and partly environmental. One of the environmental factors most likely was me, and I feel the guilt. I write to my sister. She writes back to me. I see her about once a year. We both love each other very much. At the same time, it just about kills me to see her the way she is. I've often thought that she would be better off dead. It makes me feel terrible, incredibly terrible. *(Bill stops, as if looking for support and guidance. I move in.)*

**Ruth:** Bill, will you put yourself out in front of you and see yourself as you were in those teen-aged years? Describe yourself.

**Bill:** Bill, you are passive, afraid, feeling that you always have to be good. And then something happened that gave you a great fear. Until that happened, you were able to handle being good all the time.

**Ruth:** Staying with where you are, do you want to say anything to that young boy?

**Bill:** You have just built a mountain out of a molehill. It wasn't a very nice thing. You didn't really understand. You can't take all the responsibility for what happened to your sister. The responsibility belongs to some of the other family members, too.

**Ruth:** And your own physical urges weren't bad.

**Bill:** Understand that your own physical urges weren't bad—they were natural. You had no other way of expressing those urges. You didn't know how.

**Ruth:** As you say those things to the young Bill, will you also say that you forgive him?

**Bill:** I forgive you, Bill. It is all right that you are alive and that you let yourself out. You had to let yourself out then, and you have to let yourself out now—in a different way. You can't survive if you don't. *(He pauses, takes a long breath, and looks fixedly at me.)* I want to go on.

*Bill wants to tell the whole story. Perhaps my interruption—getting him to forgive himself—is a way of taking care of myself as I feel caught up in the drama. I pull back to listening and understanding. This is what Bill asked from me.*

**Bill** *(continues)*: My last year in medical school, I got married. I still wasn't knowledgeable in many ways about sex. The girl that I married was in the same situation. On the first night we were married, it was obvious to both of us that we had made a mistake. Yet, we didn't do anything about it for 20 years. After five years, we had a daughter. My main reason for staying in the family was to give her a father. I thought of leaving, many times. And then I found a way of getting along in the situation. I remember when she was two years old and her mother would—*(Bill is overcome with tears.)* Miriam, that was my daughter's name, would cry and cry at night. It would take hours for her to get to sleep. It wasn't until she was four that we discovered she had an allergy to milk (which caused her intestinal pain). My wife would go and lie down with her every night until Miriam finally went to sleep. I felt left out of the family. I thought that I was missing out on something. I swear nothing else entered my mind.

When Miriam was 3 I felt that I should have a chance to comfort her, too. I told my wife, and she said go ahead. About half the time that Miriam cried I would go and lie down with her until she stopped. I remembered touching her. That was sexually stimulating for me. She didn't know what was going on. There was nothing more than just touching her. My wife and I were not having sexual relations. I wasn't seeing anyone else. As the years went by, and Miriam was still crying, I would do the same thing.

When she was six she realized that I was touching her, and she seemed to like it. What I'm talking about is touching, not intercourse.

When she was about eleven, we moved. I changed jobs. I wanted to stop being with my daughter that way. I knew that it was bad. I spent all my time working—that was my escape. That's the way I survived.

After we moved, Miriam gradually stopped crying. And I never lay next to her again. When she was thirteen I still felt very sad. I had no sexual life at all. I remember sitting in front of the television—which is what Miriam and I did together a lot—and I would expose myself to my daughter. I did this in a subtle way: She could pretend not to notice.

When she was fifteen I just had to move away, and I did. She was at camp at the time. My wife and I had talked for six months about getting a divorce. We agreed about this while Miriam was away. We agreed that I would see my daughter once every three weeks after that, but my wife would be sitting in the room, because she didn't trust me.

I couldn't afford to pay child support and alimony working where I was. So, we moved to Madison, and I worked harder than ever. My daughter went to college and graduated. Last year, she came and lived with us (Bette, Nick, and myself) for a year. She has just gotten married and seems very happy. I wasn't quite sure why she wanted to come to Madison. Luckily, she got a good job there in her line of work. I asked her one day why she had moved. She said, "Because I wanted to get to know my father better. I haven't seen him since I was 15 years old." I love her very much, and I know she loves me. But I still feel all this guilt. I feel ashamed, like a dirty man. I never thought anyone would understand.

**Ruth** *(after a long pause)*: I hear where you are, Bill, and I hear your story. It is important that you talked and that you find a way to end the guilt and suffering for yourself.

**Bill:** It is important to me. I have two things I could do: I'd like to talk to my younger sister, but I can't. She doesn't live in a real world. I know my daughter wants to talk, and I know I have to talk to her. She is obviously more mature, as far as looking at this, than I am. I need to know one other thing: whether other people can understand, and especially, whether my family understands.

**Bette** *(dully)*: I understand.

**Nick** *(matter of factly)*: I understand.

**Ruth:** Bette, will you share with Bill what you're feeling?

**Bette** *(to me)*: I admire his courage. I remember when Miriam came to visit—

**Ruth:** Will you tell Bill directly, not me?

**Bette:** I felt jealous of Miriam, and I couldn't understand why. And, before we were married, when we talked about how our life would be, you said your wife had been frigid. I couldn't understand how you could be as sexual as you are with me, and still have been without sex for 20 years. So I am relieved to find that you had sexual needs and impulses those 20 years. I consider this a huge relief, rather than a shame. My only questions are: What does Miriam know? What did she think? Did she know what was happening?

**Bill:** I'm sure she realized, when she was older.

**Bette:** I also remember saying to you that I couldn't understand why you and Miriam never touched.

**Bill:** Now you understand. That's why I have difficulty touching anyone.

Ruth, may I ask a question? My first wife took Miriam to see a psychologist. Miriam was disturbed by the sessions—she said it was too upsetting to go on. My wife says that the psychologist told Miriam, "If Bill was that way once, he will be that way all the time." But never, since she was 15, have I felt that way. After my divorce, my relations with women were fine. I still have this fear about touching because of what the psychologist said then, and because of what was said to me as a child.

**Ruth:** There is no truth in the statement, "If you were that way once, you'll always be that way." In fact, Bill, I think you should share what you think and feel with Miriam. Tell her that you want to have physical contact with her—to be able to give her a hug—and that you know now that you can honor those boundaries with her. I have respect for you as a man, and I am impressed by your courage.

**Domenic:** Thank you, Bill. That was courageous.

*(The trainees join in and say that Bill has been carrying a large burden. They understand his concern: he needs to know what other people will think of him after they've heard his story.)*

**Nick:** It takes guts to talk about this in front of people. I like knowing this is in the past and that you're not like that now.

**Ruth:** I am touched, Bill, by who you are.

**Bill:** Now that I've begun to share, I think I can talk with my daughter and make things right between us.

*(The session is over. The room is quiet and intense. I am quiet, and I am relieved. It takes a long while before I am ready to talk, even to Les.)*

# THURSDAY MORNING

# YOUNG PEOPLE'S GROUP—WITH LES

*I am working with the young people. We are sitting in the living room where Bill revealed his hidden past. As I begin this morning's session three things about Nick are on my mind: his need to separate himself from his mother, his relationship with his natural father, and how Bill's revealed past has affected him. Since we most likely won't be meeting again in this structure, I'm not opening up new issues, but tying up the ones relevant to the children. Nick is sitting on the stairs, in the same place Bill sat. I wonder how Bill's disclosure will affect Nick's identification with male figures and his separation from female figures. When I ask Nick how he is, his first instinct, as usual, is to cover up.*

**Nick:** I'm fine. Everything is going great for me, and for Bill, so far.

**Les:** Bill did some important work yesterday, Nick. Will you share your response?

**Nick** *(haltingly):* It was O.K. I mean, it did freak me out, but it was in the past. I figure he doesn't do it anymore. *(Nick is jiggling his foot nervously. I ask him to exaggerate the movement. This might get at his real feeling. He pushes me off.)*

**Nick:** I always do this. My Dad used to do the same thing.

**Les:** I wonder if it might be a nervous reaction to your thinking about Bill.

**Nick:** Well, this is a hard subject to talk about. I just never pictured Bill that way, but I guess it's okay. I guess it was all because of his wife—because she was frigid and everything. This can't be Bill, unless he has changed a whole lot.

**Les:** You look uncomfortable.

**Nick:** I'm a little scared of what Bill did.

**Les:** What this reminds me of is how hard it was for you to look at your real father being in a bad situation. People in your family often don't seem to want to see things the way they really are.

**Nick:** That's true. It's certainly true with my father, and it's half way true with Bill.

**Les:** And it's certainly true with your mother. She doesn't want to see anything bad in you. She doesn't want to see a single flaw in you.

**Nick** (*suddenly animated*): Like I said before, if I were perfect the way she wants me to be, I'd be boring. I think, like our coach does, that as long as I try—to the best of my ability—everything is going to be okay with me.

> *Looking back, another option would have been to ask him what he was scared about ". . . what Bill did."*
> *This probably would have led into his uncertainty about male identification figures. His coach is clearly an important role model.*

**Les:** I like hearing you give yourself permission to not have to push all the time.

**Nick:** I am trying to be the best that I can. Not for my Mom—for me. And that's not because I'm scared any longer about being like my Dad. I'll improve myself the best I can in sports. Sometimes, I like to go out and mess around with my friends. I don't have to do the best I can with that.

**Les:** During the chocolate pudding group you and your mother stayed very close and messed around.

**Nick:** You're wrong. I wanted to stay at the other side of the lawn and throw pudding at her, because she's always too neat. I wanted to see what it would be like if she was all messy. (*Angrily*) I used to be in competitive swimming. I'd get up at five in the morning to train, come home at noon for lunch, and go back to practice in the afternoon. My mother would give me rewards for winning races, like a toy parachute or a toy gun. But if I messed up in a meet, she would get really mad. I'd go to my room and punch my punching bag. Sometimes I'd get bloody knuckles. I couldn't hold it in.

**Les:** So, it used to be very hard to set goals for yourself that were different from your mother's. And, you would get very angry with her pushing you.

**Nick** (*thoughtfully*): Yes, and I can still retaliate now—do what I want to do. When I was younger, she could push me into anything. When I was only one, I had this little bathing suit that said "Olympic Champion" on it.

When I was three, she threw me off the side of the pool. I couldn't swim, of course. But, before I got to the bottom of the pool, she'd reach down and get me. I think it scared the hell out of me. My grandfather made her stop it. My father didn't know anything about it, because he was away at work. I guess she wanted to mold me into what she wanted. She can't do that anymore, because I have my own opinions about who I am and what I want to be.

**Les:** I'm glad to know that, and I support you.

*For Nick, the major goal of the week is to strengthen his sense of himself and his separateness from his mother. The remaining issues concern his identification with men. Nick's reference to his father's absence—his father wasn't there to protect Nick, because he was away at work—is strikingly similar to Bill's memory of hard times in his childhood. His father was too passive to stick up for his son.*

## PARENTS' GROUP—WITH RUTH

*As Les did with the young people, I began by reminding people that we're in the last part of the workshop. I focus on what has been opened up that needs to be finished. For the Sarnons, I wonder in my head about Bette's response to Bill's admissions yesterday. Instead Bette begins to talk about Nick.*

**Bette:** What I want to do is talk about my relationship with Nick. Nick just lied to me. He told me he hadn't been seeing a boy I don't approve of, and I know he has. I want to know the connection between that and your saying I'm forcing him to be a perfect son.

*If I were to follow Bette's lead, we'd be back to where we were at the beginning of the week, with her concern that Nick is failing her and her over involvement with him. I'm concerned with the marital relationship. I'm also concerned with not having been able to "touch" Bette.*

**Ruth:** What you're asking is important and I'll answer it, but first I wonder if it's taking away from the relationship between you and Bill. What Bill talked about yesterday was very important. I wonder if it needs to be talked about more?

**Bette:** Well, Bill and I feel a lot closer today. I wonder whether Bill has gotten out all of his feelings though. I don't think so.

**Ruth:** Bette, what I wonder more about is how you feel. One of the things I wondered about yesterday was what you felt. After Bill had shared all of that information, you showed little feeling.

**Paula Quinn:** I am confused, too. I had some good times with you both, Bette. But I'm concerned that when Bill talks, you don't hear him. I don't think you want to listen to Bill. I don't think you want to know what he's feeling. As we get to be friends, this is the one thing that bothers me.

**Ruth:** Bill, will you respond to Bette about all of this?

**Bill:** I really appreciate being allowed to do that work. I think that I'm over the mountain, and I'm going down the other side. I let myself have some feelings, and the world didn't come to an end. I've written poems over the last two years. I realize now that if I had looked at them carefully, I would have seen some of the things I uncovered here. My rational side kept everything down. I was afraid of what would happen. Now I'll say it.

**Bill:** I care a lot about you, but there seems to be a wall you put up around you and around us.

*In confronting Bette, Bill shows he is integrating his major redecisions into his actions.*

*Bette doesn't react. She sits motionless, staring at a spot above my head.*

**Ruth:** Bette, don't worry about figuring it out with words. Use your body to respond, or put some sounds to how you feel.

**Bette:** I don't know what to do.

**Ruth** (*in a kind tone*): You don't have to know what to do. It's OK just to respond. Get up and walk, jump, or make any movement that feels good to you now. What's important is that you not make yourself a stone. Bill doesn't need another frigid woman in his life.

*It's a common position for Bette—the little girl concerned about doing the right thing. She takes a few steps, then stops and shakes her head. She won't allow me to help her. After a long pause, she circles Bill and then kneels in front of him. Bill pulls her gently by the arms to encourage her to get up and move around. This is new behavior for him. At the beginning of the workshop, when Bette held onto him, he would collapse into her. I suggest that she try holding her right foot in her right hand (a bioenergetics movement designed to motivate activity). Les comes into the room, finished with the kids' group. His entrance makes a little break. Bette looks at him gratefully. She grabs the excuse to stop and return to her chair.*

**Ruth:** Les, join us. I haven't any place to go with Bette.

**Les:** I'm struck by an intense sense of sadness in the room.

**Ruth:** It has been a sad morning.

**Paula:** Bette, I think you have some prejudices about the way people are going to be. Will you forget what that boy at school said to you about being the ugly one? Could you forget about your mother being the smart one and see how sad she was in some ways? Could you forget what your lawyer's wife said to you?

**Bette:** I don't know what moving around or making sounds has to do with my family. I don't know what to do.

**Ruth:** Bette, I'll share my thinking with you right now. If you move freely, you might find out more about yourself and be able to share your feelings, whatever they are. You are a person who benefits from moving.

**Bette:** When you told me to try holding my foot in my hand, I felt as if I was being subjected to some medieval torture.

**Ruth:** Have you been expecting to be tortured here?

*Paula's comment about Bette's preconceptions led me to take this track.*

**Bette:** I was told you would probably have a negative feeling toward me. I was told that I'm not the kind of woman you like. Is there some truth to that?

*Bette had been referred by Bill's lawyer and wife who had been in a previous workshop. Obviously, the friends had mixed feelings about me, and perhaps about Bette herself. Although the couple urged Bette and Bill to come, they warned Bette that she wasn't the kind of woman I'd like. No wonder Bette has been so careful around me, doing only what she thought would give me a good picture of her. I wish she had said this earlier!*

**Ruth:** I didn't have any preconceived ideas about you. Early in this week I had some observations.

**Bette:** What were they?

**Ruth:** The same ones that I've been feeding back to you—about how tight and controlled you seem and about how important it would be for you to feel safe and let go.

**Les:** Bette, what was it like for you to come here and work with Ruth?

**Bette:** I thought of myself as coming here to work for Bill or for Nick. I didn't see myself as doing anything.

**Ruth:** That puts into words where I am with you, Bette. I see you lose yourself for Bill or for Nick. You seem to have little sense of yourself as a woman and as a person. I would like to know you, and right now I am relieved to know more about what has been going on. Sometimes I felt I was being hard on you. I questioned that for myself. Now I understand. *(Les senses that an important shift has been made. He decides to finish for the moment.)*

**Les:** Bette, will you take some time at lunch to go back and look at the videotape of yourself and then come back and share what you learned?

**Bette:** Yes.

# THURSDAY AFTERNOON

# FAMILY GROUP (LES SPEAKING)

*All the families are together this afternoon. I have just finished work with the Quinns.*

**Les:** Bette, did you look at the tape?

**Bette** *(caustically)*: I looked. I thought I was clingy. I looked as if I needed Bill. I didn't look like stone. I thought I looked pitiful. And I was surprised to see myself looking needy, because I don't feel that way.

**Les:** Did the woman you saw on the tape remind you of anyone or anything?

**Bette:** I remember my father telling me that my twin would go up to my mother again and again and say, "Mommy, do you love me?"

I'll bet my self-sufficiency comes from reacting to what my sister did. I think I might have felt the way she did, but that I decided not to say anything. When I look at the tapes, I feel as if I'm looking at my twin and not myself.

**Les:** You have put a lot of energy into looking self-sufficient and capable, being different from your twin, and not needing your mother.

**Bette:** The only time I was ever overcome with my emotional needs was after I got divorced. I couldn't stand not being married.

**Ruth:** What do you mean, overcome?

**Bette** (in a curt, put-offish way): Well, I don't know exactly.

**Les:** Continue.

**Bette** (responding to Les): I think I cried a lot and was depressed and fell apart.

**Ruth:** That sounds frightening. I understand more why you try to keep this marriage all neat and smooth, and yourself all pulled together. Did you feel out of control?

**Bette:** Oh yes. (She tightens up).

*Bette is frightened of letting out any of herself. She holds on tightly to her self-image, almost as if she will disappear or disintegrate if she lets go.*

**Les** (to Ruth): It also seems important for Bette to surround herself with people who are confident, who don't show their feelings, and don't present any threat.

**Bette:** I think that this must be hard for Nick. I think I'm going to cry. (Bill moves over to Bette with a box of Kleenex. Nick asks if she wants him to move nearer.)

**Ruth:** Bill and Nick, Bette needs to work without your protection and without your stopping her. She's not going to fall apart now. You are off duty. (Bill and Nick look at each other and pull back. Bette stares at Ruth.)

**Les:** When you were a kid, Bette, what happened in your family when you showed that you were needy? How did you get taken care of?

**Bette:** I don't remember ever acting needy.

**Ruth** (to Les): That sounds like an important, old decision—to never show her needs—to always act as if she were self-sufficient and thus to act different from her sister. We already know her mother wasn't going to respond to her.

**Bette** *(sweetly to Les)*: When I cried, mother would listen, but she wouldn't really hear me. I could talk to my twin, but she wouldn't hear me either.

> *Bette's description of being ignored by her mother and her sister reminds me of Paula's comment that Bette doesn't seem to listen to Bill. Most importantly, though, is that this is what has happened at the workshop. Bette, expecting that she won't be listened to, has actually set up that experience here. She feels unheard and misunderstood, especially by Ruth. Bette expects us to act and react as the people from her past did. Bette decided to never show herself, because no woman would listen anyway. She found refuge with her brothers and walled out her mother and sister.*

**Nick:** My mother shows me when she's needy. The way she does it is to say in baby talk, "Come over and give your Mommy a hug."
*(The general response in the group is a good-natured "Yuk." Even Bette and Bill laugh. Nick goes on a little and Bette withdraws.)*

**Ruth:** Les, I think we are trapped now. When we sat in the apartment a few hours ago, you had all these brilliant ideas about how to help Bette get unstuck. Now even you are stuck. You've been telling me about how you're going to rescue Bette, because I'm not working with her right. I've become the bad guy just like Bette's mother and sister.

**Les:** That's true.

**Ruth** *(to Les)*: I'm angry at you for criticizing me. You have gone along with Bette's idea of sides and now I'm the not-okay one.

**Les:** What I think about Bette is that she's a sad little girl with a great big protective armor around her.

**Ruth:** I agree. I also think Bette is seductive and angry. She has managed to seduce you, and you are taking care of the little girl the way Bill and Nick do, and her father and brothers did. I'm walled out and seen as disapproving and torturing like the females in her past. She gets men to take care of her, and she gets angry as hell at women.

**Bette:** I don't understand. Can you repeat that?

**Les** *(without responding to Bette)*: Ruth, I agree that Bette is angry also.

**Ruth** *(continuing to Les)*: You have to move on that, then, but you have to be on my side. That's what didn't happen at her home, with her mother and father.

> *Our talking allows us to say things to people indirectly. We outline the current drama and show how it is a repetition. Then we extract ourselves so we no longer play into the family scene. In our argument, we model a different way of acting and break the rules of both Bette's and Bill's family of origin. In both families, there was a tacit agreement not to fight. We are also really having an argument.*
>
> *Nick is delighted with Les and Ruth's argument.*

**Les** *(to Ruth)*: I agree that Bette seduced me. I'm aware, too, that Nick doesn't let out his anger at her. And that she picked a guy like Bill, who won't very often confront her. All of us men are taking care of her. Bette, what are your thoughts?

**Bette:** This is Ruth's issue. *(Nick gets agitated and starts kicking the pillow, but Bette doesn't notice.)* I don't understand her saying I get angry at women. I have many women friends. I think it's her problem.

**Bill** *(standing up in front of Bette, his posture unusually straight)*: Bette, you're almost losing the whole thing. We've just gotten somewhere and it's disappearing. I'm not going to be a quiet little boy. I am going to get mad. I can see the problem, and it's not Ruth's problem. It's your problem, Bette. Don't put it off on Ruth.

**Bette** *(shocked)*: No!

**Bill:** I'm here for me, but I'm here for you, too. I'm sorry you're throwing this opportunity away. Today and tomorrow are our last chances. You can't go back to Madison and check it out with somebody who isn't a therapist. You've talked to somebody before and you managed to block them out too. I'm mad, and Nick is mad, too.

**Les:** Hooray for you, Bill. I'm glad you're standing up that way. You said you knew what the issue was?

**Bill** *(to Bette—still loud, firm and clear)*: You never listen to me. I've told you that many times before. You've got to listen now. When we were all together last night, even Paula saw that if our marriage is going to last, you're going to have to listen, because I need that. That's as clear as I can get right now, Bette. You have a problem, too. I'm not the depressed one anymore. *(He sits down. Bette laughs and claps Bill on the shoulder.)*

**Les:** Bette, that was nasty and condescending. After Bill shares what's going on with him, you pat him and treat him like a little boy who just did a good trick.

**Bette:** All I was trying to do was think of something comforting to do to Bill.

**Bill:** I don't need comforting.

**Les:** It's going to be rough on you, Bill, because you've decided to make a change. You're going to have to maintain your momentum on your own, until Bette is ready to respond.

**Ruth** *(to Bette, softly)*: Bette, I don't know where to go. I'm afraid that you're living out what I said earlier in the workshop. You are stopping everyone. I have run out of ways to try to connect with you. You don't let me in whether I am supportive or confrontive. It's as if you make me not exist. I'm not out to get you. I don't dislike you. I'm not your mother or your sister.

> *Both Ruth and I are aware that this is day four of the workshop. Perhaps Bette will take this last confrontation as a permission to connect with some woman here.*

# MEN'S GROUP—WITH LES

> *This is the latter part of the afternoon. We have decided to finish today with men's and women's groups.*
>
> *In the men's group, Bill speaks up about halfway through the session.*

**Bill:** I want to talk to Nick. I haven't been a parent to you, Nick. I have left most of the decisions up to you and your mother. For example, whether you should be allowed to chew tobacco, which drives your Mother crazy, and whether you have the right to make that decision for yourself. Each of the three of us has had a different opinion on this. I have backed out.

*Bill again gives clear signals of the changes he's made.*

**Les:** In the last session when Bette had a difficult time, what I noticed at the break was that Bette and Nick had a lot of contact. There was almost something secretive and special about their being together. Bette needed some consoling, and she looked for it from Nick. This relationship, between Nick and Bette, excludes you. You hang back, let yourself be excluded, and then are no help to Nick.

**Bill:** I see I've helped foster that, over the past two years, by being so passive. This is between me and Bette also.

**Les:** Yes. The issue with Nick is one between you and Nick and also between you and Bette. *(To Nick:)* What do you think?

**Nick:** My mother wants me to be a mature adult. At the same time, she wants me to be a little boy she can hug and cuddle and make all the choices for. But I have my own brain. And I think I have to have my own say-so on many more things.

**Les:** You're sharp, Nick, and yes, you do have your own brain. There are a lot of things you can decide about, on your own. There are also some things you still need some adult help on. I think, at times you try to pull Bill in to get his help. It must be a lot easier for you when Bill is there.

**Nick:** That's true, all right. Bill handles things in a much more level-headed way then my mother. In fact, earlier this morning, in the group, I was thinking of telling my mother I was going to get some tobacco to chew. I was going to do it in front of everybody, so the whole group would see how she gets angry and jumps up and down.

**Bill** *(to Nick)*: I see the difficulty you have. I'm going to stop being the way my father was and your mother's father was. I'm willing to speak up and say more. Even if it's just to say more about your chewing tobacco.

*This is a good example of third stage work: The separation between Nick and Bette is outlined by Nick himself; Bill says that he will ally himself with Nick when appropriate; he will help him, and he will continue to act in a more straightforward and potent manner with Bette. I feel good about them as I watch Bill and Nick together. I still wonder what needs to happen to make the new family structure more solid. Bill and Nick have both made powerful redecisions for themselves. Is this enough, if nothing happens with Bette? Can Nick and Bill hold it together in the face of her resistance? She is very important to them both.*

## WOMEN'S GROUP—WITH RUTH

*Bette keeps quiet about herself. Her comments concern Angela and Berenice.*

**Ruth:** I appreciate your comments about Angela and Berenice.
**Bette:** It's easy for me to see everyone but myself.

*Her awareness is encouraging. Watching herself on the videotape helped Bette see the similarity between herself and her sister. Perhaps this has started Bette thinking more about herself. Maybe she let Bill in and listened to him, even though she wasn't able to show it.*

**Ruth:** There's an enormous difference in you now. You are softer. You've gotten involved with the other women here by commenting. I like having you here. *(Bette gives a genuine smile. The session ends.)*

## FRIDAY MORNING

## INDIVIDUAL FAMILIES—WITH LES

*The Sarnons and Quinns are with me. I divided the groups so that Bette would work with Paula and me. Perhaps this configuration will help me reach Bette.*

**Les:** This is the last chance to finish up what you came to do at the workshop. Think of the goals you had—as individuals and as a family—and see how far you have already gone along the path. I will then do rounds and check with each of you.

*In rounds, each person is asked to make a simple statement about what he or she is thinking and feeling now. It keeps the group focusing on the present and ensures that no one slips by.*

**Bette** *(eagerly)*: I obviously need to begin someplace, because I haven't started anyplace yet. As odd as it may sound, I thought I had no needs. Now I see that I'm probably holding in a lot of sadness. I don't think I'm holding in anger, even though other people seem to think that. I think my sadness comes from not having a place in my family.

*Bette has pulled together the separate pieces. Earlier, she couldn't accept our contact around her sadness, her fear, or her anger. I wonder what happened. I learn later that one of the trainees, Claudette, spent time with Bette and helped her to accept her sadness. In these workshops, the trainees are invaluable, particularly when people see us as negative figures.*

**Les:** I like hearing about you from you. *(Continuing the rounds, I come to Nick.)*

**Nick:** I'm feeling a little sad. I don't know what about. I'd like to talk with my mother about what Bill and I said yesterday afternoon. I feel good, because my goal was to become more of a family. We've already done that. I mean Bill and I did, yesterday.

*(The Quinns talk. Then, I return to Bette.)*

**Les:** Bette, are you ready?

**Bette:** Yes. This morning when I was running, I ran my bones off so that my guard would be down.

**Les:** I'm experiencing a new softness in you.

**Bette:** I think one of the things I need to look at is the wall that people say I put up. I don't even know when I do it.

**Les:** One of the observations I made yesterday, when I was working with Bill and Nick, is that the only time you show your feelings is related to Nick.

**Bette** *(crying)*: I start to cry when you even say his name. I'm so emotional where Nick is concerned.

*In her second sentence, Betty is intellectualizing. She is beginning to stiffen up.*

**Les:** After your confrontation with Ruth and me yesterday, you went directly to Nick for comfort.

**Bette:** You're right. I was angry at Bill. I went to Nick for support. That's the old support system. If anything could wipe me out, losing that could.

**Les:** I like your awareness of how you use Nick and of your anger towards Bill. (*Turning to Bill:*) Again, I'm reminded of your father and mother. Maybe some of the reason you hold back is to protect Nick from being used by Bette against you. You thought that's what your father did.

**Bill** (*with a look of real awareness*): You are right.

**Les** (*turning back to Bette*): Now, will you stay with the idea of being wiped out?

**Bette:** Yes, without Nick I would be wiped out and dead. I'd be nothing.

**Les:** You'd be nothing. Will you say more about that?

**Bette** (*looking away*): I don't know.

**Les:** What I notice is how attached you are to Nick. I guess you've been attached since you were pregannt with him. Will you float back to when you were a little girl? Which people were you attached to then?

**Bette:** I was joined with my brother, who was six years younger. I mothered him. He backed me up those awful times I would look in the mirror and wonder why I had the nose I did, the mouth I did, when my twin sister, Barbara, had features that were so perfect and so pretty. My brother Mark would tell me I shouldn't worry, because I had a better personality than she did.

Barbara was a loner up in her bedroom. I was left to my little brother, Mark, and my older brother.

**Les** (*putting a cushion in front of Bette*): Will you put Barbara out there and tell her what it's like for you to be close to your brothers while she stays up there in her bedroom?

**Bette** (*pauses and sighs*): I think you're being selfish (*she begins to cry*) and bossy, and not a part of things. You drew a line between us and wouldn't let me cross it. I know I could hurt you if I showed how mad I was. So, I'm just going to ignore you. I feel hurt and mad.

**Les:** Tell her about feeling hurt.

**Bette:** I think that you are cold. I don't have a sister. I tell myself I don't need a sister. (*Looking up, crying:*) But maybe I did.

**Les:** Tell her what's going on inside you.

**Bette:** You're always so perfect, Barbara. You were always neat. I was messy. I resented it when you built the wall down the middle of the room and didn't let me come on your side. So I joined my brothers and left you out. I needed to forget me *(she stumbles)*. I mean I needed to forget you.

*It is becoming clearer to Bette that when she was cut off from her twin, she lost part of herself. This week, as Bette was confronted with herself—particularly when she looked at the videotape—she recognized herself again.*

**Les:** Will you switch and take Barbara's part? Be Barbara; say what it's like to stay in the room.

**Bette** *(as Barbara)*: I don't like Mother, so I just go into my room. I hate Mother, because she always told me to go out when I went into her room. I don't like anybody. I'm just going to like myself.

**Les:** It sounds, Barbara, as if you don't feel very wanted in the family.

**Bette** *(as Barbara)*: I'm not. They don't want me, so I'm staying in my room.

**Les:** It seems as if you are the different one in the family. Everyone else is together. Is it important for you to be different?

**Bette** *(as Barbara)*: Yes.

**Les:** Will you switch back to being Bette? Respond to your sister. She says she's going to stay totally apart. Tell her what that's like for you.

**Bette:** I'm mad because you wouldn't let anyone in. You were so stiff and always so right. You drove the car, you made the arrangements for everything. You ran us. You ran me.

**Les:** Bette, I hear your anger again. I want to go back to something you have said before. Will you tell Barbara that no matter how angry you feel, you will not hurt or kill her, yourself or anyone?

**Bette** *(with astonishment and connection)*: Yes, I've always been afraid I would kill her if I was mad. *(She looks as if she is experiencing relief and thinking clearly.)* Barbara, no matter how mad I ever am, I would not hurt or kill you or anyone.

**Les:** The last part—not killing yourself—is most important.

**Bette** *(with soft tears and clarity)*: I won't hurt or kill myself, for anything.

**Les:** Do you want to tell your parents and Barbara that?

**Bette:** No. I don't need to. I am clear.

**Les** *(with firmness and gentleness)*: Good. It's important to care for, and to trust, yourself. Am I also picking up that part of you wanted to be near Barbara and needed her, especially when your mother had walled herself off?

**Bette:** Yes, I didn't really have a sister or a mother. I didn't know that until today. I only had the boys.

**Les:** The only people you could be soft and caring with, or get anything from, were your brothers.

**Bette:** Yes. I poured so much love into them.

**Les:** What you really needed and wanted was for your mother and Barbara to let you in, but you stayed as stoney as they did.

**Bette:** I think that's right.

**Les:** Will you tell Barbara that?

**Bette:** In all the years we were together, Barbara, we never really lived together. It's so sad we never lived together. *(She cries.)* I wish we could have helped each other. I wish I could have been your friend and talked to you. I wish that you had let me in and that I had let you in. I wish that you had known Mark. I wish we could have told Mother how we felt. I know Mother probably wouldn't have listened, but it would have made us feel better. I think we just shut everything out including each other. *(Deep sigh.)*

**Les:** What's your sigh about?

**Bette:** A realization. I think things between us could change. I think I have to talk to Barbara in person.

**Les:** I support that. I suspect that, as you continue to see Barbara differently, you will care more for yourself also. Are you willing to go one more step? *(Bette nods, yes.)* Will you put your brother Mark in front of you?

**Bette:** I think if anything ever happened to him, I would die.

**Les:** Tell Mark that.

**Bette:** Mark, if anything ever happens to you it would be devastating to me. You support me.

**Les** *(feeding lines)*: You're my world. I can't live without you.

**Bette** *(pausing and looking tenderly at Mark on the pillow)*: You're my world and I *can* live without you.

**Les:** Tell him again that you can live without him. Tell him what you feel as you say it.

**Bette:** You're important and I can live without you. I feel relief as I say I can live without you. *(To Les:)* I was so used to saying and doing everything that Barbara told me to do that I usually do exactly what people tell me to do. It's interesting that I didn't say exactly what you told me to.

> *In the workshop, Bette hasn't done what we told her to do. The resistance was hard for us, but it constituted a healthy rebellion for her.*

**Les:** Bette, look at Nick. Will you put Mark on the cushion at Nick's side? See how different they are?

**Bette:** Nick is not like Mark. Maybe I've been trying to make Nick into Mark. I looked to Mark to be perfect. Nick, I don't need you to be perfect.

**Nick** *(with gusto)*: Thank God.

**Les:** I think he needs to hear one more thing, Bette. That is, that if anything bad happened to him, you'll be really sad, but you'll survive. Is that true?

**Bette** *(pauses for awhile, then with much feeling)*: Nick, if anything bad happens to you, I know that I'll be very sad. But I will survive. I know that. I will not hurt or kill myself.

> *This ends Bette's work. Bette has tapped the roots of her depression. She recognizes her fear of showing feelings. She has redecided, not to hurt or kill herself or anyone else. She has made her existence separate from others. For the first time, she is truly in charge of herself.*

**Les** *(turning)*: Bill, what are you thinking?

**Bill:** I'm thinking that Bette has done some important things, and I'm very glad. There is still another piece, though, that I want to get back to and talk about, for my sake.

**Les:** Tell Bette what it is. I like your clarity.

**Bill:** Bette, you still surround yourself with men just the way you did with your brothers. These men are more or less perfect, and you're flirtatious and seductive. You also get on with their wives, because you are polite and pleasing. If a wife complains, Bette, you don't even have to defend yourself, because all the men will defend you.

**Les:** You sound mad at Bette.

**Bill:** I'll be even more direct, because now I know we can both take it. Neither of us will die because I'm talking. I'll tell you, Bette, how I used to fit in to your system. I fit into your system, Bette, when I could still play tennis and run. For you, doctors were perfect. Doctors who could run or play tennis were super-perfect.

**Les:** And are you worried now that, because your injury keeps you from running or playing tennis, you won't be as valuable to Bette?

**Bill** *(looking down, and then raising his head and speaking clearly)*: Yes.

**Les:** Is there anything you want to check out with Bette or ask her?

**Bill:** Yes. *(Turning to Bette:)* I'm not perfect; I'm just me. Nick is just him. I won't be at the right hand of God and I want you to love me this way. I want you to stop joining the boys and gathering the men.

*(Bette looks soft and is gently crying.)*

**Les:** I see Bette's response to you. Do you?

**Bill:** Yes. I'm finished for now.

**Les:** Will the two of you continue anything that is left over lunch and report back this afternoon?

*(Both Bill and Bette nod and the session finishes.)*

"I've learned that I am Angela and that I'm not bad or crazy."

—Angela Dellapietra

# 5

# The Dellapietras

## MONDAY MORNING

## FAMILY GROUP—LES SPEAKING

*All the families are in the main room with Ruth and me. I've asked everyone to think about, and then talk about, how they'd like to be different as a result of being here. The Dellapietras are in a circle on the floor. All of them seem to be moving all the time. The dimensions of the circle keep changing. Maria, 6, is jumping up and down.*

**Les:** Maria is jumping in with something to say.

**Dom:** She's dying to tell me what problems I've got and what I've got to do to overcome them. *(To Maria:)* What do you want me to change?

*(Maria and Dom are leaning toward each other, while Angela, Maria's mother, has leaned back stiffly.)*

**Maria** *(in a high-pitched, coquettish voice)*: I want you to stop smoking.

**Dom:** Look, just tell me seriously what you want me to do.

*(His voice has the same sing-song quality as his daughter's. Dom's four-year-old son, Marco, is across the room. He is on his back, on the floor, with his feet in the air. The father and the two children are acting as if being here is all play.)*

**Maria:** Stop smoking.

**Dom** *(with a childish grin)*: Well, we're going to try. No, wait, we *are* going to quit. With all this professional help here this week, I can't help but improve.

> *Dom's use of the word "we" connects himself to the rest of the family, even though none of the rest smoke. His joking tone shows condescension to the rest of his family and to us.*

**Les:** Marco looks as if he is out of the family now.

**Dom** *(shouting)*: Hey, Marco, what do you think?

*(Marco rocks and sucks his thumb.)*

**Angela:** We're not here to be silly. We're here to work.

**Dom:** Hey, Marco, give me a kiss.

*(Marco comes from halfway across the room.)*

**Angela:** Maria and Marco, sit still.

*(She starts to explain to Maria why they're here.)*

**Dom:** Come here, Marco.

*(Marco doesn't respond.)*

> *Both times now, Dom's moves undermine Angela's: she says "sit still" and he says "come here." His actions seem to support Angela and calm the kids, but his tone, affect, and words incite different behavior. He hasn't, physically, moved an inch.*

**Les:** Dom, did you actually want Marco to move?

**Dom:** Yes. One of the reasons we're here is because our kids run us. When I put the kids to bed, they get up again a few seconds later.

**Angela:** After I say something five or six times, I get frustrated and say, "Okay, forget it."

**Maria:** I'm not going to do anything I don't want to.

**Marco:** I'm not going to do anything I don't want to.

*(Marco's little echo gets up a peal of laughter in the room, from all but Angela and us.)*

**Angela:** They don't take me seriously.

*(As if to confirm that, Marco and Maria go on so loudly that it's hard to hear Angela. They're flinging their hands around. Marco is acting 2, not 4. Maria is mocking her mother.)*

**Les:** I certainly see that they don't listen and I have some idea how come, already.

**Angela:** There sure is a lot of chaos here, but when the kids are just alone with us, we enjoy each other.

*I made a move to support Angela. She immediately moved away and became defensive. Dom supports the kids' "chaos" and undermines Angela's attempts at order. While she is talking, Dom is smiling and patting the seat next to him, indicating that the kids should move next to him.*

**Dom:** Aren't there a lot of things in the day?

*This doesn't make any sense and only adds to the confusion, but Maria responds vehemently, as if she were joining her father in a secret language.*

**Maria:** That's not the way it is. I just hate it. I just hate to clear the table.
**Angela:** Are you really upset, Maria, or just showing off because you're in front of people?
**Dom:** Come here, Marco.
**Marco:** No.

*Dom ends up moving over to Marco. The exchange between Angela and Maria never gets finished. Angela's comment that the chaos is painful for her has been buried. Every transaction is incomplete.*

**Ruth:** It looks and sounds like what we're going to help you do this week is to make clear who are the parents and who are the kids, in this family.
**Angela:** Mostly, it's when we're with other people that this trouble comes up.

*Ruth attempts to restate the problem and define the treatment goals. Angela is defensive and wards her off.*

*(We talk for a moment to another family and then return to the Dellapietras.)*
**Ruth:** How do you discipline your children?
**Angela:** I don't. I can't because they don't take me seriously. (She begins to cry. Marco comes over.)*
**Marco:** Don't cry, Mommy, it's bad.
*(Maria also comes over and puts her arm around her mother. Marco retreats to a corner.)*

**Ruth:** So they don't take you seriously, and then you give up on them?

*(Maria wipes the tears off her mother's cheeks. Angela doesn't respond to Ruth.)*

**Les:** Right now, Angela, what do you think Maria is doing?

**Angela:** Showing how much she cares about me. But she only shows it when I get to the point of crying, and then I don't want it anymore.

> *The picture is a strange one. Maria is on her mother's lap, wiping away Angela's tears. Marco is in the corner, inattentive and disconnected, flailing his feet in the air. Dom is sitting back, looking inappropriately pleased. I am puzzled.*

**Les:** What are you feeling, Dom?

**Dom:** I feel happy and relaxed that my wife and daughter are closer, and my son is doing his thing, and I'm playing my role: listening and letting them be free.

> *Dom's response has nothing to do with Angela's sadness. It is out of place. It diverts attention from serious emotion, and thus, like Angela's comments, avoids defining a problem. It occurs to me that it must be hard for Maria, whose mother is crying and whose father's response is inappropriate, to decide what is real.*

**Ruth:** Angela, what I notice is that no matter what you do, someone moves in to stop it. Every time you show feeling, Maria, in effect, wipes away the tears, and things don't get finished.

**Angela:** Maria is sensitive. She doesn't want me to have problems.

> *Ruth's comment was an attempt to point out her sense of how the family moves away from saying anything concrete about a problem. Since we're searching for a way to get some agreement on any issue, Ruth goes on to focus on the one thing Angela and Dom might be able to concur on, the only problem they've raised: disciplining the children.*

**Ruth:** Maria, come over and sit next to me. *(Maria runs over looking pleased.)* What I suggest working on is having Maria not be the stopper in this family, but you, Angela and Dom, be in charge of what gets done.

**Angela:** It's because Maria has a strong personality for a six-year-old.

**Dom:** What can I do?

**Angela:** I don't know.

**Maria:** You can stop smoking.

*The family has again stopped any agreement regarding the problem. They have not accepted anything we've said and continue to exclude us. With Maria's repetition of her parental response, we're really back to go. Angela has grabbed her knees, closing up. Dom and Marco are playing like a couple of four-year-olds.*

**Les:** You have a hard time, in this family, finishing anything.

**Dom:** I know I need to discipline. I spent a lot of time getting my family the material things they needed. I couldn't relate to my two-year-old daughter and my newborn son. Now they're suddenly six and four. They need more of me. I see my daughter getting on her bicycle and zooming down the street. I can see it's time for Dad to get his ass in gear.

My wife and daughter need me. I don't need to be motivated. What I need is professional advice about which way to go.

*(Marco is roaming around the room, occasionally kicking furniture.)* This little terror is going to need something from me, too.

*(Dom talks about Marco's misbehavior with a smile and a delighted tone.)*

**Les:** My professional advice for right now is that you, Dom, need to help Marco get quiet when it's appropriate for him to be quiet.

*The session ends with the only contract coming from Dom (in his adaptive, good-boy self), putting forward a good image, as the father who wants to do more. Ruth and I have also stated our opinion that a significant family problem is finishing things, but we have no agreement from them.*

# MONDAY AFTERNOON

# INDIVIDUAL FAMILIES—WITH LES

*In the afternoon, I'm alone with the Dellapietras and Gerry and Margaret Ann Barker. Dom has been talking about his drinking. He says that, in the last four months (since Angela threatened divorce), he has had almost no alcohol to drink.*

**Dom** *(hostile)*: I've been over all these details before. I'm ready to start on new work, but what?
**Les:** Will you and Angela talk together about that?
*(They begin to talk. Angela's chair is close to Dom's, but Marco has squeezed into it—between them—and is kicking, and singing loudly. Maria is far across the room.)*

*Every time I attempt to get the parents together, one or the other of the children interrupts them.*

**Dom:** We need to have good days with the kids.
**Angela:** I have good days with the kids, and I don't have to come to a week of therapy to get that.
**Les:** Will you tell Dom what it is you do want, then?
**Angela:** I'd like to clear up the difficulty we've been having—mostly between Dom and me. We're very tense with each other.
**Les:** Will you tell this to Dom, Angela? I like that you're beginning to define something for yourself.
**Dom** *(interrupting before Angela speaks)*: Our pace is fast. I've had a big drinking problem.
**Angela** *(to Dom, and with determination)*: I'm not going to carry the whole burden of the family anymore. It was only when I went to a lawyer that you decided to make the marriage work. Only now you have begun to do some of the disciplining with the children.
**Les:** I still don't know what the difficulty is.
**Angela:** I don't know either. I don't know anything. I had a strong commitment to get Dom out of the bar. Now that I've done that, I don't know what's going on.
**Les:** Are you saying that you had this commitment to get Dom straightened out, and now that he has stopped

drinking, you don't seem to have a clear direction for the relationship for yourself and Dom?

**Angela** *(responding as if Les were blaming her)*: It's hard to change.

**Dom:** You're not trying hard enough, Angela.

> *Dom is joining me in what he perceives as an attack on Angela. As Angela grew up, she was repeatedly accused of being the* bad one *by her alcoholic mother. Her husband, believing he has gained an ally in me, is now blaming her, as her mother did before.*

**Angela:** I am very angry. I'm mad at Dom. I've had to go a long way to get him to pay attention to me. My pride is hurt.

*(Marco and Maria are bouncing around the room, playing with the curtains, and making a lot of noise at the windows.)*

**Angela** *(turning to Dom)*: I'd like our kids to be present here mentally—or not present at all.

**Dom:** I think you've been really good, kids.

> *This again, openly, but indirectly, contradicts what Angela has just said. It seems to be Dom's way of responding to direct confrontation. I decide to respond directly and throw my weight with Angela.*

**Les:** Dom, you sound angry. You are really undermining what Angela just wanted with the children.

**Dom:** Marco, don't you think what I'm saying is right?

> *Dom attempts to pull in the kids as allies, avoiding both Angela and myself.*

**Les** *(with emphasis)*: Dom, you don't respond directly to your wife or to me, but you bring Marco in instead!

**Angela** *(coming in to defend)*: We believe that asking the kids' opinion is a way of showing respect for them.

> *So far, any attempt by Ruth or myself to have contact with Angela or Dom has quickly been rebuffed. It is apparently not alright for us to take sides, regardless of whose side. Any attempt at contact, in whatever form, is quickly rebuffed. They also avoid*

*directly supporting each other. Instead, they support one or both kids.*

**Maria** *(bouncing and giddy)*: When is it over? When is it over?

**Dom:** I feel backed into a corner with the kids. The only way to go is spanking or physical abuse.

*(He tries to get Marco to sit down, but the child is stubborn and insists on standing. Dom gives out an awful, strained laugh.)*

> *Dom's bitter laugh expresses his mixed dismay and excitement at Marco's stubborness. There is a marked incongruence between what Dom says and what he shows about how he feels. Marco takes permission to be rebellious from Dom's laughter. I speculate that he's supporting Marco in doing the things he couldn't do as a child.*

**Les:** I suspect, Dom and Angela, that you are not yet ready, or feeling safe enough, to proceed with anything else, other than the problems with parenting the kids. Let's go back there, for now. Angela, it will be real important to come back to the relationship between you later.

**Angela** *(backing away again)*: I think some things are better left alone—unknown or unsaid. I hate having to analyze everything. If you look at everything with a microscope, pretty soon somebody's going to start thinking you're a candidate for the funny farm.

> *Angela has just expressed the basis of her fear: being labeled crazy and, perhaps, actually being crazy. We'll come back to this.*

**Les** *(loudly, and walking to a different position himself)*: Here we go again! It has been twenty minutes since we started. Lots of topics have been discussed and nothing has been finished. Your job now, Angela and Dom, is to order these topics and to decide something about how you want to proceed in this week.

**Dom:** Angela, what I want to get out of this week is to control the kids.

**Angela:** That's the main reason I came—to understand them. It's important for me to know my children because I didn't have any respect for my own family. My father was a strict disciplinarian for the short time he was with us.

*This is the first time they have both agreed on anything.*

**Les:** I like your clarity now. Parenting the kids seems to be number one on your list of priorities. It would be hard for you, Angela, to get the children to listen to you if you operated on the basis that you had to understand everything that was going on with them, before you could discipline them. Do you do this?

**Angela:** Yes, but you've got to let them get away with some things.

**Les:** One of the things you can learn here is that you can gain better control and say what you want to say to your children, even though you don't understand everything completely.

*This constitutes a minor contract for Angela. It is a small step in the overall contract of changing how she parents her children.*

**Angela:** Dom is blustery, but he's never tough with the kids. He doesn't have a tough bone in his body.

*Angela's father was a tough disciplinarian; she sees her husband as not having a tough bone in his body. Angela's mother beat her daughter. We hear that Angela puts a lot of energy into defending against the possibility of repeating these things in her present family. She is still keeping me away from her.*

**Dom** *(spouting information)*: I'm the youngest of three brothers. My grandfather started a trucking company that I own now. My four uncles are all alcoholics—

**Les** *(interrupting)*: You're another typical man in your family, then?

**Dom:** Yeah.

*Dom uses his family-of-origin dynamics as a cop-out, saying, in effect, "How can you expect any more from me?" He is also proud of his typical-man position in the family line.*

**Les:** Dom, it seems like you have some idea, then, about what you want to do with your kids now. Do you want Marco to be another typical, alcoholic man in the Dellapietra family line?

**Dom** *(soberly)*: No.

**Les:** On the other hand, Dom, you seem to have no sense of how you and Angela are going to resolve the difficulties between you. Everytime Angela has brought it up, you deflect the issue in some way. Part of becoming a different kind of father will be learning not to avoid your wife and not to undermine her with the kids, no matter how angry you are.

**Maria** *(in a provoking, sing-song attempt at helping her Dad out)*: I don't have to listen to anything, because nobody's talking to me.

**Les:** Dom, did you hear me?

**Dom:** Yeah!

**Les** *(turning)*: Maria, what do you think when you hear your parents talking about how hard it is to be good parents?

**Maria:** I don't have to listen to anything. I don't want to hear anything. *(She puts her fingers in her ears.)*

**Les** *(to Dom)*: I'm not surprised she doesn't want to hear anything. It would be new for her to listen. When you continually fog the issues with your goodie-goodie intentions and your undermining of Angela, then Maria learns how to avoid responsibility and listening.

**Dom** *(with a sardonic laugh)*: Well, sit down here, little girl, and hear it all.

**Les:** That's one of the ways you give her permission not to listen. You seem to get serious, and then you laugh and make a mockery of things.

**Dom** *(with a sharp change in tone to seriousness)*: You could be right.

*(Maria then sits down quietly next to her father. A minute later, however, she bounces up again. I signal [as I'd arranged earlier] to the play therapist to take Maria and Marco outside.)*

**Gerry Barker** *(speaking to Dom)*: I have to say that none of the stuff that you are talking about touches me. I think you're just trying to take over.

**Dom:** What?

**Les:** You get off on your own thing, and you don't seem to pay attention to other people. That must be hard for Angela.

**Angela** *(nodding)*: He's always bouncing off the walls with his own things. He doesn't accept anything in other people.

**Margaret Ann:** If I were you, Angela, I couldn't stand it. All I've wanted to do for the last fifteen minutes is to tell Dom to shut his mouth.

*(Angela avoids Margaret Ann's eyes, refusing to acknowledge and accept her support.)*

**Gerry:** Both of you, Angela and Dom, have avoided anything with other people, even with each other. Angela, have you given up trying to get through to Dom?

**Angela:** I've always been a fighter, but it has been hard for me to have any impact on Dom. I've had to file for divorce to get him to stay home.

**Les:** It seems that another one of the things you may want in this workshop, Angela, is to learn how to have some impact on Dom. Is this so?

**Angela:** Yes, but, I'm worried that people here will think I'm a bad parent.

> *Angela's responses continue to be related, but not directly responsive, to the issue. It takes my continual effort to keep on track. I have decided not to confront her, until she appears to feel more comfortable here.*

**Les:** There's a similarity in your position of not being sure you're getting through to your kids and not being sure you're getting through to Dom.

**Angela:** Other people don't take me seriously either. No one ever has. I thought that it was because I look younger than I am.

**Les:** I want you to know that I've heard how important this workshop is to you and how important it is to you that Dom and the kids take you seriously. That is an essential issue this week, for you. *(Angela nods, looking relieved.)*

**Barbara** *(a trainee)*: I'm touched. I have respect for the effort you're willing to make.

**Margaret Ann:** Me, too.

**Angela** *(warmly)*: Thanks.

**Dom:** You're okay, Angela.

*(He shows a glimmer of warmth, but then spins off to talk about himself.)* I see our problem with the children as coming from my problems when I was a kid—

**Les:** Dom, stop! You're acting like you haven't heard Angela at all. Angela, tell him directly, "What I want out of this week is that you take me seriously."

*(Angela directs her statement to Dom. He nods. This is a good place to end our first day's contact with the Dellapietras.)*

# TUESDAY MORNING
# PARENTS' GROUP—WITH RUTH

*The group is divided into parents and children. I have the parents group, including Angela and Dom. The Dellapietras are quiet all morning: neither of them volunteers to begin anything. Then, fifteen minutes before the session ends, Dom and I have an explosive contact.*

**Ruth:** Is there anything from anyone, before we finish for the morning?

**Dom** *(from his lounging position)*: It has been interesting for me to sit and keep my mouth shut. I talk a whole lot, as Margaret Ann said yesterday. I decided not to talk, and I felt a lot come in all of a sudden.

> *On the surface, this sounds like a positive reaction to what happened yesterday, but there is an edge of hostility in Dom's voice that leads me to think he's making a counter-attack.*

*(Dom, in a very general gushing way, tells how he felt good as he listened to others.)*
**Ruth:** Would you be specific and tell me how many times you've been touched by what someone has said and which instances moved you?
*(He is silent. Ruth continues.)* There is a difference between keeping your mouth shut and being affected by what you hear.
**Dom** *(stammering)*: Well, I thought it was good to listen.
*(He continues, speaking vaguely. He doesn't specify what he means or what he wants.)*
**Ruth:** Share with specific people what they said that touched you.

*Dom's lack of specificity is another way of avoiding contact and discounting other people.*

*(Dom begins, again in a general way, to talk to the others in the group. He doesn't remember anyone's name. He tries to muddle through by making a joke out of it.)*

**Ruth:** Ask each person's name, and use their name when you talk to them.

*(Dom begins. He asks Bill Sarnon his name and speaks to him first.)*

**Dom:** Bill, I see you as someone who works hard, but who gets frustrated because he's not treated like a male and a strong man. I can relate to that.

*(After two sentences, Dom becomes vague. He gestures nervously with his hand and jokes in a desperate way.)*

**Ruth:** Would you say directly to Bill: "I let you in"?

**Dom** *(condescendingly)*: I definitely let you in.

**Angela** *(glancing at Dom)*: I respect the way Bill has been straight.

**Ruth:** Dom, I have some unfinished business. Part of me liked hearing what you had to say, and part of me thought it was all bullshit.

*(Angela lets out a sharp laugh, then quickly covers her face with her hands.)*

*Dom's way of relating is common with alcoholics. He takes a superior position in order to defuse, or disengage, with people whom he perceives as threatening.*

**Dom** *(squirming in his chair)*: I think the bullshit part is wrong.

**Ruth:** I think I'm right. I think you're doing it right now. What I mean by bullshitting is that you're not making a genuine response to other people, whether the responses are of fear, gladness, anger, frustration, whatever.

**Dom** *(again in a superior tone)*: You have a right to your own thoughts, Ruth.

**Ruth:** I'm concerned that you have the ability to slip through the week on bullshit alone. You could do what's right on the surface, and never get an inch down into what's going on with you. I hope you won't do that. I'm going to go on letting you know when I believe you're bullshitting.

**Dom:** Yes, I've been aware this morning that I could take the position of just sitting and not listening.

**Ruth:** I quit now. What you just said is significant. You're right, unfortunately, you most likely will take that position, and then you and your family will not get what you need.

*(Angela has been looking at the floor, with her finger raised to her smiling mouth, seemingly to keep herself quiet.)*

# TUESDAY MORNING

# YOUNG PEOPLE'S GROUP—WITH LES

*Maria Dellapietra is here with me and the other older kids. Marco is outside with Kitty, the play therapist. We are meeting in one of the condominium's living rooms.*

**Les:** Maria, what's it like for you being here, right now?

**Maria:** One of my big problems is I don't like it when my brother bugs me. I also don't like it that he's not here.

**Les:** Will you show me the picture you drew?

*(I had asked everyone to think of a time when things weren't going well, and to draw a picture of their family at that time. To my surprise Maria's picture, which she readily produced, shows her mother, her father, her brother, and her maternal grandmother all holding hands and dancing.)*

**Les:** It looks like a happy picture. Maria, is that so?

**Maria** *(vigorously shaking her head, no; her voice is high-pitched and fast)*: I don't like it when they dance. I don't like it, because when they're happy they want to leave me out. I don't draw well. There are lots of things I don't like.

*(Her manner of speaking is similar to her father's.)*

**Les:** You're talking so fast that it's hard to hear you or to say anything to you. Is this what it's like for you, in your family?

**Maria:** They don't want me to be there or to say anything. I don't feel very important.

*(She suddenly looks very sad.)* Mom pushes me away every time I come near her. Mom hits me, and I don't like that.

**Les:** Maria, you look sad. What goes on inside you when that happens at home?

**Maria** *(with voice level rising)*: I don't think Mom likes me. I think she hates me. I hate her, too.

**Les:** How come you think your mother treats you that way?

**Maria:** Boys are better than girls.

*(She squinches down and looks very little, and very frightened as she speaks.)*

**Les:** So, you think your mom hates you, and that boys are better than girls? Do you also think it's easier to be little than to be big?

**Maria** *(covering her ears)*: I don't want to talk about that.

> *Maria has stated, very clearly, what she thinks and feels about herself. She has shown some of her pain. Our goal will be to help her change this sense of herself, and to help the family change their way of reinforcing that self concept. Right now, it is important to back off.*

**Les:** You've done really well talking, so far. Now, I would like you to go back to your picture and change your picture to the way you want it to be.

*(As I move on to David Quinn, Maria turns back to her drawing. She wrings her hands, but never picks up a crayon.)*

**Les** *(later on)*: Maria, will you show the group your picture and what you changed?

**Maria** *(loudly and directly)*: I didn't change anything.

**Les:** I bet it's really hard for you to change anything. You draw a pretty picture of your family, but you don't seem to feel pretty about it, inside you. One thing I know is that people in your family don't easily say when they are angry. Is it also hard, or scary, for you to say if you are angry?

**Maria:** Yes.

**Les:** We will be able to help you this week to not feel so scared and angry.

*(Maria looks relieved. I decide to leave her, without adding anything.)*

> *There is a combination of things with Maria that will be important for us to get to. I feel a little like*

*Angela in wanting to understand what the reasons are
for Maria's behavior before I act.*

## TUESDAY AFTERNOON

## CHOCOLATE PUDDING—WITH RUTH

*The afternoon is warm and sunny. The family members
chosen for the chocolate pudding group are sitting in a
circle, on the lawn, with a large piece of plastic under them,
and with five big metal bowls of pudding around. Angela is
the only member of the Dellapietra family involved.*

*We include Angela in the group to explore the ways she
makes, or doesn't make, contact. Also, she has said she is
afraid of physical contact with other people because of the
horrendous fights she had had with her mother. Finally,
Angela described herself as intolerant of messes, because her
mother was an awful housekeeper.*

*Angela begins the group, sitting cross-legged on the
plastic, with her eyes wide and frightened and her back
stiff. She, very slowly, begins to put pudding on her arms
and holds back from putting pudding on anyone else. She
tries to stall her involvement by asking a lot of why
questions: "Why me?" It's only gradually that Angela
experiments with putting pudding on her body. Other group
members—especially Nicholas and Bette Sarnon—are
throwing it around.*

*Paula Quinn, one of the more neat and careful members
of the group, finally started Angela playing with the
pudding by tossing a little blob onto her foot. By the end of
the twenty-minute session, Angela is covered with
pudding—face, hair, arms, and legs. One of the metal
bowls is turned upside down on her head, and she is
laughing.*

**Angela:** Wait until Dom sees me. Wait until Marco and
Maria see me. *(Uproarious laughter.)* They've never seen
me messy.

*(At the end of the session, Angela goes upstairs and
inside without washing any of the pudding off. She takes
some delight in kissing Dom. Both children howl with
laughter when Angela rubs her cheek on Dom's.)*

# DURING CHOCOLATE PUDDING—WITH LES

*While the pudding group is outside, the remaining group is inside, with me. Maria and Marco keep rushing to the window to watch their mother. Dom stays seated and does nothing.*

**Les:** Why haven't you gotten up to take a look?
**Dom** *(sarcastically)*: Oh, I'm just tired.
**Les:** You sound angry, Dom.
**Dom:** Oh no, everything's just fine.
*(David Quinn complains about not being outside with the pudding. Maria mocks him:)*
**Maria:** I'm angry. I'm not in the fun.

*Like her father, she does a lot of pretending.*

**Berenice:** I see Melissa in the group. She's going a little too far. I'm so worried.

*Berenice is exaggerating, as she often does.*

**Dom** *(sarcastically)*: I'm not too concerned about it.
**Berenice** *(to Dom)*: I'm sick and tired of the way you constantly upstage other people and go after them.
**Dom** *(in an acid voice)*: I'm terribly, terribly sorry!
**Berenice** *(loudly)*: I don't believe you. You're never straight.
**Maria** *(screaming)*: I want to get out of here. I don't want to hear that lady talk to my Daddy like that.

*For years, Angela has covered up for Dom. Maria has never seen her mother confront her father about his sarcasm, evasiveness, or his alcoholism. Angela made excuses for Dom's coming home late at night, as she made excuses for her wayward father when she was a girl.*

**Les:** Maria, sit down here by me. Marco?
*(He's in the middle of the room, twirling and hitting people with an encounter bat.)*
Sit down where you are, next to Barbara. Maria, it's

important for you to know that people sometimes do have bad feelings—that doesn't necessarily mean that anyone will get hurt.

Dom, this afternoon so far is an example of how you avoid parenting the kids and how Maria runs away from feelings. She quickly gets the message from you, when you make everything nice, that it's not all right to have feelings and look at them.

**Dom** (*very casually*): I don't see it that way.

(*Dom then becomes disruptive, loudly asking the kids to bring him the Polaroid pictures Barbara has been taking of the chocolate-pudding group. I turn and talk to Berenice, but she can barely hear me.*)

*There's a pattern in the way Dom handles confrontation. Instead of responding, he smoothes over any disturbance, backs away, and then gets back later with some kind of acting out. Ruth suggested to me, on Monday night, that this might be the pattern Dom's drinking takes. (He drinks whenever he feels angry and hasn't realized it.)*

**Dom** (*attacking Margaret Ann*): You know, I don't think you were careful enough with Little Gerry yesterday at the swimming pool.

**Margaret Ann:** I do the best I can. I think he was safe.

(*Maria is hanging on Dom's neck as he attacks Margaret Ann. He then halfheartedly pushes Maria away as he placates Margaret Ann.*)

**Les:** This is an exact example, Dom. Whenever anyone says anything to you that you don't like, you get back at them later, like now, with Margaret Ann. You make it not okay for people to tell you what's on their minds. People can never trust that they will be safe with you. It must be hard for your family never to be able to trust you.

*What is unfinished, at this time, is a response to Maria and Dom's nonverbal interaction. As I talk to Dom, Maria runs her fingers through her father's hair. When I say the words "not okay," Dom pulls Maria across his lap, as if having her sitting across him is a device he uses to comfort himself and to ward me off while I confront him.*

# WEDNESDAY MORNING
# WOMEN'S GROUP—WITH RUTH

*I'm meeting with the women in the living room of one condominium. Most of us are clustered on pillows on the floor. Maria is across the room, playing. Angela volunteers to work. I'm delighted she wants to start. We have done alot of talking in the training meetings about how to make contact with Angela. Our hope is that the women's group will be a safer place for her. I've come to the group with an agenda for her.*

*It has been difficult, so far, to get any separation between Angela and Dom. They work together to make sure that no problems get defined or solved. I will work to get Angela to define herself, and to find out more about what she thinks and feels about herself.*

**Angela:** I want to talk about some things, privately. They would be harmful to Dom, and I don't want to hurt anyone.

**Ruth:** I'm glad that you want to talk, and I am ready to listen. I also have a list of some things I would like to bring up with you.

**Angela:** I meant privately, with you, alone. There are some things, still, that I don't want to hurt Dom with.

**Ruth:** Have you ever thought about how often, and in how many ways, you protect Dom? What Dom needs, and what you and your family need, is for you to stand up for yourself and be open with what is going on, rather than hiding your thoughts and feelings about things like his drinking.

**Angela:** I know I do hide things. It's hard for me to stand up to anyone.

**Ruth:** I watch you unable to stand up to Maria, and Dom in particular. I understand some with Dom, because when someone stands up to or confronts him he always gets them back in some way, later. I imagine he gets you back by his drinking, and in many respects, it is unsafe for you to stand up to him.

**Angela** (*sadly and intensely*)**:** You are right.

**Ruth:** Where did you learn to hide things and to be so frightened of standing up for yourself? Will you tell us about yourself as you were growing up and where you think this comes from?

**Angela** *(looking terrified)*: I can't.

**Ruth:** Okay, I see your fright. *(I decide to back off.)* I have some current things, then, I'd like to talk about. Maybe they will help you make some connections.

**Angela** *(relieved, and looking like she is back in the room again)*: That's alright.

**Ruth:** I'd like to talk about sexual issues.

**Angela** *(laughing)*: I knew you were going to bring that up. That's a personal subject. I'm very nervous talking about it.

**Ruth:** I'm concerned that it's not so personal and private as you think. Watching Maria, I see there's a real seductive element in her interactions with people, particularly with Dom. Also, Kitty had some observations about her time with Maria and Marco that I have asked her to tell you about.

*(Maria moves across the room to her mother, sits on her lap, and puts her face in front of her mother's so that they're almost touching noses.)*

**Angela:** Maria, I'm talking and I'm going to go on talking. Go back and play or sit here beside me, as I go on.

**Maria** *(in a whining, infuriating voice)*: I don't want to move.

**Ruth:** Angela, I like the way you're being consistent and firm.

**Angela** *(to Maria, and at the same time moving her)*: Sit here or go there, whether you want to or not.

**Ruth:** It's my sense that there are a lot of public sexual issues in your family.

*(Turning to Maria, who is sitting beside her mother and still wiggling and whimpering.)*

Maria, there might be some things that you, as a girl, would want to talk about in this group. Things you wouldn't feel easy talking about with boys or men around. There are for sure things that are important for you to listen to, like right now. Kitty, will you tell Angela what you observed?

**Kitty:** Yesterday, I had Little Gerry and Marco together. Marco had said he was very tired, and he asked if he and I could be alone for a while. I said sure. We went out to sit on the grass. Marco had a stick in his hands, and he tried to put the stick up my skirt, saying he wanted to touch my vagina and my boobies.

**Angela** *(eyes wide)*: Are you kidding?

**Kitty:** I am not kidding. I said no, and he looked extremely surprised and hurt. Later, Maria told me that Marco often comes into her bedroom at night and lays on her bumping up and down.

**Maria** *(in a firm, mature voice)*: Marco bugs me.

**Angela:** Maria, why didn't you tell me that? I can't help you if I don't know what's bothering you.

**Maria:** If I tell you, you'll just tell him to stop, and then he'll go on anyways, and I don't want to wake you.

**Ruth:** Maria, you're talking to your mother very clearly. I like the way you're sitting quietly and paying attention now.

Angela, what are you thinking and feeling as you hear all of this?

**Angela:** I feel uncomfortable. It was my decision to be open with the kids in discussing sexual organs. I wanted things different in my house, with my children. When I grew up, discussing sex was absolutely not allowed, with the one exception of my mother calling me a slut and a whore.

*(In tears)* I wanted my children to have a different picture. I hadn't thought what was going on with Marco and Maria was serious. I thought it was normal exploration. In fact, I hadn't seen what Kitty's telling me about, or Maria. *(Her voice drops, and she looks away.)*

**Ruth:** I support your wanting to make a different atmosphere in your house now than the one you grew up in. It is important, though, to look at the line between being open and not noticing what may be overstimulation.

*(Angela looks very defensive.)*

**Angela:** There isn't any overstimulating going on at my house!

*Angela again tightens up and moves back. It is difficult to say anything to her that she might construe as making her look bad. The difficulty that I have maintaining a connection with her must be something Dom and the children experience, too.*

*(There's a lot of tension in the room centering on Angela and Maria. I call a five-minute stretch break, to let people move around a little and to give others the space to connect with Angela.)*

**Ruth** *(back from the break)*: I want to shift issues a little, now, and then come back later to finish up the sexual things. Angela, you commented yesterday that you see yourself as being a candidate for the funny farm. Are you afraid of going crazy?

*Les had shared with me Angela's comment and his sense of her fear about being like her mother. In the training meeting, we decided that this was an essential belief about herself that we needed to respond to and to help her change.*

**Angela:** I don't know.

*(She is very strained: her voice is cracking, her neck and shoulders are very tense.)*

**Ruth:** I don't believe you are a candidate for the funny farm.

*Using the same words Angela herself used is important as a way of keeping contact with her.*

*(Angela laughs nervously. Maria crawls onto her mother's lap.)*

**Maria:** Mommy, I want to sit by you.

**Ruth:** Maria, come over and sit by me, instead. Your mother is doing fine right now.

*I want to keep Maria from taking care of her mother's feelings, and free Angela from having to refocus on Maria. This is also an action to take care of Maria, who is obviously anxious.*

*(Maria crawls across the room, and climbs into my lap, with a contented sigh.)*

**Angela:** All I can think about, when you ask me about feeling crazy, is my childhood, and how unhappy it was. I put a lot of energy into holding those memories away. I don't want to go back.

**Ruth:** I understand your fear of going back to parts of that awful time. You were really strong to have made it through all that. I also know you're spending too much energy, now, attempting to keep things pushed away. It's by opening up some of those issues in your past, that there can be a resolution to the problems now.

**Angela** *(in tears):* I know I put a lot of energy into avoiding having other people suffer. I don't want others to feel hurt, so I brush things off.

*(Maria slips off my lap and back to her mother, again trying to wipe away Angela's tears.)*

**Angela:** I'm all right, Maria. You can get yourself taken care of someplace else. Also, don't get in the way of my talking.

*(Maria crawls a few feet away and sits staring at her mother.)*

**Ruth:** Tell us in your own way, and at your own pace, some information about your past.

**Angela:** I can't.

**Ruth:** I think you can. Just take it slow.

**Angela** *(hesitantly, but available):* The problem was the violent fighting between my mother and me. My mother would hold me by the hair on the back of my head and hit me in the face. My little brother had to watch.

> *The same kind of antagonism is developing between Angela and Maria. Maria doesn't listen to her mother. She frequently pushes at Angela, infuriatingly.*

**Angela** *(continuing):* As I got bigger, I swore I wouldn't take that. I decided that, if my mother chose to fight and never to talk, then I was going to bust her right back. *(She slides to the floor.)*

> *One reason Angela pulls back and doesn't stand up for herself and what she thinks, is that she's concerned about really hurting the people she fights with.*

**Angela** *(crying profusely, huddled on the floor like a little girl):* It was so awful. I hate myself for what I did, although I know I had to protect myself. Everyone said I was bad and that I ought to be sent to reform school. They said my mother ought to get rid of me somehow. The week I turned 18, I said good-bye, and I haven't been back to my mother's house again. I see my mother sometimes, but we don't talk about any of the important things between us.

*(Clearly, without tears, and now looking up:)* I hate my mother. She can suffer all she wants to. I hate her. I hate her. I hate her. I don't want her to influence my children. It makes me sad that I hate her so much, though.

> *I wonder if Angela also keeps Dom, who is an alcoholic like her mother, and who attacks Angela verbally, from influencing the children.*
> *When we were talking outside of a session, Angela said she used to have nightmares about people screaming and beating each other up. She's afraid that looking at the past will start the nightmares again and that she will break into pieces.*
> *I decide to repeatedly confront Angela's internal belief system about herself. I will also facilitate group support and encouragement, for her.*

**Ruth:** When I think of you as a little girl, I feel sad that there was no one there to help you. There was no one to tell you that you weren't bad and that mothers shouldn't behave the way your mother behaved.

*(Angela looks soft and sad. She moves back into her seat, away from me.)*

**Angela:** I know my mother was wrong, but I also know that everyone else thought I was wrong, and that if I fail in my marriage, or as a mother, everyone will say "Well, what could you expect? Remember what kind of a kid Angela was." There's no one who will be surprised if I fail. They'll all go on saying that I was the one to blame.

> *Angela's position, "I'll show them I wasn't bad, no matter what I have to put up with," shores up her fragile sense of herself.*

**Ruth:** Do you sometimes get scared that you can't make the distinction between anger and violence?

> *Her fear that her own rage may turn to violence is what seems to prevent her from moving into the past. I'm remembering that a couple of other people in the workshop have told me they're afraid Angela could*

*become physically abusive with Maria, particularly since Maria acts as if she's asking for it.*

**Angela:** No, because I think my decision to make it not like it was when I was a kid will keep me from being violent.

**Ruth:** That is an important decision.

*Angela's firmness about making the decision not to be violent rests on top of the volcano that is her fear of herself. For her, to admit that fear would be to admit that she might be bad and make her fear for her sanity.*

**Maria** *(in a two-year-old voice)*: Hit him. Hit him. Hit him.

*(She's talking to one of the stuffed bears in the corner.)* It was the bear that said, "Hit him," not me.

**Ruth:** What have you been feeling, Maria, as you hear your mother and me talking?

**Maria:** My Mommy was sad. When she gets sad, I get sad. Then I try to help my Mommy.

**Ruth:** You try to help your Mommy by being sad and angry?

**Maria:** Yes, that's the way it is.

*(She has the bear next to her. I pick up another bear and talk to Maria, bear-to-bear.)*

**Maria** *(making her bear jump up and down and roar)*: I'm the Mommy. I'm the Mom, and I'm mad.

**Ruth** *(bouncing her bear)*: My bear wants to know how come you are the Mommy? You don't look like the Mommy.

**Maria:** I won't tell. I won't tell.

**Ruth** *(roaring)*: I'm mad, too.

**Maria:** I still won't tell. I won't tell.

**Ruth:** My bear says, "When you're ready, I'm ready to hear what you have to say. Now I'm going back to talk to Angela, the real Mommy."

**Maria:** My bear is laughing. *(She bounces it across the room.)* My bear says, "I won't tell you. I won't tell you."

**Ruth:** Angela, what are you thinking at this point?

**Angela:** I'm thinking about Marco.

**Ruth:** We can get back to Marco, a little later. It's important to stay with yourself and Maria, right now.

*(Maria is playing with the bear and making it sing, "No, no, no. I'm not a baby, baby, baby . . . I'm a Mommy, Mommy, Mommy.")*

**Angela:** Okay, maybe it's too hard to think about Maria. She takes over my place, and I give up.

**Maria** *(chanting)*: Yes, yes, yes, yes.

**Ruth:** I am concerned about what might be occurring now. As I watch you and Maria, she doesn't listen to you, she fights you, she's high-strung. Maria seems to believe, also, that she is the Mommy. She interferes, and you are unsuccessful at stopping her. Finally, she and your husband have an alliance, a twosome that has some real seductive sexual elements.

**Angela** *(quietly)*: I guess that's right.

**Ruth:** Sometimes, no matter how strong our conscious decisions are to not be like our parents, we act like them anyway, outside of our awareness.

**Maria** *(giving a big sigh through her bear)*: You're right.

**Ruth:** The other thing is that in families where parents decide not to be like their own parents, they frequently tend to make their children into their parents in order to maintain their position in life—that predictable, usual position created by their early decision.

*As Angela listens, I can see her posture go from defensive to open and back to defensive. When I see her moving away, I support her. Because I want her to keep listening, I balance information and support. Then I leave an empty space for the other women in the group to offer their comments to Angela.*

**Bette Sarnon:** I really admire your ability to listen.

**Berenice Barker:** What I see is that you've survived through very difficult situations.

**Angela:** You have all gotten some idea of what was going on with my mother. No one ever saw it when I was little, because my mother was so good at making things look all right, on the outside. The only one who ever saw was my brother. He was so frightened that he had to keep his mouth shut.

**Ruth:** You weren't bad, and you weren't the crazy one.

**Paula Quinn:** Your mother did an awful thing.

**Angela** *(shyly)*: Is what's going on with Marco normal or something I should be concerned about also?

*One of the ways, again, that Angela protects herself from contact and support from other people is to shift onto Marco. This time, I am ready to let her go with it.*

**Ruth:** It is something you should be concerned about. But, before we switch, have you heard the other women's support?

**Angela:** Yes, and I don't believe it.

**Ruth:** We'll return to that.

**Kitty:** I think you should be concerned, too.

*(Maria, in the corner, with her bear, begins to make growling sounds.)*

**Angela:** I have been concerned about Marco's behavior. He has been on what I call the booby trip. I told Maria she should slap him in the face if he touches her where she doesn't want to be touched.

*(Maria giggles a low giggle through the bear, and a high giggle on her own.)*

**Ruth:** Les and I will be available to talk to you about Marco, in many ways, during the rest of the week. We will have some suggestions for you. To begin with, I think it would be better if you didn't slap him in the face and if you didn't tell Maria to slap him in the face.

**Angela** *(stiff and frosty)*: What would you suggest?

**Ruth:** Tell him to stop what he is doing.

**Angela:** That's what I say, and then I slap him.

**Ruth:** You need to learn to come across clearly, without having to slap Marco. You need to stop slapping and stop Maria from slapping. Remember when you reported earlier how your mother would slap you? Don't you do that, and don't have Maria do it.

**Angela:** Oh, okay.

**Ruth:** Dom has a part in this also, and you need to let him have his part. When the family is together this afternoon, we will focus on that.

**Maria:** No, no, no. My Daddy doesn't! He doesn't! He doesn't! He doesn't!

**Ruth** *(firmly to Maria)*: Yes, he does Maria, and it's okay to talk about it, and for people to be angry at him.

**Angela:** I need to talk about how things are with Dom.

**Ruth:** Yes. I was glad you brought this up at the beginning of the group. I'm glad you want to follow through on it now.

**Angela:** I talked after the session to Paula and Robin yesterday, and then Dom said that I needed to practice what I preached and that I hit Maria too much. I was angry at Dom last night, because he thinks that because I punish the kids, I'm like my mother.

**Ruth:** That must leave you feeling like the bad guy again.

**Angela:** Yes.

**Ruth:** I think this is one of the setups in your family. Dom is the nice guy and does nothing, and you are forced into the opposite position, because you do something. Dom can set you up to be the bad guy, but you're not. You need to be sure you don't let yourself get set up that way.

**Angela:** Dom doesn't listen. I need help with that.

**Ruth:** I've noticed that, too, and I'll help you.

*(There's a murmur of agreement in the group.)*

**Paula:** Dom bullshits. That is what I know to be the alcoholic style. I may be wrong, but I think I'm quite aware of how Dom treats you and of how it must be at home.

**Berenice:** Angela, you're right to stand up to him. If I were you, I wouldn't worry so much about being harmful.

**Ruth:** Angela, what's most important is that you not perpetuate the scenes you had with your mother. That is, that everything looks fine on the surface, you get the hell beat out of you behind closed doors, and then you're the one who's labeled as bad.

**Angela:** What I had on my mind at the beginning of this session was that I don't want to continue with Dom at all. I'm amazed at all the crap he's spouting here about everything being great. I can't be happy, and I'm not happy at all. I would like to find a way to end it. That's what I'm also here for. To find a way to end my marriage to Dom, so that none of us gets hurt. *(Laughing:)* I've come to the workshop to figure out how to get rid of Dom. I'd like to get rid of him without having to run and without having to hit. I don't know how I can do it without feeling I'm the bad one. The goal of my life has been to prove that I'm not the bad guy and that I'm not crazy. Once, in the past, when his drinking was unbearable, I moved out. He was so devastated that I moved back in.

**Kitty:** Angela, I want to ask you about something Maria said. Maria said that during your separation, Dom threatened to kill himself in front of Marco and her.

**Angela:** That is true. He was crying and told all of us that he would kill himself if I didn't come back. *(Crying:)* How can I help but be the bad guy when this is going on? When my children were saying, "Mommy, Mommy, you're going to make Daddy do this. You're going to make Daddy dead." All I could figure out was that I had no choice.

**Ruth:** You weren't the bad guy as a child, and you aren't now. When we start the couples' session, tomorrow morning, will you be willing to talk to Dom directly about where you are and let me work with him, so that he doesn't pull this devastated stuff and the guilt games? I know that's risky for you, because you can't know what Dom will do.

*(Maria bounces her bear on her mother's lap and says "Hi, baby, Hi baby," as if taunting her mother into being grown up. Angela finally has to shush her.)*

**Angela** *(looking at me, and around at the group)*: Okay, I think I can do that tomorrow. Dom will be embarrassed and ashamed. I haven't wanted that to happen.

**Margaret Ann:** Let him be embarrassed. You have to do what you need to do. Let him be the bad guy for once. Maybe you can even do it, so that there isn't a bad guy.

**Angela:** He's not so awful. Oh, God, here I go defending him again.

*(Maria starts shouting, "Hi, baby," to the women in the room, and waving her arms and shaking her hands.)*

**Ruth:** Maria, stop what you're doing. Come and sit down. Every time we talk about your father, you begin acting weird.

**Angela:** It's hard for Dom and me to even begin to talk, because Maria is always right there in the middle.

**Ruth:** Maria, it's not okay for you to act funny and do strange things. It's not okay for you to take on the job of stopping the talking in the family and getting things off the track. Maria, I think you're smart. You can think. You can handle your feelings in a way that makes sense. Your father is also smart. He needs to learn to take better care of himself. That's his job and not your job. You are not the Mommy to Angela or the Mommy or wife to Dom.

**Angela:** Maria, you're an interesting and fun person to be with when you act like yourself. I enjoy being with you, and I like you as my little girl. From now on, I am going to stop you from some of these other things you are doing. I am the Mommy.

**Berenice:** Maria, I can tell you're smart. I've seen you figure out hard things.

*There are similarities between the way six-year-old Maria acts and the way thirty-year-old Angela acts. Maria is constantly setting herself up so that other people have to reprimand her. She creates interactions that say, "you're bad." In another way, she reflects Angela's fear of being a candidate for the funny farm.*
    *Many things are now clear with this family, but so much needs to be done. It is already Wednesday, and we have only gotten through enough to clarify the problems. How we shall proceed, so that one issue gets finished, is now my concern.*

# WEDNESDAY MORNING

# MEN'S GROUP—WITH LES

*All of the men (be they 3 years old or 53 years old) are meeting with me in one of the condominium living rooms. Marco and Little Gerry are playing in the corner.*

**Les:** Dom, is there any difference for you in this group, as compared to any of the other groups we have done here so far?
**Dom:** Being with men who are fathers reminds me that it's hard for me to be a good father. I think I'm too authoritarian, that I feel as if I always have to be in control.

*More important than what Dom says is the way he says it. He's talking in his sing-song voice again, eager to be saying and doing the right thing. It seems to me as if he wants to get through this workshop unchanged, hoping only to mollify Angela.*

**Les:** Dom, one of the things you said you wanted was feedback about your parenting. I'm ready to do that. In the last day and a half I've noticed some inconsistencies.
    Yesterday, Marco found a caterpillar outside and brought it in to the room in a paper cup. You seemed not to want him to play with it. What you told him, however,

was to take the caterpillar outside, give it something to eat, and that the caterpillar would be there when Marco went back outside after the session. I think you must have known, Dom, that wasn't true. The caterpillar wouldn't still be there.

**Marco** (*with tears and baby-talk*): Ya, he was gone, but I fed him good.

(*Dom looks very sheepish. Marco returns to his game.*)

**Dom** (*quickly*): Sure, I'd like to look at that, but I don't really see any purpose.

> *Again, Dom doesn't honestly take responsibility for his own actions. Treatment does not proceed unless we can facilitate this responsibility taking.*

**Les:** Shit, Dom, you don't take responsibility for anything.

**Dom:** Yeah.

**Gerry Barker:** Dom, every time anybody says anything to you, you act like you're being criticized.

**Dom:** Whenever anyone talks to me, I get defensive.

**Bill Sarnon** (*slowly and carefully*): I don't want to hurt your feelings.

**Dom** (*joking skittishly*): I'm not reacting that much, am I?

**Bill:** I think you're afraid of making a mistake. Everyone is entitled to make mistakes. We call it experience.

(*Dom doesn't respond. Edgar volunteers to talk about how he got along with his parents. I turn my attention to him. As Edgar talks to his mother, via the Gestalt two-chair technique, Dom listens closely.*)

**Dom** (*as Edgar finishes*): Jesus, that's sad.

**Les:** You seem sad now, yourself. Was that important to you?

**Dom** (*shrugging it off*): Sure, yeah. I want to get down to work, too, I guess, but I don't know what to talk about.

**Les:** You never filled out the history questionnaire. You never took even that responsibility. I need some more information about your mother. Let's start there.

(*The background Dom then gives us, is that his mother and father lived together for twelve years, and then divorced. Dom's father was his mother's second husband. He had a stepfather for eight weeks, who decided as soon as he got married that he didn't want to be married. Dom's mother then had several boyfriends. She was married for a year to another unstable man, and then remarried her first husband, who was the father of Dom's two older half-brothers.)*

**Dom** *(suddenly angry)*: She kept saying, "Say, 'Hello,' to your Dad, Dom," with every one of her boyfriends. I said to myself every time, "This isn't my Dad."

*(He laughs embarrassedly.)*

She wanted me to make all those Dads my Dad. Because I was the youngest, a lot got laid on me. I was the father and the husband to my mother for a long time. *(Grimly)* I didn't like being an adult around that house.

*(He then smiles and pushes away his feelings.)*

**Les:** I like sensing some of your realness, Dom. It's important for you to allow yourself to stay for a longer time with what you feel.

**Dom:** I'm not ready to forgive my mother.

*(He starts into his own version of Edgar's two-chair work.)*

I'm not ready to forgive you for being so blind to me and your sons. It's hard to forgive you for always asking me for advice about your boyfriends and husbands, and then not listening to me when I gave it to you.

I used to be in the bar all night with my father when he was drinking. I don't want to be like my Dad.

*(He sits back and wraps things up in a perfunctory way.)*

I feel better about that.

**Les:** You really stuck with your feelings until almost the end. That's the longest period of time that I've heard you do that.

**Bill:** Talking like that, Dom, you seem like a different person. In fact, that's the first time I've ever believed what you said.

**Edgar:** I've had feelings like yours, Dom, with my mother.

**Gerry:** I had the sense, when you were talking, about how ripped off you must have felt when you were a little boy.

**Dom:** I'm just starting to see that.

**Les:** I have another thought to share with you, also, Dom. I heard you say you didn't like being the adult around that house. I can understand that, when you were really a kid. Now, though, I still see you not willing to be grown-up and take your responsibility as a parent. I also see your son frequently keeping himself littler than he is.

**Dom** *(in his put-off way)*: Um-hum. I guess I am angry about all that.

**Les:** I feel put off again. If you want to accomplish anything here, Dom, you will have to stop shining us on.

*(Marco is making sputtering sounds in the corner. I decide to leave Dom and move on.)*

> One of the major issues for Dom is his rebellious, angry position to not give his mother what she wanted, and, in that way, not to grow up. This is harmful to him and his family when he doesn't take appropriate responsibility and acts out by his drinking.
>
> I am discouraged. I doubt if we will even come close to him this week. In the training session, we will need to talk about other approaches to Dom and his righteous rebellion. If Angela moves some, perhaps she will help open things up.

# WEDNESDAY AFTERNOON

# INDIVIDUAL FAMILIES—WITH RUTH

*Our Wednesday afternoon session is short, so that the families can take a stretch away from the workshop. I am meeting with the Dellapietras and the Sarnons in the living room of one of the small condominiums. Les is with both parts of the Barker family, and the Quinns.*

**Ruth** *(addressing everyone)*: We're halfway through the week, now. Think about what you've already accomplished, and think about what you still want to achieve.

The time off, this afternoon, is an important opportunity for a breather. Check to see if you're acting to support the changes you've decided to make or if you're doing something to undermine the changes.

Be aware of how your family is operating. This will help you clarify your goals for our remaining time.

*(Dom and Angela are sitting on the sofa. Maria and Marco are banging around the room restlessly.)*

**Dom:** I'm pleased with myself and what I did for me this morning.

**Ruth:** Beginning from there, what do you want to do this afternoon?

**Dom** *(in his nice, evasive manner)*: I'd like to work with Angela about being better parents.

*(As he says this, Maria shoots over from across the room, sticking her face right in front of him and patting his lap.)*

**Maria:** Don't make Momma cry. She's already cried once today.

**Dom** *(hesitantly)*: It's not so bad to cry, Maria. *(To Angela:)* You can see I'm uncomfortable being a father.

**Ruth:** I'm glad you turned to Angela. Go on talking with her.

**Dom:** It's hard for me to be a father in this family. For one thing, I can't bear to make mistakes.

*(Maria starts to hum loudly and continues to hover around. She leans over the back of the couch and puts her head between her parents, making funny faces. She leans on her father's shoulders, with her hands draped down his front. Marco is increasingly agitated, pounding on the pillows piled in the corner.)*

*This scene clearly exemplifies the parenting issues. Sensing that their parents will begin something between them, the two children, their anxiety increasing, are also increasing their disruptive behavior. Maria's behavior is extremely seductive. Dom is encouraging her through his own actions. Angela looks as if she is getting more and more irritated, and yet says nothing.*

**Dom:** Angela, I really want to be a better father.

*(Marco comes over and boldly plops himself down next to his mother. As soon as Marco does this, Dom calls Maria from behind the sofa.)*

**Dom:** Sit next to me, Maria. Sit close to me.

*(Dom is now on one end of the couch; Angela is on the other. Maria is nestled next to Dom. Marco is cuddled next to Angela.)*

*Each parent uses one of the children as an ally against the other parent: Marco for Angela, Maria for Dom. Each child is used as caretaker and comforter.*

**Dom:** I'd like to take on more of the jobs that a father should do.

*(Maria puts her hands over her ears and shouts.)*
**Maria:** I don't like to hear my Mom and Dad talking to each other.
**Dom:** I'll go on, whether you like hearing it or not.
**Ruth:** Good, Dom.
**Maria** *(yelling)*: I'll plug my ears even more.
*(She picks up the couch end pillows and puts them over her ears.)*

*I now decide to attend to Maria, even if it is reinforcing her disruption. I want to know more of what goes on with her.*

**Ruth:** Unplug your ears, Maria, and say how come you don't like hearing your Mom and Dad talk. I don't understand that.
**Maria** *(her voice is sad and querulous)*: They fight when they talk. I know they're going to fight now. I know they're going to fight now.
**Ruth:** What goes on inside of you when you hear them fight?
**Maria:** It's bad, because I think they're going to hurt each other when they get really, really mad.
**Ruth:** Have you seen them hurt each other when they fight?
**Marco:** I've seen them hurt each other—the time when Mommy knocked down two pictures and a lamp.
**Maria** *(in loud chorus with Marco)*: She broke the lamp *(and then on her own)* and almost broke a glass table. It scared me, and I thought the house was going to burn down. That's why I don't like fighting.
**Marco:** I go outside.
*(He's getting littler and littler, curling up like a one-year-old, with his thumb in his mouth.)*
Don't hurt Momma, Dadda. Don't hurt Momma, Dadda.
**Maria** *(defensively)*: I never saw Daddy hurt Mommy. *(To me:)* When I get scared, I cry and hide.

*Marco is Angela's child; he comes to her defense. Maria is Dom's child; she comes to his defense. Marco and Maria fight with each other, each defending his or her allied parent. Angela and Dom do nothing clearly.*

**Ruth:** Maria, I wonder if one of the things you do is to make yourself the big one and try to solve the fight.

*(Maria, cuddled up with her father, nods.)*

**Maria:** Either I'm the boss or my brother is. That's the only way its ever gonna work.

**Marco** *(in a big voice)*: Uh, huh.

*(Since she has the floor, Maria takes the chance to switch topics.)*

**Maria:** Marco never goes to sleep at night. He bugs me, too.

*This is back to the sexual play between two children who believe they need to be grown-up. I wonder what I can do to pull all of these related pieces together and help them establish a different order.*

**Ruth:** It sounds important that you, Dom and Angela, find a way to be the bosses in your family. Right now, it doesn't seem as if Maria or Marco feel very safe.

**Marco** *(with a baby shriek)*: No, I'm scared Maria might throw me over the bench if she's the boss.

**Ruth:** So you get scared that Maria might hurt you?

**Marco:** Yes. *(He rolls around, feet in the air, goo-gooing.)*

**Maria:** Marco and I get mad at each other and fight a lot.

**Ruth:** I wonder if the two of you do what you see your Mom and Dad do sometimes?

**Maria:** Yes.

**Marco:** No.

**Ruth** *(to Marco)*: I'm glad you share what you think, even when you disagree with Maria. *(Turning:)* Dom and Angela, you need to listen to what happens with the kids when they fight and to what they're saying right now.

**Maria:** Now they'll know, and so they won't fight again.

**Ruth:** I think they've heard what you said, but that doesn't mean they'll never fight again.

**Maria:** They won't fight now, because now they know that we'll get scared.

**Ruth** *(to Maria and Marco)*: Parents need to listen to kids, but what they hear doesn't control their feelings or their behavior.

*(To Dom and Angela:)* You need to learn how to fight, so that it's not dangerous for the kids.

**Maria:** Fighting is always dangerous, because it's hitting.

> *There's no intervention I can make, at this point, that would be satisfying, or safe, for Marco and Maria. What is most striking to me is that neither Angela nor Dom has made any attempt to show that they're listening to anything.*

**Ruth:** Dom and Angela, I keep trying to get back to you. Will you share with each other what you're thinking and feeling, right now?

**Dom** *(speaking to the whole room, rather than to Angela)*: It's nice to hear my daughter open up. I really enjoyed having her speak about her fears.

*(Maria is in her father's arms. She is running her fingers up and down his leg. Dom is caressing Maria's neck and shoulders. Marco is sitting with Angela, gazing up into space.)*

**Angela** *(also to the room)*: I have no doubts that Marco and Maria have fears. But I also see that Maria likes the spotlight and that she'll say what she thinks people want her to say. She says things that are exaggerated, or confused, or wrong.

> *Neither Dom nor Angela responds to the children's fear. Dom brushes things off and makes it all nice. Neither parent relates to Maria's current inappropriateness. Angela does not confront Dom.*

**Dom** *(in a booming voice)*: I heard no lies in anything Maria said.

**Angela:** That's true. It was just exaggerated.

**Bette Sarnon:** Dom, I support Angela's view of Maria's behavior. I've noticed that, several times, she has greatly exaggerated what has been happening.

**Ruth** *(with voice raised)*: Dom, if I were Maria and I heard your comment about enjoying hearing about my fears, I am sure that one of the things I would do is exaggerate things.

Maria is hungry for your attention, and she protects you. I'm aware also of the mutual satisfaction the two of you get from being in physical contact with each other. *(Maria makes a whimpering sound.)*

**Angela** *(sounding bolder)*: At home, Maria frequently blows up her emotions and lies about things. She'll cry very hard, with no tears, and say she hurt herself. When I ask what happened, Maria will finally say she wasn't really hurt. This has happened so often that a lot of the time I don't take Maria seriously.

**Maria:** But remember the time I was learning to ride my bicycle? I really got hurt then, didn't I?

**Ruth:** Dom, Angela is correct about Maria. This is a good example of one thing the two of you parents need to get together on.

*I decide to keep the pressure on Dom, by continuing on Angela's side. I want to get back to the contract for the afternoon, which was that Dom wanted to learn more about being a father.*

**Ruth:** Will you talk together about what has just happened and what you need to do to handle Maria's exaggerations and her seductive behavior?

**Dom:** Yeah, Angela.

*(He jumps in to say, "Yeah," but then goes ahead and acts without consulting Angela. He speaks in a loud, ingenuous tone.)* Okay, Maria, be quiet. Sit here with me and let me talk.

**Maria:** I don't want my parents to fight.

**Dom:** I've heard that. Now you need to sit down and listen.

**Ruth** *(directly)*: Dom, you didn't talk to Angela about Maria. Will you include Angela?

*It requires continuous direction on my part to keep them on track.*

*(Maria is rubbing her father's head. Dom ignores me, and continues to talk to her.)*

**Ruth** *(louder and firmer)*: Dom, you are not dealing with the issue! You are excluding Angela and you are not parenting Maria appropriately.

Angela, it's obvious how you get forced to become firmer and firmer with Maria. Then you're the bad mother and Dom is the nice father.

**Angela** *(crying in frustration)*: This happens over and over again. I get angry now and I don't know what to do.

**Ruth:** Continue with your husband.

**Angela** *(to Dom, in a stumbling, tearful voice)*: You don't act firmly with Maria. You are constantly being only loving with her. Right now you should tell her to stop it, and if she doesn't, you should spank her.

**Dom:** Okay, okay.

*(He does nothing. Maria continues to pat her father's head.)*

**Ruth:** Angela, you are certainly right. He doesn't listen to anyone. Will you tell him, again, what's going on and what you want?

> In the morning, I worked with Angela and her feeling that she was being made into the bad guy by her alcoholic mother. Angela was open about her willingness to take the blame and her unwillingness to stand up to Dom.

*(Angela turns to Dom, but can't talk. She looks down.)*

**Angela:** I feel lost and frustrated. I can never get through to him.

> This is Angela's position with her mother. At this point, I can either help Angela make the tie-in with her past, or go on working within the current family. I decide to stay with the here and now. Early work done with Angela, at this point, might reinforce the family setup that Angela is the bad one who needs help.

**Ruth:** Continue, Angela. Tell Dom.

**Angela** *(in a meek voice)*: Dom, you step around everything. You avoid—

**Maria** *(interrupting)*: Mommy, why didn't you get another lamp?

**Angela:** Stay out, Maria, that's not the subject right now.

*(Maria continues to have Dom's attention. They're whispering together.)*

Dom, you don't make any sense when you talk to the kids. I have to get harder and harder. I don't even think you're listening to me now.

**Ruth:** I don't think he's listening, either. Will you see what you can do to get him to answer you? What can you do with Dom, instead of getting harder and harder with Maria?

Do you see what's happening, Angela? Dom isn't there at all. You set up yourself, then, to become the one who talks harshly to Maria, and you avoid Dom.

**Angela:** I do see. But I know Dom can't follow his own train of thought when Maria is sitting there patting him.

**Ruth** (*loudly*): You're only making excuses for him. Dom is the grown-up. Maria is only a little girl. Dom hasn't even attempted to tell Maria to stop or to move her off his lap. It's almost as if he is enjoying mocking you, and he uses Maria to help him.

**Angela:** I tend not to take him seriously when he lets this go on.

**Ruth:** Angela, when you tune Dom out, you get mad at Maria and come down on her much harder than is appropriate. Then you look like the bad one, and Dom looks like the nice one. Dom sets up the trap, and you fall into it. Then, finally and worst of all, Maria doesn't get the limiting and protection a little girl needs. This sounds like what we were talking about this morning. Your mother never got the blame. Do you want to repeat that for your daughter?

**Angela** (*softly and sadly*): No.

**Ruth:** Then what you need to do is to find a way to continue to deal with Dom rather than coming down harder on Maria. That's the old setup. Find a way, now, to help your daughter and confront you husband.

**Dom:** I'm just becoming aware of this: that I don't give Angela any help. I am willing to start being a parent.

**Ruth** (*to Angela*): Right now, Dom could come in, and you wouldn't have the chance to follow through with what we have been saying. Do you want to let that go?

**Angela:** No! It is your fault Dom. You don't even listen to me. You are always encouraging and playing with Maria. I want you to stop that. We have some big problems in our family, and I can't do it all alone, especially when you are always making me bad.

**Dom:** I'm here, aren't I?.

**Ruth** (*to Dom*): Are you sure you're ready to do this? It means you're not always going to be the nice guy, with a smooth voice and loving hands all over your daughter.

**Dom:** Yes, I'm ready. I've taken the easy way out all these years. For years, I've stood back and done nothing but be very critical of Angela.

**Ruth:** Tell Angela what you're willing to do.

**Dom:** I'm willing to keep my eyes open, to listen more, and to sometimes be the heavy.

*(Marco gets louder, and begins to talk about "ka ka" and "pee pee." Maria moves away from the couch.)*

**Angela** *(disbelieving)*: All right.

**Ruth:** Dom, I'm glad to hear you want to take more responsibility, and I know that the only thing that will count is what you do; not what you intend to do. Also, I get a little scared when you talk about becoming "the heavy." I believe you really can be hurtful sometimes, particularly when you're drinking.

**Dom:** I'll take the responsibility to not be hurtful and also to be more involved.

**Ruth:** Dom, will you and Angela talk to your children, right now?

*(Maria is playing in the corner. Dom calls her over. She comes and sits on his lap.)*

**Dom** *(stroking her leg)*: Maria, have you been listening? I want you to know that I'm going to be . . .

**Marco** *(interrupting in a loud, squeaky voice)*: A kid!

**Ruth:** Dom, stop touching Maria on her leg! It is inappropriate for you to be touching your daughter like that.

**Maria:** I don't mind it.

**Dom** *(following Ruth's directions)*: I'm going to work harder at being your father.

*(He stumbles and looks lost. Maria gets up to wander away. Dom yanks her back, slaps her rear, and sits her down on the couch. He speaks in a soft, coy voice.)* Listen to me, will you, Maria? Will you take me seriously?

**Ruth** *(in a loud commanding voice)*: Stop! Stop, right now! You're demonstrating exactly what we've been talking about. First, you haven't included Angela. Second, it is confusing for a child to go from one minute in which you have your arm around her and stroke her leg to the next minute when you jerk her around and whack her backside. One moment you act as if you are her lover; the next moment you are hitting her. How is a six-year-old supposed to know what to do, or how to trust you? Do you understand what I'm saying, Dom? *(He nods.)*

Do you understand, Angela? *(She nods. They look at each other in agreement.)*

**Angela:** I was beginning to get mad, Dom, because you were saying, "Listen to me," in a begging sort of voice, and, "Will you take me seriously?" in a very unserious voice.

**Ruth:** You're right, Angela. I'm glad you're pointing that out to Dom and that you're letting yourself in. You need to get in there, over and over. You need to notice and help stop the seductive play and also the inappropriate limiting. Don't let yourself be excluded. You need to be helping Dom to behave differently with the children.

**Angela** *(clearly)*: I know.

**Ruth** *(now standing and walking around)*: How will the two of you, Dom and Angela, set it up right now—even the physical setup—so that you are dealing with Marco and Maria from a grown-up position and so that you're dealing with them together?

**Angela** *(to Dom)*: The first thing I'd do is take Maria and Marco's toys away so that the distractions are limited, since it's important for them to be listening.

**Dom:** Okay.

*(Both parents gently, but firmly, tell and help the kids to put away the toys.)*

**Ruth:** That is appropriate. Now will you discuss how you will ask the children to sit in a structure that will make it clear who are the grown-ups and who are the children?

**Dom:** Well, Angela, you and I could sit on the floor with Marco and Maria on the couch.

**Angela:** If anyone is on the floor, it should be Marco and Maria.

**Ruth:** That is wise, Angela.

*(In a firm way, Dom and Angela show the children where to sit. Both Marco and Maria are feigning protestations.)*

**Angela:** Most of the time, I've come down to the children's level to talk with them. I had never thought, before now, that there needed to be a distinction between the levels. Dom and I need to maintain a more grown-up position, even physically.

**Dom:** Hey, that's neat.

**Ruth:** Yes, that's neat, Angela. Tell your children what you've decided.

**Dom** *(in a stilted but clear voice)*: Maria, I am the Dad, and your Mom is the Mom. We are making some things different so that you can get more of what you need and so that your Mom gets better things for herself, too.

*Dom is acting like a parent for the first time. His tone and posture are in line with his message to Maria. As Dom does this, Angela leans over and touches him in a warm way.*

**Angela:** Marco and Maria, I love you and your Dad and I are the bosses. You will do what we say and we will help things to be safer for you. We'll all get along better when this happens.

**Dom:** It's not just your Mom who's the boss. It's both of us now.

*It's a relief to see that Dom and Angela aren't undermining each other.*

**Angela** *(to Maria):* Your father and I are the bosses. That means that we will take care of your brother. We are his parents, and the way he acts is not your responsibility. You may come to us when he is bugging you and when you need something. This is different from tattling, and you can trust me to help you know the difference.

**Dom:** You children can come to your mother and you can come to me.

*It is a joy to hear how Angela has included the work from the morning session—Maria's telling her about the disturbing things she said Marco had been doing with her.*

**Ruth:** Angela, I like the caring way you respond to your daughter. I also appreciate how well you remembered what we talked about this morning. Dom and Angela, will you tell each other what you're thinking and feeling, right now?

**Angela:** I feel good, and different.

**Dom:** I do, too. I intend to stick to it this time.

**Ruth:** Dom, I like the difference I see in you in the last ten minutes. You seem to be beginning to integrate what you did in the men's group about being responsible and grown up. The thing to look out for is moving back into being the super-sweet, good guy and setting Angela up to be the bad guy with the children. She is not your mother. This is a good place to stop. And a good way to send you off for your afternoon together.

*(Marco is talking as a four-year-old about the games he wants to play outside.)*

# THURSDAY MORNING
# PARENTS' GROUP—WITH RUTH

*I have the parents and Les has the kids. After Wednesday's sessions, we met with the trainees and planned to support Angela in continuing to talk to Dom directly. She hadn't told him that she intends to seperate. We also want to reinforce the division between parents and kids and the realignment of the teams. We decided to split parents from kids to facilitate the realignment process.*

*When we get to this session, I know what's coming and so do the trainees. Angela volunteers to start, moving to the center of the room and asking Dom to sit opposite her.*

*I pull up a chair to make a triangle with them. Leaning back, drinking my tea, I let Angela begin.*

*As Angela begins, in a cracked and unsteady voice, I wonder if her decision to separate comes from a real need to be apart or whether it's a reaction to the possibility that the family could change. Dom has actually been more responsive to Angela this week and more willing to share the responsibility for the kids. Is Angela moving away from Dom as he gets closer to her and acts more like a husband and father? Is she moving away because of someone else? Again, I decide not to focus on this latter possibility as the necessary changes are the same whether or not another relationship is part of the issue for Angela.*

**Angela** *(clearly and directly)*: What I want, and what I need, is for the kids and I to live for awhile without you, Dom. I've spent the last eight years with you refusing to listen to me. I am glad that you are here, but I don't trust you. *(She looks to me, in an appeal for help.)* This is so hard.

**Ruth:** It's okay to go on. Say what you want to say. *(Dom is leaning back on his hands, his legs crossed in front of him, his chin jauntily up in the air.)*

**Angela** *(weaker and more tearful)*: The difficulty for me, Dom, is that I have so much resentment toward you that I don't think I can recover. I resent the fact that when we split, you threatened to commit suicide in front of the children. I resent the fact that you called my mother and said I kicked you out. I resent the fact that throughout our marriage, I haven't been able to do anything on my own without your acting very suspicious. I couldn't do try-outs or see an agent or a photographer. I hope the two of us will go on getting help so that we can take care of the children, but I feel smothered all the time. When we go home from here, I want you to leave for, at least, awhile.

**Ruth:** Angela, stop for now. Dom, what are you hearing Angela say, and what are you thinking and feeling as you hear her?

**Dom** *(in his usual, cocky voice)*: I know I'm suspicious and difficult. I know I'm all over the place. But at this point I'm much closer to understanding that I have been in the past. Angela, you're wrong! *(Pointing his finger.)* You're the one that's lost. You're the one who doesn't know what you want. I'm concerned about the kids. If you're the one that's unhappy, then you're the one who should leave, 'cause I don't want to.

**Angela** *(to me)*: This is where we get stuck.

**Dom:** Yes, this is where we get stuck. I'm not leaving.

**Ruth:** Dom, would you share directly with Angela what goes on inside of you when you hear her say that she wants you to leave?

**Dom:** I'm hurt. *(There's a brief moment of real sadness before he switches back to accusing her.)* I've helped Angela through a lot. I came here and wanted to do what we decided yesterday—to be a parent with her.

**Angela:** I want and intend to go on being parents together. But I don't want to live with you. What has happened, Dom, is that you come back to me only when I threaten to leave, and then you're all nice and responsive, and you expect me to accept everything as okay. But you weren't there for eight years, and that counts more than this. It feels very unnatural now. You have been a good father in providing financially.

**Dom:** Angela, you're wrong and you're running away.

**Ruth:** Dom, will you talk about yourself? You keep going after Angela rather than saying where you are. It must be hard for you to let yourself and other people know what's going on inside of you.

**Dom** *(tearful)*: I made a million dollars. It's all a waste if I don't have my children and my wife.

*Angela is leaning back, crying quietly. She is sympathetic to his pain, but she's not letting herself be drawn into acting angrily and taking all the blame.*

*Dom tries to shift attention away from himself and focus on Angela, the kids, and money. Dom does everything possible to avoid any self-confrontation. His usual way to avoid his thinking and feeling is to be drunk.*

**Ruth:** I hear how important the kids and Angela are to you. I also hear that they are the only reason you've kept yourself going.

**Dom:** You're right. I haven't done anything that hasn't been for Angela and the kids.

**Ruth:** Are you saying that the only reason you've kept yourself going—maybe even the only reason you've kept yourself alive—is that you have your family to give to and to take care of?

**Dom:** The only way I know my life is worthwhile is because I have two beautiful kids.

**Ruth** *(softly and firmly)*: You need to find out that you are a worthwhile person whether or not you live with your wife and your two children. *(Dom begins to sob. Angela is also crying, as are many in the room. I am sitting forward in my chair, getting ready to be more involved with Dom. He looks at me imploringly and I move to the floor, a little closer to him than to Angela.)*

**Ruth:** Dom, the most important issue is that you decide to keep yourself alive no matter what.

*His basic belief is that, if things get bad enough or if he gets angry enough and if all else fails, he will kill himself. He has finally opened the door to that part of himself.*

**Ruth:** I feel stuck and stopped by you. When I try to connect with you, you bring in the kids or Angela. My major concern is that you take care of your own life—and that you not use the kids to take care of you. That's not okay for either one of the kids. It's not fair to them. It's not being a good father. It's doing to them what your mother did to you.

**Angela:** I am resentful of Dom using the children. I remember driving down the freeway with Dom having a hysterical fit, telling the kids that he's going to end it all, and after he's gone they should remember that it's all their mother's fault.

Dom, I think this is part of what Ruth means. I don't want our kids to grow up with that burden.

I think you're also always putting blocks in my way. You gave me an unusable car, you took away all my credit cards, all the while proclaiming to the children that you were doing these things to help their mother.

**Ruth:** Dom, did you do those things?

**Dom** *(head bowed):* Yes.

**Ruth:** It's not okay to abuse your kids in that way and to manipulate your family that way. It is those things that have to stop.

*(Dom nods.)*

You need to be clear that you won't hurt or kill yourself for any reason and that you won't threaten your wife and your children with hurting yourself or anyone else. Your mother and father played those games—don't you. *(As I talk, Dom is shaking his head no.)*

**Dom:** I won't.

**Ruth:** Turn to Angela and tell her that you will not hurt, or kill, yourself for any reason, at any time.

**Dom:** Angela, I . . .

*He forgets, and hems and haws in a joking manner. I have to feed him the same words three times and repeatedly confront his lack of seriousness to get him to make a clear statement to Angela.*

**Dom:** Angela, I won't hurt or kill myself. Whenever.

**Ruth:** Is what you've just said true?

**Dom:** No, it's not.

**Ruth** *(firmly and loudly):* Do not hurt or kill yourself or anyone else for any reason.

The most important issue is that you keep yourself and other people safe.

Angela, will you move out of the center? Sit in the circle, beside someone you feel comfortable with.

*(Angela moves next to Bette. I move, so that I am facing Dom squarely.)*

Unless you're willing to be clear and honest about not hurting yourself or anyone else, you are likely to go on using this threat and being abusive to Marco and Maria.

**Dom** *(after a long pause, speaking in a loud and steady voice)*: Angela, I will not hurt or kill myself, for any reason, at any time. You can be sure of that, Angela. I will not threaten anymore. I will not hurt my children.

It is important not to hurt myself just because I am angry at you or someone else.

*It was Dom, on his own, who initiated turning to Angela. His serious demeanor matches his serious words. I believe him now.*

**Angela:** I believe you. I'm pleased and relieved to hear you say that. I know the children need to know that.

**Ruth:** Angela, you're right, they do need to know. I like the way you look out for your children. I like you keeping things straight between you and Dom right now. This is a change for you.

Dom, I agree with what Angela said. I think it will be important for you and Angela to talk later with Marco and Maria about this.

I know that you are a determined man and that you've done a lot for yourself in your life. You've met many challenges that have been put in front of you. One of the biggest challenges for an adult is to be a responsible and responsive person.

I believed you when you told Angela you wouldn't hurt or kill yourself. I believed you for the first time.

As a way of pushing a little further now, for yourself, will you think back to one of the first times in your life when you wanted to, or threatened to, kill yourself or someone else?

*Saying the words has prepared him to do the work.*

**Dom** *(with tears in his eyes)*: When I was very little and my father and mother were still together—that was one of those times.

**Ruth** *(bringing out two cushions)*: How old are you?

**Dom:** I am six.

*This is Maria's age now. On her questionnaire,
Maria mentioned suicide, writing "I would be good. I
should kill myself. I should throw myself over a cliff."*

**Ruth:** Be a six-year-old now and stay with your
feelings.
*(Dom becomes six easily. His head is bowed, but he looks
very different from the hang-dog expression he wears, as a
grown up.)*
**Dom** *(to his mother and father)*: The only way I think I
can get out of here is if I die. And I don't want to die.
**Ruth** *(talking to the little boy)*: Tell them what you
mean when you say the only way you think you can get
out of here is to die.
**Dom** *(sobbing)*: Nobody ever is around. You're boozed
up all the time, and you just pat me and nothing else. I
don't know what to do.
**Ruth** *(putting a hand on Dom's arm)*: Tell your parents
again that you don't want to die.
**Dom:** I don't want to die, and I don't want to be here
with you. *(He pauses.)* I won't die just to get away from
you.
*(Dom suddenly switches, in posture and voice, to an
older age. He goes on angrily.)*
Mother, I hate you, because you always wanted me to
pat you and to treat your new husbands and your new
boyfriends like they were my father.
**Ruth:** Tell your mother you won't hurt or kill yourself,
no matter how angry you are!
**Dom:** Ya, Mom, I won't hurt or kill myself just to get
you. And Dad, what a loser you've always been. You've had
your head in a bottle your whole life, and I'm not like you.
**Ruth:** Tell your father, "I'm not a loser like you. I'm
not going to hurt or kill myself with alcohol or any other
thing."
**Dom:** I'm not going to keep my head in a bottle like
you did and like every other man in the family. I'm not
going to hurt or kill myself with alcohol or any other
thing. Ruth, may I bring in someone else?
**Ruth:** Go ahead with what fits for you.
**Dom** *(picking up another pillow)*: This is Angela's
father. I am pissed off at you, because you left, and Angela
has spent her whole life wanting you. I'm not going to cop
out on my job of being a father like you did. Even though

Angela and I may be separated, I'll go on being responsible for my children and in contact with them. I won't be like you, or like you, Dad.

*(Dom settles back and looks at me.)*

**Ruth:** It is important that you keep yourself alive.

*(Dom goes on, for awhile, sharing angry times from his past. He has real emotional contact with himself; he's not just putting on a show.*

*(One particularly dramatic memory involved his mother living for three years with a man who wouldn't work. She gradually sold most of her possessions, getting rid of all the gifts Dom's real father had given her. When the money ran out, the man left.*

*(When Dom finishes, he looks settled. The tension in his face is gone.)*

**Ruth:** Are you finished?

**Dom:** Yes.

**Ruth:** Angela, what are you thinking and feeling?

**Angela:** I feel sad. I don't know anymore right now.

**Dom:** Can I say one more thing?

*(He looks around at the other members of the group.)*

Thank you for supporting me in something difficult.

> *In this work, Dom decided to stop tyrannizing his family with his manipulative feelings of worthlessness. He redecided not to hurt or kill himself. These individual changes are necessary in order for him to follow through with being a responsible parent.*

# YOUNG PEOPLE'S GROUP—WITH LES

> *Kitty, the play therapist, and I have a short but productive time with Marco and Maria. Kitty reported to me earlier this morning that Marco was still behaving in a provocative way and that Maria expressed more of her feelings of being unwanted and worthless.*
>
> *Our work so far has revealed many of the bases for Maria believing about herself that she is worthless. She and her father share a very close and relationship. She identifies with him. Dom felt it would please his parents if he died and that the only way out was to kill himself. Dom was asked to be his mother's confidant and "man" when he was very young. Maria holds the same position in her family.*

*Dom and Maria are also alike in their mannerisms: they alternate between hostility and covering up with niceness. Also, Angela reacts to Maria as if Maria were Angela's mother, and then pushes her away or rejects her. In response to being pushed out, Maria tries to leave her mother out.*

*Angela remembered a similar dynamic from her childhood. In her family, she never felt safe. It's not surprising that Maria doesn't feel secure either or that Angela doesn't know how to help her feel safe.*

*It is difficult to work with Maria, because although she's only six, she has two highly developed defense mechanisms. We've seen her put her hands over her ears and say several times, "I'll plug my ears up, and I won't listen." She blocks out facts and anyone else's opinion. Maria's second defense is to become very dramatic. Her father reinforces her "free expression"; her mother retreats in exasperated anger.*

*We interrupted the way the family reinforces her. Then, by being sympathetic, I helped her to express her anxiety. One of the things that had previously came out was Maria's five-year-old belief in magic. "Now that I've told you about it," she told Kitty once, "My Mommy and Daddy won't fight any more."*

*Melissa and Maria are watching the trainee Barbara, who is an amateur magician. She brought some of the props for her tricks. Melissa and Maria are learning to palm coins.*

**Les:** Maria, what are you thinking and feeling, as you play?

**Maria:** I'm just having fun.

**Les:** I'm remembering the picture you drew, in which it seemed that the people were having fun, but you couldn't join in.

*(A cloud comes over Maria's face. I pick up the teddy bear, the same one Ruth used with Maria in the women's group.)*

**Les:** This is the Daddy Bear. Will you tell the Daddy Bear what you're feeling?

*(Maria looks scared. She calms a little when Kitty puts an arm around her.)*

**Maria:** Daddy Bear, I don't like it when you fight.

**Les** *(moving a second bear into the picture)*: This is the Mommy Bear. Will you tell her what you are feeling?

**Maria:** I don't like it when you fight. I think you're going to hurt me. I don't want you to hurt me.

*(She is shivering with fear. Kitty rubs her arms.)*

**Les:** Would you tell the mother bear that she's the Mommy and you're the little girl and she's not supposed to hurt you because you are important and okay.

**Maria** *(brightening up)*: That's right. You're not supposed to hurt me, Mommy Bear. I count, too.

**Les:** Would you like to tell that to your real Mommy?

**Maria:** Yes, I would.

**Les:** Would you like some help with that?

**Maria:** Yes.

*(She nods and relaxes . . . Marco puts down the truck he was playing with. He is unusually quiet as Maria talks.)*

**Les:** I bet you get scared in the house, too, sometimes, Marco. *(Marco gives a tiny nod, no words.)*

**Les:** I also bet, when you're scared, it's hard for you to act like a four-year-old.

*(Marco is listening intently, taking in what I say.)* One of the things I think it is important for you to learn to say to your Mom and Dad is that you're scared. You can say it to them, rather than trying to show them by acting like a baby. Would you like to practice that?

**Marco:** Yes.

*(I put the two bears in front of him.)*

**Les:** Tell the mother and father bear that you're four years old and not a baby and that sometimes you get scared.

**Marco:** I'm four years old. I'm not a baby. Sometimes I get scared.

**Les:** Just for practice, would you say it again.

**Marco** *(louder)*: I'm four years old. I'm not a baby. Sometimes I get scared.

*(He's speaking louder, his head and back straight.)*

**Les:** Just to make sure you have it, say it again.

**Marco:** I'm four years old, and I'm not a baby. I get scared sometimes, though.

**Les:** You really look four years old now. *(Marco beams.)*

# THURSDAY AFTERNOON

# FAMILY GROUP—LES SPEAKING

*All the families are together with Les and me in the large meeting room. Paula told David about his father, ending the time of secrets and unreality in her family. Dom, Angela, Maria, and Marco were spellbound. Dom wept when*

*Paula described times when her alcoholic husband might have hurt her infant son David.*

*Bette Sarnon works next. Ruth is impatient with her. Angela reacts in a revealing way.*

**Angela:** I think you've all been very unfair to Bette. I think you've given Bette a raw deal.

*(To Ruth:)* If it had been me, I would have gotten up and hit you with one of those bats.

*(Turning:)* Bette, it made me mad that you didn't stick up for yourself.

> *Angela identifies with the underdog. The whole group gets involved.*

**Bill:** Angela, I know Bette has a lot of good qualities. It's also important that my wife get in touch with things she needs to look at. I didn't see hostility in the way Ruth talked to Bette. What I saw was Ruth trying to help Bette move.

**Angela** *(softly)*: Bill, when I look at it through your eyes I see the helpful side of the exchange between Ruth and Bette.

I'm always sticking up for the people who won't stick up for themselves. I've always done that.

**Ruth:** Who did you stick up for when you were a child?

> *Here's another example of the benefits of the multiple family setup. It was Bill who helped Angela to start working.*

*(Angela becomes tearful.)*

**Ruth:** I know how uncomfortable it must have been for you in the past as you experienced yourself and watched people get hurt.

**Angela:** I've always been on the side of the loser.

**Ruth:** Who was the loser in your family?

**Angela** *(with great sadness)*: My father.

**Ruth:** How was your father the loser?

**Angela:** In every way. When he left I was 13. My fights with my mother began just after my father left.

*(Angela looks restless, as though she wants to move away. I encourage her to stay here and to keep her mind on the issue of her support of the underdog.)*

**Ruth:** Would you describe your father?

**Angela** *(speaking up)*: He was handsome and always right. He was sensitive, but he never showed it. I saw him cry twice, and that was devastating to me.

**Ruth:** What were the scenes when your father cried?

**Angela:** When I was nine, my father fell out of a boat tied up at a dock. I was supposed to be holding a rope taut to keep the boat still, but I let it move. He broke his arm falling between the boat and the dock. It really hurt. He made me go away so I wouldn't see him cry. It was my fault that my father got hurt.

**Ruth:** Is that the most important part for you?

**Angela:** Yes, the most important part is that it was my fault—that it was me who made my father cry. I didn't take good enough care of him. When he cried, he sent me away.

*(Angela begins to become rigid, her voice gets colder. She acts a little angry at me.)*

*On a hunch, Ruth switches to the next question.*

**Ruth:** Was your father ever angry at your mother?

**Angela:** Yes, sometimes.

**Ruth:** How was that expressed?

**Angela:** Sometimes my father physically abused my mother. On a few occasions, I defended my mother, but then my mother got mad at me for trying to defend her. My father would also get mad at me for stepping in.

*(She begins to laugh. It turns into a belly laugh.)*

Everybody ended up mad at me, and all I was trying to do was help.

**Ruth:** Everybody ended up mad at you, and all you were trying to do was help.

**Angela:** Yes. And this is what just happened with me right now when I defended Bette. I see it. That's like with the rope too, all I was trying to do was help, and I ended up mad at myself, thinking it was my fault.

**Ruth:** Angela will you put your nine-year-old self out in front of you and tell you it wasn't your fault?

**Angela** *(hesitantly)*: Yes. Angie, it wasn't your fault. It wasn't your fault.

*(Angela quickly pulls back.)*

**Les:** I like that you were willing to put the pieces together for yourself.

**Ruth:** Les, I'm delighted with Angela making that connection, and I also wonder if Angela has to create turmoil around her sometimes.

**Les:** I agree. Maria also attempts to be in the same kind of control. She's constantly moving into the middle with her parents, only trying to help, as Angela once did.

*Ruth and I talk out loud to each other. Angela can listen without having to respond. We avoid, as much as possible, the risk of her getting defensive.*

**Dom:** Angela, why don't you and I go at it with those red things?

**Angela:** But I don't want to hit you.

**Dom:** Has it occurred to you that I might still be angry at you? I'd like to be able to let out my anger that way.

*(People in the room laugh and cheer, supporting Dom's directness. Angela and Dom move into the center of the room with the bats. Angela continues to say she doesn't want to hit Dom. They cautiously move around each other, taking a couple of halfhearted swings that miss.)*

**Ruth:** Angela, I understand that doing this isn't your idea or even something you like to do.

It's important though that, as you finish this week, you experiment and find a middle ground for yourself—some way of expressing your feelings that's not extreme.

**Angela** *(looking frightened and little-girlish)*: I understand.

*Angela ends up in the unmoving position that she saw Bette end up in. She is frightened of other people's anger, her own anger, and her ability to control herself.*

*During the break, Ruth and I discuss our next move. We decide to give the kids the rest of the afternoon off and to separate into men's and women's groups. This will be the last chance for members of a couple to work separately.*

## WOMEN'S GROUP—WITH RUTH

**Ruth:** Angela, what are you thinking and feeling?

**Angela:** One of the things in my mind is what we talked about Wednesday afternoon. I became aware of how I sit back and let myself get very, very angry until I have to explode. I tend to explode at Maria more than anybody.

**Ruth:** I'm glad you're aware of that. Can we talk further about it?

**Angela:** Yes.

**Ruth:** I've been concerned about the possibility of your being hurtful to Maria. Maybe even abusing her in a way similar to what your mother did to you.

*I'm proceeding very cautiously, because the material is so important and because I know how quickly Angela can pull away.*

**Angela:** I've tried very hard to make myself go exactly the other way. I don't see myself as getting violent with the kids, although I know I get angry and spank them.

**Ruth:** I'm concerned that maybe you let your anger build up. That seemed so in your exchange with Dom this afternoon and in the way you talked about Bette.

When you say you're not angry, sometimes people looking at you and listening to you don't believe you.

**Angela** *(angrily)*: I know that. I also know the likelihood of abused kids becoming abusive parents. I will not be an abusive parent. I will not do that to my kids, no matter what.

**Ruth:** That's good. I admire you for saying that. Stick with me a little longer now, though. *(I pull out a chair.)* Put your father there, and tell him two things. First, that you're not going to fight his battles for him and, second, that you aren't your mother.

**Angela** *(looks at me and then looks at the empty chair. She pauses for a full minute)*: Dad, I love and honor you, but I will not fight your fights.

I also want to tell you something that you know very well: that I am not my mother.

**Ruth:** Tell him what you feel as you say those things.

**Angela:** I feel sorry. I think you lost a lot when you left us kids. I feel the suffering now. I miss you, and I'm not going to get out of your life.

I can understand why you didn't want to live with her. She was a witch. I would have left, too, if I could have.

**Ruth:** Angela, do you know why he didn't take you with him?

**Angela:** Yes. Because he didn't want me. *(Caustically:)* He said it was better that I stayed with her.

**Ruth:** You sound bitter.

**Angela:** I don't think I am.

**Ruth:** What are you feeling about being left?

**Angela:** Just nothing I know. I never felt anger about my father not being there. She was such a witch.

**Ruth:** How come you so easily accepted the idea the he didn't want you?

**Angela:** Because I went along with anything he said.

**Ruth:** Tell your father why you went along with whatever he said. As you do that, listen to the tone in your voice!

**Angela** (angrily): I went along with you simply because you were my father.

**Ruth:** Your father—love him, honor him, obey him, respect him, no matter what?

**Angela:** With him, yes.

**Ruth:** Tell your Dad why, no matter what he does or says, you'll always go along with him.

**Angela:** I don't know, Dad. I just always took whatever you said and considered it was always right. I respect you and love you. I always will.

> Angela speaks with an air of finality, as if she wants to finish things up. I want to see if I can help her move with her feelings about her father by speculating a little and putting my guesses into words. I guess about Angela's meaning and put my guesses into words. I ask Angela to repeat these words and let me know if they match her internal experience.

**Ruth:** Stay with him a little longer and let me give you some words. My fantasy is that if you were to deal with your father, or with Dom for that matter, in any different way, it would seem to you that you were like your mother. What I know already is that the most important thing for you has been to prove that you're not like her. And you don't want to treat people the way she did.

**Angela** (to her father, softly but determinedly): Dad, you always would agree with me that I wasn't like her. And yet you would say that she would take care of me. I didn't understand that. But the most important thing to me was the assurance that I was not like her. When you said it, then I knew it.

*(To me:)* I've always said that my goal, my only goal in life, is to be the opposite of her.

*If Angela were to doubt her father, she would have to doubt her sense of herself. His confirmation of her was life saving.*

**Ruth** *(very softly, aware of how vulnerable Angela has made herself)*: I do understand. I understand that in letting out your anger at your father or Dom, you would experience yourself as just like your mother and then not really know who you are.

**Angela:** Yes.

*(We're sitting very close. The people in the room are involved. The atmosphere is intense.)*

**Ruth:** I respect your decision and determination to be different. I know, also, that when people make decisions to be the opposite of one or both of their parents, sometimes that decision gets in the way of their developing for themselves.

It gets in the way for you, Angela, because so much energy has to be put into making sure that each thing you do is different from what your mother would have done. Sometimes there's not much room to stop and think and be for yourself.

Angela, put your mother out there for a moment. Look at her and say several times, "I am not you. I am me."

**Angela:** I am not you, Mother. I am me. I am not you, Mother. I am me. I am not you, Mother. I am me. *(Looking at me)* I am not you, Mother. I am me. I'm finished. I understand.

*(We smile at each other. After a long pause, I move on to work with Berenice.)*

*Her nonverbal expression tells me that this has been important for her. In confronting her early decision to be absolutely not like her mother, Angela made the redecision that she is herself. In doing this she also underlined that she isn't bad and she isn't crazy.*

*(Just before the afternoon is over, Angela volunteers some information.)*

**Angela:** I'd like to talk about something I've been thinking about. Earlier, I was rubbing one of the kids in the group, and I realized I was being too rough. It was Melissa. Then she told me I was rubbing her neck too roughly.

Sometimes I am too rough, and I don't realize it. *(To me, with a smile:)* Thank you.

I've also been thinking about whether, by separating from Dom, I might be setting up for my children exactly the family situation I grew up in. I don't want to do this. I have to think about it.

**Paula:** You know, I've had some experience with physical violence. It's difficult, I know, when you don't know your own strength and how hard you can be. I've had to watch it so I don't get too rough with my kids.

## MEN'S GROUP—WITH LES

*When Dom began, he started with generalities about a woman's place.*

**Les:** Dom, you sound angry.

**Dom:** I am angry. What I'm angry about is that I don't get any recognition. I certainly don't get any from Angela. *(He begins to shift uncomfortably in his seat.)*

**Les:** After this morning, I guess that you must also be sad and scared, and it seems as if all you're focusing on is blaming Angela.

**Dom:** Maybe. I'm certainly beginning to believe that she's serious now about leaving. I keep saying to myself, "Okay, Dom, get your ass in gear."

**Les:** What Angela talked about his morning was the real possibility of a divorce. In fact, a likelihood. It seems as if Angela's holding the reins now. How are you going to take charge of yourself?

*I am determined to keep focused on how Dom deals with unpleasant feelings, especially anger and sadness. In the past, he has always turned to drinking.*

**Les:** Dom, will you share what you know about how your father dealt with the divorce from your mother?

**Dom** *(with a barking laugh)*: He didn't deal with it. He drank more. He showered my mother with presents, but he never talked to her.

**Les** *(putting a pillow in front of Dom)*: Tell your father what this was like for you.

**Dom** *(his voice cracking with sadness)*: I was really discouraged with you. You know one of the things that's helping me get my act together now is the fact that you never did. Nobody in our family ever did. We have all been too attached to the bottle. Even now, I think you always go back to the old times. You keep saying, "Any minute now, it will all come together." Dad, you're wrong. You've been on your death bed for many years. I'm sure not going to get myself there. *(He gives a big sigh.)* I don't think my father would ever talk about these things.

> *This work is significant for Dom. It is virtually spontaneous. With only a little bit of nudging from me, he has picked up the thread of thought himself.*

**Les:** Dom, it looks as if Angela is getting ready to act. How are you going to handle this differently from the way your father did? He tried denying it, giving your mother gifts, and keeping his head in a bottle. How are you going to take care of yourself?

**Dom** *(in a grown-up, reflective tone)*: I'm going to continue to work, although I know it's going to be the pits.

**Les:** What about alcohol?

**Dom:** I don't think about that. I'm not worried about going to the bottle.

> *The alcoholic denial is still there. The alcoholic mechanism of not thinking is very clear.*

**Les:** Dom, that sounds just like your father, and I know you've said this to yourself before. Every time you've had serious stress before, particularly when Angela threatened to leave, you've gone back to the bottle.

*(Dom shakes his head no.)*

It seems to me that you forget that even though you stop drinking, you're still an alcoholic.

**Dom:** That's true.

**Les:** What are you going to do for support?

**Don** *(a trainee)*: I'm worried about you, Dom, particularly if you don't get involved in Alcoholics Anonymous.

**Dom:** I don't go for that kind of stuff. It's too much of a religion.

**Les:** You know, Dom, there's that twelve-year-old part of you. He's always around when you're drinking. One of the things I know about twelve-year-olds is that they think they can conquer the world without any help.

Do you think you might be conning yourself right now, when you say that you can stop drinking without any help?

**Dom:** You may be right. I'll have to think about that.

*I don't know whether Dom is putting me off or whether he has really decided to think. I don't want to go any further now: I don't want to distract him from thinking about his father's reaction to being left by his wife.*

**Les:** I'm glad to hear you'll think about that. I like the work that you did for yourself. I feel encouraged for you if you are willing to think and not drink.

# FRIDAY MORNING

# INDIVIDUAL FAMILIES—WITH RUTH

*On Friday I tie up the loose ends. I emphasize attaining a new equilibrium within the family. I build in support to maintain the changes made in the week. The Dellapietras and the Barkers are with me.*

*I wonder how much of the Dellapietras' work is real. I still have unfinished business, particularly with Maria.*

*I begin the session with rounds: I go around the room and ask each person to share what he or she is thinking and feeling. I am struck by the regression in the Dellapietra family: Marco is curled up in a chair talking baby talk and humming; Angela is next to Marco, looking sternly ahead; Dom is making irrelevant wisecracks; and Maria is standing up, pulling on his hand. I come to Marco first.*

**Marco:** I think I'm such a good boy now, because now I let Maria sleep. And my Mommy's so pretty, and my Dad is so handsome.

**Angela:** I don't have much to share.

**Dom:** Angela and I might share our good feelings about wanting to help each other throughout our lives to come.

*My heart sinks. It's apparent from Marco's babyish behavior and Dom's slickness that there's a lot of anxiety being covered up. How do I proceed this morning, so that this family leaves in a solid and different place for itself? What we know is that the separation issue has not been clarified.*

*(Immediately after rounds, Dom volunteers to work. He pulls Angela into the center. Marco continues his infantile singing. Maria is sitting on the edge of the sofa, watching nervously, but appropriately.)*

**Ruth:** Dom, something's not right around here this morning. You sound like you have been making a testimonial speech at a retirement party.

*(As I finish talking, Angela closes herself up by pulling Maria over to her and wrapping her up in a hug.)*

**Ruth:** Dom, will you cut the bullshit and say what's really going on?

**Dom** *(with saccharine sweetness)*: Come on, Ruth, there's nothing hidden. We're going to help each other. We've learned so much.

**Ruth:** Dom, you're putting me on. The worst thing that could happen for you and your family is for you to seal over your feelings and make a lovely, sweet, nice package out of yourself.

**Dom:** Perhaps I am sealing over things. Going home and being separate will be hard for us all.

**Ruth:** That's what I'm concerned about.

*(Angela looks frightened and questioning.)*

**Ruth:** Angela, what's going on with you?

**Angela:** I don't know.

**Ruth:** I don't know either. But yesterday you were talking to Dom about separating, and today it seems as if you have let that, along with the issue of managing the kids, just go under the rug.

Marco has been acting two years old this morning, and neither of you has noticed him or talked to him. In some ways, you've even been supporting his babyish behavior.

I noticed, too, that, Dom, you came down hard on Maria. This was exactly the family pattern you wanted to change.

**Dom:** Maybe you're right, Ruth.

*(He then settles back, as if that finished things. Angela lowers her head. She looks very depressed.)*

**Ruth:** Angela, what's going on?

**Angela:** I'm very frightened about things being the same when we leave. I'm especially frightened because now I have to consider the possibility of my being an abusive parent. I spent all last night in my room alone, crying.

*This is the key to the family regression. Angela gets frightened and cries, and everyone closes up in the old ways.*

*(Maria moves close to Angela. Dom moves back; right now he's being the observer.)*

**Ruth:** Angela, as you recall the feeling you had last night, will you remember a time from the past when you were feeling the same way?

**Angela:** Yes, I was very down on my mother. I felt the same way as I do now when I'm down on me.

**Ruth:** Are you willing to continue some work with her right now?

**Angela** *(with a grimace)*: Yes. But it's hard for me. I've spent most of my adult life trying to block out those memories from the past, and I've brought up so much already this week.

*(I put a chair in front of Angela and make sure she is sitting up in her own chair with her two feet flat on the ground. She had her legs folded under her. Angela moves her head back and to the side and puts a hand up, as if she's warding off a blow. This reminds me of Maria putting her hands over her ears. Angela looks and sounds young.)*

**Ruth:** I'll help you. Start with what has just happened. Start with telling your mother how you immediately pull away from her.

**Angela** *(panicky)*: I don't know how to start. I don't want to be here with her.

**Ruth:** Begin with these words. "When I see you, I immediately pull away from you, because I'm afraid of you."

**Angela:** When I see you I, immediately pull away from you, because I'm afraid of you. And, I'm afraid of the feelings I have when I'm around you.

**Ruth:** Tell your mother about those feelings you have when you're around her.

**Angela:** I'm not afraid that you'll hit me.

**Ruth:** Tell her what you are afraid of.

**Angela** *(very slowly)*: I'm embarrassed that I hit you. I don't believe I should have hit my mother. I'd rather just stay away.

**Ruth** *(noticing Angela's panic)*: Be the age you are now, and tell your mother that the only way you can handle yourself is to stay away from her.

**Angela** *(relaxing and strongly shaking her head, yes)*: The only way I can handle myself now is to stay away from you, very far away. *(Her hands are pushing her mother away.)*

**Ruth:** Put some words to the motion you're making with your hands.

*(Angela looks with surprise at her hands.)*

**Angela** *(to her mother)*: Stay away from me. That's why I moved out of town. I don't want your influence. I don't want my kids to be influenced by you. It's over. All of that old stuff is over. *(Her hands continue to hold her mother off.)* It's over now. I know that. I won't take it anymore.

**Ruth:** Keep going with your hands, and tell her what you won't take and what you're feeling as you say that.

*(Angela looks to me, tearful and frightened).*

Stay with it. You're okay.

**Angela:** Mom, your bitterness and your unhappiness is your problem.

**Ruth:** Tell your mother that you're not the cause of her problems.

**Angela:** I'm definitely not the cause of your problems. It's not my fault that Dad left. It was your problem and his, not mine. I resent being made into the one who made him go—the one who caused all the trouble. I'm not the one who caused all the trouble. I was just a kid trying to grow up.

**Ruth:** Angela, tell your mother, "I'm not the bad one."

**Angela:** I'm not the bad one.

**Ruth:** Say it again.

**Angela:** I'm not the bad one. It's not my fault. It was never my fault. I wasn't bad.

**Ruth:** Continue to tell your mother about how things are now.

**Angela:** I'm not the bad one in my life now.

*(She takes a full, breath from deep in her middle. Her face tightens.)*

I'm not like you. I'm not like you. I'm not the bad one. And I'm not—

*(She stops abruptly and there is a thick silence in the room.)*

And I'm not crazy. I'm not crazy.

*(She looks at me with a shocked expression and then speaks firmly.)*

I'm not crazy, Mother.

**Ruth:** Tell her again.

**Angela** *(with a large smile and much relief)*: I wasn't crazy then, and I'm not crazy now. I'm not a bad person, and I'm not crazy.

> *This is the redecision work that we've been moving toward all week. Angela is reorganizing her image of herself.*

**Angela** *(beaming)*: I understand it now.

**Ruth** *(smiling)*: Will you check out with yourself and see if there's anything more you want to say to your mother now?

**Angela:** I'm going to do it my way. I'm not the opposite of you. I'm me. I'm going to do it my way, and that's all right. I'm not going to hurt my children the way you did me. And I'm not going to make my daughter into a bad one.

*(I touch Angela on the shoulder, and we look at each other. There is silence in the room. Marco and Maria, both of whom have been watching their mother intently, are quiet and a little tearful.)*

> *It is good that Marco and Maria are here. They are having an opportunity to get a new sense of their mother as she integrates herself differently.*

**Ruth:** If you're ready, I'd like to nudge you a little further.

*(Angela nods. I pull up another chair.)*

Put your father here.

**Angela** *(laughing)*: What a week this has been. I haven't talked to these people in so many years. It has been an even longer time since my mother and father sat next to each other.

*(The room explodes with laughter.)*

*I am including Angela's father now because her "bad" image of herself is related to him as well as to her mother. To make Angela's work complete, we need to bring in her father and the other members of her family who where present when she made her first decisions about herself.*

**Ruth:** Tell your father what's going on with you.

**Angela** *(perkily)*: I'm Angela, Dad. I'm not Mom. And I'm not the opposite of Mom. I'm Angela. I love you, because *(she begins to cry)* . . . because I love you.

**Ruth:** Stay with him. Tell him what your tears are about.

**Angela** *(to me)*: He was so hard to connect with.

**Ruth:** Tell that to him.

**Angela:** You were so hard to connect with. Besides that, I genuinely do love you. Also, I love you because nobody else did. *(She becomes quiet and looks at me.)*

**Ruth:** What are you thinking and feeling?

**Angela:** I never stood up to my father before. I never said anything straight to him before. It feels good.

**Ruth:** Is there anything else to tell him about you?

**Angela:** No, not now.

**Ruth:** Now that you are standing up and being straight, there are two other people we need to bring in. Bring in your little brother and your older sister, and see if there's anything that you need or want to say to them.

*(Angela looks to one side, at her sister, and to the other, at her brother. Looking at her brother, she begins to cry again.)*

**Angela** *(to her brother)*: I didn't want you to have to watch all those terrible fights between Mom and me.

**Ruth:** Will you tell him that you're not bad and you're not crazy?

**Angela:** I know now that I'm not bad and I'm not crazy. I'm embarrassed if you hurt, and I'm sorry for you, but I'm not bad and I'm not crazy. *(She looks at her sister and hesitates.)*

**Ruth:** Go ahead.

**Angela:** I love Dad even though you didn't. *(Angela sighs and pulls back, indicating she is finished.)*

**Ruth:** You've done a lot this morning. I think you're a fine woman. I like you and I respect you. I respect your bravery and your willingness to take a look at yourself and to change the things you need to make better for yourself and your children.

**Dom** *(who has been appropriately quiet and close to the children while Angela has been talking)*: May I go on?

**Ruth:** Sure.

**Dom:** I'd like to state to you, Marco, and you, Maria, that I do not have a desire to hurt or kill anyone including me, and I won't ever do that.

**Ruth:** Dom and Angela, I think Maria has something to tell you two also.

**Maria:** Ya.

**Ruth:** Do you want help?

**Maria:** No. Mom and Dad, I'm important here, and I'm just a little girl.

**Angela** *(with tears)*: Yes, and we want you always to care about yourself. I think you are the most wonderful daughter a mother could ever have.

**Dom:** Me too, Maria.

*(Maria is quiet and radiant.)*

**Ruth:** Dom, you look like you want to go on.

**Dom** *(in a gruff voice)*: Yes, I also feel that when we separate, the kids should be with you, Angela. I want you to know, Angela, that you will not have any problems from me about that.

*(Maria, next to Dom, moves nervously. Marco, on Dom's lap, gets agitated. Angela gently puts a hand on Marco, who becomes quiet.)*

> *Dom's statements have been spontaneous. Both of us are glad to hear him speak clearly and directly.*

**Ruth:** Right now, I believe what you're saying, Dom, because you're talking like a grown-up. Like someone who is aware of other people outside of himself.

I'm still concerned that if you get into the little-boy position of not thinking and drinking you will have trouble.

> *Both Dom and Angela are appropriately and quietly attending to Marco and Maria. The agitation with the children is decreasing, even during my confrontation of Dom. I remember Maria's previous agitated defending of*

*Dom. Today she has kept her distance from him and acted more grown-up.*

**Dom:** Angela and I have discussed the idea of having continuing therapy work. We've even thought of staying here another week if we can.

**Ruth:** It's not possible to stay next week. It is possible to come back for a week in August.

I think it's time for a break now. I have an assignment for you. Spend the break time deciding, first, what you're going to say to the children about how your family is going to operate when you get home, and, second, what your plans will be for coming back or not.

*(During the break, Dom and Angela talk with each other outside. After the break, they set up the seating so that Marco and Maria are facing them.)*

**Ruth:** I like the way the two of you have taken command and arranged your family.

**Angela:** Marco and Maria, put your cookies aside so that you can listen better.

*(Dom helps the children lay the cookie box down.)*

**Dom:** Marco and Maria, when we get back home there will be something different in the family. There will be something different for two reasons. The first thing is that we, your mother and I, have decided that we are going to come back here in four weeks to continue the work we have started.

*(Marco and Maria clap their hands and say, "Yea.")*

What we've also decided is that when we get home, your mother and I are not going to live together for a while.

**Angela:** We don't know how long that while will be.

**Maria:** Who's going to babysit for us?

**Angela:** We may not need anyone to babysit, because I will be home. That will not be different for you.

**Ruth:** Be more specific with them.

**Dom:** The change will be that I am going to live in another place.

*(Marco's thumb goes into his mouth. He begins to curl up in a ball like a caterpillar that has been poked. Maria's head goes down.)*

**Maria:** I am sad.

**Dom:** I hear you, Maria. The reason we're doing this is so we can be a better Mom and Dad.

**Ruth:** It's important, Dom and Angela, not to set it up so that the children feel responsible for the separation. Marco and Maria need to know that the main reason their parents will be living in different places is that you two need to find a way to be a different kind of husband and wife.

*(Angela puts her hand on Dom's arm. Maria sticks her hand into her father's, interfering with the contact between her parents. Both Dom and Angela gently stop her.)*

**Angela:** Marco and Maria, your Dad and I have problems together, and we've decided to stay away from each other for a period of time. We will talk, so there's a possibility that we'll be able to work things out better. No matter what the situation is, your Daddy and I are still the bosses of the two of you.

**Dom:** Marco, you're not the father or the husband in this family. You're the little boy. Maria, you're not the mother or the wife in the family. You are a little girl, and you are my daughter.

*(Angela gives Dom a fond and approving look. Maria smiles broadly, with giddy laughter. Then both children protest in unison.)*

**Marco and Maria:** No. No. We're the bosses.

**Maria:** We can be the bosses if we want to.

**Angela:** No, you cannot! Marco, you are my little boy. You are four years old and I love you very much for being Marco and for being four. When you were a little baby, I loved you as my little baby boy. Right now, you are four, and I love you as my four-year-old boy, not as a baby anymore and not as a grown-up man.

*(As Angela talks to Marco, Dom does a good job of keeping Maria from coming between mother and son.)*

**Angela:** Maria, you are my six-year-old daughter, and I love you as my six-year-old daughter. You are not my mother, and you are not me. I love you for being Maria. It's important that you are alive and here with us, in our family.

**Ruth** *(smiling)*: You have made their places clear. You have taken care of them well.

**Dom:** Maria, I am your father and you are my daughter.

**Maria** *(impatiently)*: I know that, Dad.

**Dom:** And it's important that you are alive and here.

**Ruth:** Dom, I remember that you have done some important work about being here yourself. Will you share that again with Marco and Maria.

**Dom:** I want the two of you to know, no matter where I am living, that I will not hurt or kill myself or anyone else. My deciding to live somewhere else is not your mother's fault; it is something that the two of us have decided together.

**Ruth:** Maria, have you heard what your father just said?

**Maria** *(impatiently)*: Ya! Dad, can we do the "just friend" handshake?

*(Dom, with a big smile, does a slapping handshake with her. This is their special device. Maria dances over to Angela and does the handshake with her, then with Marco. Maria and Marco slap hands, and finally, Angela and Dom do a slow version. Maria and Marco try to do the handshake faster, get messed up, and fall down laughing.)*

**Ruth:** I think this is a good place to end.

*(Dom and Angela agree. The family moves back from the center of the circle, with applause and laughter from the group.)*

_____ *6* _____

# Ending with the Families

*On Friday afternoon, all the families are in the main
room together. The room is filled with a sense of excitement
and of traveling on. This is the last opportunity to finish
the therapy work that families and individuals came to do.
(Tonight is reserved for a party; Saturday, for saying
good-bye.)*

*Gerry and Margaret Ann are on the floor. Gerry is lying
down, and Little Gerry is sitting on his father's hip. It was
Gerry who began talking on the first day, but then he began
by talking about someone else. Today he sticks to himself.*

**Gerry:** At lunch, Margaret Ann and I decided that we
are ready to move out of the therapeutic community. I
don't want to be my parents' therapist. Just hearing my
parents talk about their problems helps me to carry their
load around with me.

I've also decided to move out of my grandmother's
business. I think once I get out of that negative work
environment I won't need the constant support of the
community anymore. I'm big enough to solve my own
problems.

**Les:** I like hearing what you have said, and I
particularly like the way you and Margaret Ann shared
the decision.

**Margaret Ann:** I feel good about this. It's the way I was leaning for a long time, anyway. Also, we went on to discuss other options for therapy.

*(We're reassured that the decision to leave the community has been thought through. The group makes positive comments praising Gerry in particular for thinking for himself. Little Gerry is no longer moving between Berenice and Margaret Ann. He looks anchored with his own mother and father.)*

**Les:** Edgar, what is there left for you here this afternoon?

*(Edgar is across the room from Berenice. He turns to her but keeps his seat.)*

**Edgar:** I no longer want to be married to you. This week I've worked on my anger and loneliness. Now, I want you to know that I no longer choose to be married to you.

*(Berenice has been sitting on the floor. Now she picks herself up and sits in a chair, both feet sturdily on the floor.)*

**Berenice:** I think I've known this. I feel really sad about it. It would be much easier for me to go back home with you. I wanted it that way, and I know it won't be that way. I accept that reality.

> *This is a clear, appropriate response from a woman who, four days ago, reacted with hysteria to any confrontation from a member of her family. "I'd be better off dead," she said when she felt blamed by her family on our first day of therapy. Perhaps Berenice's new calm aids Edgar in talking to her directly.*

**Berenice** *(to Edgar)*: I haven't liked the role of your wife and being labeled the nonresponsive bitch. I haven't liked the idea: "If only I would change, then Edgar would respond to me." I'm glad you made the decision. I appreciate your being clear with me.

*(To Gerry:)* I've decided to leave the community, too. It would be more difficult for me to do what I want to do, if I was there.

*(To everyone in her family:)* I'm going to start a program that's beginning at the university for a master's degree in counseling. I think the kind of people I'll meet there are the kind of people I could use to get some support. My old system of support is not right for me.

*(Back again to Edgar:)* We've done a lot this week. I

feel pain now because we've shared a lot in our lives. Some of that was really good. I know, and I want you to know, that I'll make it. I think when I reach the next plateau, there will be exciting things there for me. I wish you well.

*(Edgar stands up, walks across the room to Berenice, and holds out his hands to her. He has a relieved, grateful look. Berenice takes his hands and turns to Melissa. She pauses and takes a minute to compose herself.)*

Melissa, I don't think we're finished. When we get home, I'd like you to continue with Jim's counseling group. And when the family things come up, you and I can go in together. Will you do that?

*(Melissa, looking angry, mumbles softly.)*

Melissa, will you answer me?

**Melissa:** In a minute.

**Berenice:** What's going on?

**Melissa:** I'm thinking about all the other times we've worked on things. It's never going to be different.

**Les:** Melissa, that same belief that it's never going to be different is something you still need to look at. It was your father's belief and it doesn't have to be yours.

You have just heard for the first time that you and your father will not be living together. What do you think and feel about that?

**Melissa:** Nothing.

**Ruth:** Edgar, will you say something directly to Melissa?

**Edgar** *(looking discouraged, with a sigh)*: Melissa, I'm not going to live with you anymore. That doesn't mean I don't love you. You're very important to me. I won't stop loving you, and I hope you won't stop loving me—although my happiness does not depend on you, and yours does not depend on me.

**Ruth:** I think what she needs to know is that she'll have your support.

**Edgar:** Melissa, you will have my support and your mother will have my support. I'll make sure I give her what she needs, financially and otherwise, to take good care of you.

I made a promise to your mother yesterday to be with her when she confronts Gertrude. I will do the same for you if you need help with your mother.

**Berenice:** I'm glad, Edgar. Thanks.

*(Melissa has tears in her eyes.)*

**Edgar:** The separation is not your fault, Melissa. And there isn't anything you can do to make it different.

**Les:** One of the final things she needs to hear from both of you is, not only did she not cause your breakup, but there's nothing she can do to salvage your relationship. Maybe she needs to hear clearly again that there's no way that damaging herself will pull the family together.

**Edgar:** Don't hurt yourself. Don't kill yourself.

**Melissa:** I won't.

**Berenice:** Don't hurt yourself or kill yourself.

**Ruth:** Melissa, will you share with me what you're thinking?

**Melissa:** They might not like it, but I feel a whole lot relieved.

**Berenice** *(softly)*: I'm glad, Melissa.

**Gerry:** Melissa, it may appear from the decisions I've made that you're going to be abandoned by me and Margaret Ann. I want you to know that I don't choose to be your father, but I'll still be around to be your brother.

**Margaret Ann:** I want to be your sister-in-law. I look forward to developing a neat relationship.

**Melissa:** I know.

**Les:** Berenice, I think you've handled what you just heard splendidly. You've been compassionate to each of your family members.

Maybe Melissa is deciding that the best way for her to be protective of herself is to remain angry and distant.

**Berenice:** So what's my next move?

**Les:** You've done everything you can possibly do, and you've done it well. Melissa's anger is not your anger. I think you've done the right thing in urging her to go ahead in her therapy. Also, you've done right in deciding you'll be involved only if she asks you to be there. I have respect for you and respect for your ability to do what's right for your family. You'll figure out when you get there what the next steps are.

It will take a while for Melissa to learn to handle herself. It takes a while for any teenager to develop a sense of who she is. Melissa, in particular, seems to be having difficulty with that. She needs to hang on for awhile to her old ways of being.

**Berenice:** Okay.

**Ruth** *(to Melissa)*: Remember, Melissa, not every teenager has to have an adolescent crisis.

**Melissa** *(bright and spunky)*: That's funny, I didn't know that!

**Ruth:** And I want to share with you, Berenice, that I think you're a fine woman. I felt sad, and proud, as I watched you.

*(Little Gerry goes over a picks up Chocolate Moose—a huge brown stuffed animal he has been playing with. He walks across the room and gives it to Melissa.)*

**Ruth:** Melissa, I have one other thing. Come into the center and sit down across from me.

*(Melissa comes and sits down crosslegged. Ruth sits crosslegged right in front of her.)*

**Ruth:** I've looked forward to this. I don't often have an opportunity to perform a ceremony like this. I have been appointed, by the powers that be, whoever they are.

**Les** *(yelling, from the back of the room)*: It's me! It's me!
*(The entire room roars.)*

**Ruth** *(emphatically and embarrassed)*: That's not true!

Melissa, the powers that be, still unknown, have given me the honor of performing this ceremony. I, Ruth McClendon, crown you, Melissa Barker, as the leader of the new Barker line of women.

*(Ruth takes a silver-pointed paper crown entwined with yellow daisies. She holds it above Melissa's head. Melissa beams.)*

The new line, I hope, will take a completely different direction. The direction will be to freedom, joy, love, warmth, caring, prosperity, and success.

**Melissa** *(smiling and loudly)*: And nondominating grandmothers.

**Ruth** *(laughingly)*: Anything else you'd like to put into this?

**Melissa:** Just totally okay people.

*(Ruth rests the crown on Melissa's head. All the families burst into clapping, laughing, and congratulations. Melissa is beaming.)*

**Gerry:** I have an idea for a new T-shirt for Little Gerry—"The Powers That Be."

*With this, the last session ends for the Barkers. In the course of the week, they have separated themselves out from the mass and done the individual work each needed to do. Today they have had a moving reintegration, in which they decided how they would be together in new ways.*

*(We turn now from the Barker family to the Sarnons. Bill begins talking loudly and in a clearly projected voice.)*

**Bill:** Over lunch I was interested in continuing the discussion about my anger with Bette, and the jealousy I sometimes feel. I was tentative in talking to Bette, I still need to change some of that. I admit I sometimes have a hard time getting to the point, but here's what I think and said. Bette's system is composed of 90 percent men, and I want her not to be afraid of being a woman and being with women.

**Bette** *(emphatically)*: Bill, I'm not afraid or anything else about being a woman. It was Barbara who always told me what to wear, and what to do and what to think. I don't need you, Bill, to do that. I now can think and say what I am.

*(Everyone claps for Bette. Bill smiles knowingly.)*

**Bill:** And now I want you to also listen to what I think and who I am. I am your man. Nick is not your man and neither is anyone else.

**Bette:** You are right and I know what you are saying. I understand it now.

**Ruth:** Nick, what's going on with you?

**Nick:** It feels good hearing Bill talk to my mother like that.

**Ruth:** Tell Bill that.

*(Nick turns to Bill and there is a warm contact between them.)*

**Les:** You're smiling now. You were looking sad earlier in the morning. Do you have any piece of unfinished business?

**Nick:** I remember when I was looking sad, I was thinking about how confused I am with that stuff about my Dad. How can I like and respect him but not be like him? How can I even like him when my mother doesn't?

**Ruth:** What's important for you about your feelings about your Dad?

**Nick** *(quietly and contentedly)*: You are right. I think I can work it out in my own head, or by talking to Bill or someone else. I know I am myself and that I can feel what I want, no matter what.

280

*(The group claps in support of Nick.)*

*This week Bill may have made the greatest move of his life; he is no longer suffering in silence. Bette has claimed her life and begun looking at the way she acts and the way she feels. Nick has disengaged himself from his mother.*

**Ruth:** You all now sound finished for this week. Am I hearing correctly?

**Bill** *(again clearly and distinctly)*: That is correct for me.

**Nick:** Um-hum.

**Bette:** I'll speak for myself. Yes, I am finished.

**Ruth** *(to Les, with a smile)*: Shall we move on?

**Les:** I'm ready.

**Ruth:** Paula and Robin, will you both come and sit in the center and Bob, will you join us for awhile?

*(Throughout the week we've known that Robin wanted to go back to school, and that Bob, the community mental health worker who referred him to us, would be able to continue therapy with him. Bob and Robin have met outside our sessions, and Robin knows that Bob has been talking and planning with us.)*

**Les** *(to Paula)*: You seem continually to be trying to make up for what did and what did not happen in those early years with Robin. We've talked about this here. Right now it's important that you sit back, knowing that you've done all you can, and begin trusting Robin and someone else. We know that Bob is a fine therapist, and that Robin likes him. Let Bob do the work from now on.

**Paula** *(crying)*: I know it has to be done. I've found out that Robin and I get too messed up and he is old enough now to direct his own life.

*(Paula moves toward Robin and speaks tearfully and softly.)*

The past can't be undone or redone, but I want you to know that I'm sorry for all that happened with you when you were little. I've tried to overcompensate for that. I see that I've been doing that, and I see that it's too much for all three of us. It's time for me to let you do things on your own, and for you to begin your own life. You don't have to take care of me or David any longer. I'm not drinking and I'm managing well. You need to take care of yourself and get yourself going ahead. I will be there when you want me or when you and Bob ask me.

**Robin:** I understand, Mom.

*(Bob, who has been sitting back a little, is invited to move in.)*

**Paula:** Bob, I trust you. In fact, it's a relief for me to know that Robin will work things out for himself and with you.

**Les:** Robin, will you say what you're thinking?

**Robin** *(to Bob)*: This feels good to me. You've helped me a lot.

**Ruth** *(sitting removed from the three men)*: Paula, will you move back here with me?

*(Les, Bob, and Robin outline a plan for Robin and Bob to work together as Robin goes back to school and lives away from home. Paula watches with Ruth from a distance. When they are finished, Ruth turns to Paula.)*

**Ruth:** Paula, is there anything more you want to finish up with David?

**Paula:** Yes, just one thing. Again, David, you don't have to take care of me, and I will take care of you as my eleven-year-old son.

**David** *(sitting in Les' chair and smiling)*: That's good, Mom.

**Ruth:** Dom and Angela, you and your family look quiet and content.

**Angela:** I think we've completed what we came to do.

**Dom:** We may come back for another session, or we may just keep in touch.

**Ruth** *(turning and speaking to Les)*: I agree I think that they have come as far as they can come for now. The critical element for the future is whether or not Dom follows through with AA and stops drinking. Nothing else really will make any difference for them from here on out.

**Les** *(loudly)*: You are correct, Ruth. Dom is in charge. He will either do it or not do it. It's up to him.

**Angela** *(quietly)*: I think so, too.

**Ruth** *(with zip and energy)*: Hey, it's time for a break!

*This is the last official break of the workshop. We let it go on for about half an hour. There is noise, excitement, and movement in the room and in the area outside, where people are talking together and the kids are running and playing. Trainees intermingle with the families. Les and I are more distant and separate from everyone. Our way is to move back now and let whatever be, be.*

*After we call to begin again, people take many minutes to reassemble. Everyone knows we are close to the end. The room is different from the way it was at other times during the week: it's smaller and there are fewer people. Of course, that's not really true—it just seems that way.*

*This last part of Friday afternoon is a time when we have each family, along with the two trainees who have been assigned to follow or work with them, go off and do a special exercise. Designed to help cement the changes and gains the family has made during the week, it teaches families how to relate to each other in a new and positive way. People are appropriately and positively recognized and appreciated for growth, change, and who they are as people. Each family member gets a chance to be "it." The rest of the family members and trainees give the "it" all of the positive strokes they can think of. Positive strokes are verbal and nonverbal appreciations for the other as a person and for what they do. As "it" the person is to accept and let in all that comes their way. Finally, "it" is to ask for two more specific strokes that they want and have not yet received. This part gives permission to ask for what one wants and needs.*

*During this exercise the trainees help family members in noticing, sharing, receiving and asking. They aid family members in doing this clearly and separately and at the same time creating and/or reinforcing the new communication and interacting styles. When each family is done with this exercise they are finished for the afternoon. For most families this last part of the afternoon takes 1½ hours or so. For all families this is a solidifying and nourishing way to finish "the work of the week."*

*When the families and trainees are bringing about this ending for themselves, Les and I move off to our own place to be together and begin our own debriefing. It has been a long and extremely intense experience for us. We finish whatever family business there is and then do the exercise ourselves.*

## FRIDAY EVENING—LES SPEAKING

*David, Melissa, Nick, and Robin had volunteered to arrange for the Friday evening celebration. Dom and Bill supplied the adult input. Emerging from a week of growing up and taking responsibility, the four kids decided they wanted to have an old-fashioned birthday party. Everyone was to come dressed as a five-year-old. Ruth brought a teddy bear. She wore braids and big freckles. Many of the other women wore short skirts and ribbons in their hair. Most of the men wore short pants.*

*Everyone participated. We played Pin the Tail on the Donkey and Blindman's Bluff—with prizes, of course. Melissa and Robin made a giant cake; Nick and David brought ice cream. A special part of the party was devoted to celebrating David's eleventh birthday. I bought him a baseball hat identical to the one I had been wearing all week—lots of jokes were made about that hat during the workshop. During cake and ice cream, I presented it to him. It was a moving and close moment for us both. David wore his hat proudly up until our last goodbyes.*

*The party, lasting for three hours, included a talent show: Dom, our professional musician, bought instruments for all, wrote songs, and acted as master of ceremonies; Barbara, the trainee who entertained the children with magic, performed a traditional act of magic; Bill Sarnon read a poem that he wrote for his daughter when, as a child, she had brought him a bouquet of droopy, browning roses. At first he had gotten angry at her for making a poor purchase. Then, together, they trimmed the stems of the roses and filled the vase. As Bill finished reading the poem, he laid the paper down in front of him, looked up at the group, and said, "And this is what happened to me this week."*

*Finally, there were the impersonations of us: Melissa perched glasses at the end of her nose and played Ruth; David wore my baseball hat and asked, "What are you thinking and feeling?" As the two children (in a very kind way) put us in our place, the group laughed, expressing release and relief from the tension of the week. In this "roast," they divested us of the super powers they had given us earlier.*

## SATURDAY MORNING—RUTH SPEAKING

*Everyone is sad but excited as they prepare for these last. contacts and connections. During this week, families and people have been transformed. Each of us has been witness to many of these intimate changes. Finishing up with each other and with the experience of the week is vital to maintaining these changes.*

*We ask people to sit together with their own family members. Each person in the room is to think about how they and their families are different now from when they arrived six days ago.*

**Ruth:** And now that you have those thoughts, will each one of you, in your own time and way, share with us what you would like in order to finish up with the group. This includes trainees. When we are done with this, we will all take the opportunity to say our own personal good-byes to each other. When you are done with this personal connection, you are done with the workshop.

**Les** (*looking at Ruth and then slowly around the room*): Anyone may begin when he is ready.

*(The room remains quiet. Even the little kids are caught in the mood. Families are sitting together. Yet each family picture looks different from the way it did on that first morning when we began. Trainees are interlaced throughout the room. Les and I sit together but not in our working chairs.)*

**Bethany** (*a trainee*): This experience this week is equal to none other in my education. I learned. I felt and I gave. My special good-bye and caring to you, Melissa. You deserve to live a good and full life.

**Dom** (*clearly and concisely*): I feel good. For the first time, at thirty-three years old, I feel as if I have some direction in my life. I've gotten something from everyone in this group, but mainly I've gotten some gifts from myself to myself. The gift I've given me is my life. I wish I'd been a little quicker in getting to things for myself. I'll do it differently if we come back or however I continue. I don't know yet about AA. I'll decide that after I'm home. As for my family, I can't describe the changes I've seen in them.

*(Many of the people in the room now speak up to thank Dom for his contributions to last night's party. Some mention how different he is now. The atmosphere is markedly different from the first time Dom spoke, when nearly everyone bristled with irritation.)*

**Angela:** I'm ready also. I feel good, and a little overwhelmed by how much I've learned. I've learned that I am Angela and that I'm not bad or crazy. I've learned that there's a part of me in many people here. It's new for me to feel I can be close to people and not have to push them away to feel safe.

*(She looks calm and self-assured.)*

**Les** *(turning to Marco who is playing quietly on the floor in front of Dom and Angela)*: Marco, will you tell us about you?

**Marco:** I'm going home on the airplane. I want to go through the clouds again. Bye, everybody.

**Maria** *(sitting next to her mother)*: Me, too. I especially want to see my own teddy bear when I get home. *(She picks up the teddy bear she has used during the workshop.)* Good bye, bear. I'll see you if I come back. You helped me a lot and so did some of the people, especially Kitty.

**Kitty:** As always, I've learned a lot about kids, grown-ups, and mostly myself. I am ready to go home to my husband and two sons. They'll find me different.

**Don** *(a trainee, who is a pastoral counselor)*: Dom, don't forget AA. For myself I have grown in knowing and love. I am inspired to continue my work.

**Bette** *(sitting next to Bill, looking softer than before)*: I feel relieved. The first relief is knowing that I have my own life and I'm not twined with anyone. The second is knowing I'm not actually happy all the time and that I don't have to be. My third relief comes from knowing that Nick doesn't have to be perfect to keep me alive, and in letting Nick know that.

*(Then, turning to Bill:)* I love you.

*(Turning to the group:)* I enjoyed meeting everybody.

*(To Helen, a trainee:)* I have to admit I had an instant, negative reaction to you. You knew that, I could tell. How I acted was an example of the way I functioned. I didn't allow any contact. I was wrong. As I watched you, I saw how you played, how relaxed you were, how warm you were with Nick. Then I let down my guard, which is an unusual thing for me.

*(Sitting back and tearful:)* I'm finished. Thank you all.

**Bill** *(tearful)*: What I feel goes so deep I can hardly say a thing. I vacillated about coming to this workshop. I can't express how I feel now except to say I think I lifted the weight of the world from my shoulders.

Before this week, I would have died rather than talk about what I did. Now I know I am okay, that I can talk.

I can't think of any other setting where I could have

done what I had to do. I've been touched by a lot of you. Thank you.

*(Everyone is silent for a while. Many are tearful and involved with Bill. After a moment, I turn to Nick. He is sitting next to Bill.)*

**Ruth:** Nick?

**Nick:** I'm glad we've been helped to become a different family. *(With a smile:)* I want you to know this is a much better place than any place else we've ever been. I found my own mind here.

*(David is sitting on Nick's other side. They exchange smiles.)*

**Barbara** *(a trainee)*: This has been an incredible week for me. It will take me months to let myself know how much I've learned. Personally, I've been touched by each and everyone of you. Thank you for letting me become a part of your changing lives. Thank you for liking my magic.

**Terry** *(a trainee)*: I'm going back to my home and family in Australia with some new ideas for my practice and most importantly with a different look at myself and my own family. I am ready to be leaving now.

**Paula:** I have a lot of mixed feelings today. Mostly I feel good. I like wiggling my face and being real. I'm ready to go home with David and live a real life now. I support Robin in being himself.

**Robin:** When I came here I was almost too scared to be with people. I feel good now. Thank you all for getting me to face myself.

**David** *(in his baseball hat)*: I like being here. It has been fun. There's nothing else I want to say except I want you to know that I'm all grown up to eleven years old now.

**Bob** *(trainee)*: What I've learned about Robin, his family, and how to work with them has been invaluable. My style of working will be different. I think I've learned more about therapy and families here than in all of my other education and training.

**Anna** *(trainee)*: I am taking some wonderful pictures back to Germany with me. The pictures I got here are of people and families as I have never seen them before. Thank you all for giving me this.

**Gerry:** I remember starting the workshop, thinking of all of us as one big family. It was a revelation to me that the easiest way to change was for me to remove myself from the one large family and put myself where I belonged. I got that out of the week.

I feel happy and grateful to know that I can't do it and that I no longer even have to fantasize about carrying the burden of the world. I'm glad my parents and Melissa are starting to carry their own loads themselves. It's better for all of us.

I feel separate, I feel different. I feel like a grown-up son. I am a man.

**Margaret Ann:** I came with a jumbled mind. I knew I didn't like the way things were going, but I didn't know what to change. Now, I feel stronger about myself. I feel a lot closer to the whole family, because we have divided it. I'm out of the middle.

*(Little Gerry is holding the stuffed moose, jumping up and down for attention.)*

**Ruth:** Little Gerry, you look ready.

**Little Gerry** *(to Ruth)*: Bye.

*(To others):* Bye.

*(To Moose):* Bye.

**Les:** Melissa?

**Melissa:** I felt caught. Now I can move. There aren't going to be any more domineering grandmothers in my life.

*(She smiles at her mother.)*

**Berenice:** I'm full of feelings. I'm sad about the end with Edgar. I'm also relieved because we have finally resolved something.

I'm going to have to take care of myself for the first time in my life. Deep inside I have some excitement about being grown up and on my own.

**Edgar:** I know I can be myself. I have the strength to act on what I feel from now on. I feel sad about separating, but I know it's what I need to do.

*(Melissa and Berenice are sitting close, on one side of the room; on the other side Gerry, Little Gerry, and Margaret Ann are cuddled up together on a sofa; Edgar is in a chair separated, by himself.)*

**Claudette** *(trainee)*: It's been a good week for me, and I am ready to go to my home. I think I've learned a lot, and I know I'll know that later.

**Helene** *(trainee)*: What is most important to me is that I know, when everyone in my family can speak English, I will bring my family from Belgium here to do what you have done. You have given me courage.

**Ruth:** I am happy, sad, and tired as we finish. I feel proud of myself and of you Les. We have done our work well. I have respect and honor for each of you who have found so much of yourselves, been willing to face yourself and each other, and then change what needed to be changed. I am sad and glad as you leave and move on in different directions. I feel enriched for your having been here.

I am ready to rest and be quiet for awhile.

Les, I love you.

**Les:** For me its been a good week. Difficult at times, but good. One of the pleasures I get as a therapist is watching people change, and I saw a lot of that this week. I liked our working together, Ruth. I learned a lot from you, as usual, and I am also ready to be done.

*(After the final embraces—verbal and physical—Les and I go around the workshop site together, just as two conscientious janitors cleaning up. We move chairs back to their proper places and empty wastebaskets. Physically setting things straight helps us finish the week.*

*(Then we go lie on the floor of our apartment and listen to music. We say little to each other until sometime later, when we move on.)*

# _____*Epilogue*_____

Two summers have gone by. After the workshop, we waited to see which families would contact us. Before writing this epilogue, we decided to write to or call the families who had not gotten in touch with us.

These final pages say what we know about each family. Since the workshop—just as during the workshop—some events have been excellent, some have been good, some not so good. Some people are changed, some are not, but all—each family, each member, each of us—have moved on with our lives.

## THE SARNONS

The Sarnons did not contact us directly. We heard how they were doing from the lawyer who had referred them to us. Approximately a year after the workshop we went to Madison, Wisconsin to do a training workshop for a community clinic. We wrote to Bill and Bette in advance, and they responded enthusiastically. We met for a glass of wine.

Our greeting was warm and exciting. After reconnecting, we learned that Bill was to get the award for Best Athlete Comeback of the Year from his fitness center. He had just begun some walking at the end of the workshop week at Lake Tahoe. He later figured out a way to run—putting weight on his toes rather than on the balls of his feet. In three months, Bill had gone from walking to running. By Christmas he was running four miles a day on an indoor track. Now that spring had finally arrived, he was up to ten miles a day around the lake. We were astounded and thrilled. Bill had clearly decided to suffer in silence no longer but to move on with his life. The accident and problems about his past were left behind.

During the workshop, Bill had felt unhappy with his job but would not risk losing medical and retirement benefits by changing jobs. He was now getting a loan to start a consulting firm, using his computer and medical knowledge to advise companies on exercise programs for their employees.

Bill was neither speaking softly nor holding his head down. He said what he wanted to. We knew he was no longer withdrawing from us or from Bette.

Bill had worked out a new relationship with his daughter. He had developed ("in my way") a new, different, and closer relationship with her. Bette now felt much differently about having Bill's daughter around. The mysteries were gone. New relationships were developing.

Bette looked radiant. After our meeting she left to be the chairwoman at an athletic-awards banquet. She was very involved with the athletic center as well as her teaching. Bette had tried to contact her twin sister but felt rebuffed by Barbara's consistent avoidance of any meaningful connection. Bette's relationship with her younger brother was "different." She no longer depended on his being happy for her to feel alive. All in all, she felt freer, more alone, and more alive.

We didn't see Nick, but both Bill and Bette revealed brief information about him. (Bill seemed more involved with Nicholas than Bette did.)

Bill and Bette had not been happy about Nicholas's grades. Bill had warned Bette about getting too involved—that her insistence might make Nick stubborn. They hired a college student to tutor Nick. It seemed to be working out well; Nick was now looking forward to getting into a small private college.

For a while, Nick and Bette had had some very stormy times. Nick wanted to assert himself as a separate person. Nick's continued and even increased interest in his father was also hard on Bette. All in all, though, Nick was being adolescent and doing well.

The evening ended with Bette going off to her awards dinner, Bill and Les having dinner together, and Ruth meeting some other people for dinner. Les had several contacts with Bill following this evening. These centered around some computer projects that they had talked about the previous evening.

## THE QUINNS

Six months after the workshop, Les, on a trip to Nevada, met with Paula and David Quinn for breakfast. We had received news about Robin and from Bob (the social worker who attended the workshop). Robin had done all right for about six months. He had continued to see Bob after the workshop. He seemed more settled. He had gone back to school but experienced a lot of pressure from the course work. The goals Robin had set for himself overstrained him. He had also had some contact with his father. This added to his stress and he again became symptomatic. There were a few months that were quite stormy as he tried to continue at school in spite of the strain. Finally, with continued support, he decided to quit school and take a full time job as a recreation director in a small town not too far from home. Since that time Robin has been doing well and David, told Les that he had had some good visits with him. Robin continues to drop us a few lines every now and then.

At breakfast, Les learned that Paula was working as an office manager for two young men and a young woman who renovated old houses. She was a motherly figure for them. Paula thought herself to be doing well. She was taking much better care of herself. She knew she was going to "make it." Robin's problems had been hard on her. But, she said, "I kept myself separate and free from guilt and responsibility." Paula looked different, too. She seemed younger and much softer. Her face even moved a lot as she talked.

About the same time as Robin was reexperiencing difficulties, David's teachers reported that he was having reading and discipline problems. They suggested that he leave school and study under a private tutor. At the time of the breakfast meeting, Paula was faced with making this decision. Les suggested that Paula work out a compromise in which David had a reading tutor in the morning and attended some afternoon classes and sports. The following fall, David went back to school at grade level.

David had quickly moved up to the next level in the Little League—second base in the Pop Warner League. His throwing and catching had gotten much better. For the first time, he felt part of a team.

David appeared, wearing Les's baseball hat. He reported that he keeps it on all of the time. He even stays late afternoons during spring practice to throw with a new kid who was going to be catcher and could not throw from home to second base.

David said: *I like making some friends, and I can do that now because I don't tease other kids so much. I still tease sometimes. That's what Robin did to me. Maybe I tease them so they won't tease me first.*

Finally, Paula told us that she had left David at home alone for a couple of weekends—her next-door neighbor had him over for lunch and dinner and telephoned him at bedtime. These times away were good for Paula.

"David even empties the kitchen garbage now," she said. "Do you remember when he wouldn't clean up the milk he spilled at Tahoe?"

## THE BARKERS

Berenice wrote to us periodically. She has given us permission to print these letters. One year after the family workshop, Melissa and Berenice attended a women's workshop with us.


May 17, 1980

Dear Ruth and Les:

I want to bring you up to date on the Barker families. The Gerry-Barker family is a separate unit from the Berenice-Barker family, which is separate from Edgar Barker, who doesn't seem to be a part of any family right now, and that's sad.

Edgar and I are divorced now, and Edgar is living by himself in Tucson. He makes infrequent contact with Melissa and Gerry. My contact with him is limited to problem-solving things about the divorce. That is the way I want it. He has indicated a desire to resume some kind of social relationship with me, but that is not something I want.

Gerry quit working for my mother's company and started working for a smaller company twenty miles away. Two months after he left the family company, his grandfather died. For a while, he was very guilty about that. He started in a sales job at the new company and was not doing well and started drinking again. But then he asked to be made production manager of the shop—getting to solve problems and repair mechanical hitches. He is much happier now.

Margaret Ann seems to be taking care of her own needs and for a while ignored Gerry's drinking. I haven't seen her alone for a few months, but the last time I did, she was weighing whether to go on being Gerry's wife or to get a divorce. A good sign lately is that she and Gerry have been busy doing repairs on their house.

Little Gerry started nursery school in September. After some tears and timidity at first, he settled in and made friends and very shortly began to speak in full sentences. He and I get to play together about once a month. We go swimming or to the park or to the zoo. We both look forward to our visits together.

Melissa swings back and forth, like a pendulum. She is class treasurer, band captain, on the track and volleyball team and honor society. She's in the spring show at school and working at the science center. Her last report card had four *A*'s and two *D*'s—the D's were in her best and favorite subjects, which was weird. She also is smoking pot, drinking, dating a twenty-year-old, and got caught smoking in the boy's bathroom at school. I have her in a local therapy group, but Melissa is clever and has the group going just the way she wants, to cause herself the least amount of discomfort.

Since the Lake Tahoe workshop, I have taken my graduate record exams and enrolled in, and completed, a year's worth of credits in the community-college rehabilitation-counseling program. I've also gotten my divorce, painted and cleaned the whole house inside and out, bought a new car, and am working part time as a graduate assistant at the college. I am doing a work term at school that includes one-to-one counseling at a shelter for abused women. In working with these women, I'm learning more and more about my own manipulations to stay dependent—and also seeing how far I've come.

I'm going out with a guy about as different from Edgar as anyone can be. He feels, cares, laughs, and cries with me. He hangs in and fights, too. When I push, he pushes back. What a great feeling! But he is so financially irresponsible that he barely keeps his head above water himself, so I can't lean on him for support. That's good for me, too, because I still need to prove that I can support myself.

I still have sad days, scared days, angry days, but they don't come as often or last as long. I'm concerned about the rest of my family, but I don't feel a need to suffer for them or to fix them. Though I do feel the need to find a way for Melissa to fix herself.

I forgot to mention that I did confront my mother. I told her that Edgar and I were divorcing and that I didn't want her advice or to listen to any garbage about how awful Gerry and Margaret Ann are but I did want a friendly relationship with her. I stayed with her while her husband was dying and took her to a musical for Mother's Day. She thought I should sell my house and that Melissa and I should move in with her. No way! Surprisingly, she hasn't put down Edgar or Margaret Ann lately. Now she puts down her maid and her lawyer—that I can live with. She got an electric alarm system installed in her house to ease her fears when I wouldn't stay with her. She found a friend to go away Memorial Day weekend with her when I chose not to go. She didn't fall apart and she didn't quit caring about me. And I don't feel used. Is it really this easy?

Thank you both for getting these changes underway. Without your assistance, we would still all be stuck in the muck.

With love, Berenice


August 4, 1980

Dear Ruth:

Thanks for your letter. I do want to do a workshop with Melissa, but since my divorce my income is about one quarter what it was last year. Do you know of a place where I could work part of the cost out serving meals or cleaning rooms, whatever?

If I can't swing a workshop, perhaps you could recommend something here in Arizona. I do feel it's important that Melissa and I do some kind of therapy. Theoretically, I know the ways of being a good parent, but in practice I come down on her, and she shuts me out. It was my feeling that, of all of us, Melissa was the least affected by last summer's workshop. I don't think she ever did take down her guard. Even when I do reach out to her, I can't get through her shell. All of which really wouldn't matter if what she was doing was working for her. But she seems unhappy, sullen, and alone. Her grades slipped badly this last quarter, her friends rarely call anymore, and she's into pot heavily now. I want so much to change things for her.

I don't communicate with Edgar. He doesn't even call or come by to see Melissa, and that is probably part of her problem. I guess he's doing okay, but my guess is that he's an angry man. My wish is that he find a woman he can take his defenses down with.

Gerry is very happy with his new job, being a troubleshooter. When a machine doesn't do what it's supposed to he finds out why and fixes it. He and Margaret Ann are getting along well. Little Gerry is talking a blue streak and visits me twice a month.

I feel better than I ever have in my life. I enjoy working as a graduate assistant to six professors and hardly ever feel anxious or scared about going to work. My second work term is at a halfway house for "chronic, institutionalized schizophrenics." They only have a five-percent recidivism rate. I'm continuing my work that I started last quarter with the women's group at the abused women's shelter, and I'll finish my requirements for my M.A. next year.

Except for my relations with Melissa, things are smooth at home. I talk to Mom every few days and see her once or twice a month. She still tries to tell me how to live my life, but she rarely hooks me anymore. She really isn't someone I want to spend time with, so I don't.

I find that I try some of the same old manipulations with my boyfriend, Joe, that I did with Edgar. They don't work with him. He would indeed turn me over his knee and spank me if I threw a two-year-old's temper tantrum, so I don't. I'm slowly and painfully learning to be straight and so is he. When the fights are over, they're over, and then we're free to make love and have fun.

That's how things are with me and my family. Thank you for helping us get where we are.

Love, Berenice


November 19, 1980

Dear Ruth and Les:

Enclosed are some pictures. Things are going well. I have three more weeks of classes and am up to my ears in term papers and exams, also in winding up my last three weeks as a graduate assistant. Then I'll begin a counseling internship.

Melissa is showing slow but steady signs of change. She made Honor Roll this grading period (after $D$'s and $F$'s as well as $A$'s, last year) and has a steady job babysitting. She's still dating the twenty-one-year-old nerd (but I'm dating a forty-five-year-old nerd, so shut up, Berenice) and still getting stoned regularly and still avoiding me. We've written a list of what is and isn't expected of her at home along with rewards and punishments. We've both stuck to it well, and it has been months since I've yelled at her or hit her.

The big success in the family is Gerry. He's doing well in his job, but looking for something with more chance for advancement. He is staying sober and not running around. He and Margaret Ann do wonderful things together like going fishing and hiking, and they just built a back porch on the house.

Little Gerry is enjoying kindergarten and is talking nonstop. He says that porcupines are called pokeypines because they poke you with their sharp things.

Don't see Edgar to know how he's doing, but I know he has joined a golf club and has a girlfriend he visits, so he's getting some pleasure out of life. And so am I—me and the nerd go dancing and camping whenever work and school permit.

Thanks for helping us find our paths.

Love, Berenice

October 6, 1981

Dear Ruth and Les:

I feel an urge to bring you up to date on the Barker
clan. First, Gerry. He's doing so well I scarcely know where
to begin. He opened his own business, repairing all kinds of
appliances. He has almost more business than he can
handle. And he is remodeling his home. And he doesn't
drink anymore. And he and Margaret Ann are getting
along beautifully, and, when they don't, they work it out.

Margaret Ann is doing Gerry's paperwork, helping with
painting the house, and continuing her job at the law firm.
She has just been promoted to personnel manager, and she
looks terrific. Both Gerry and Margaret Ann have
developed a network of friends. They enjoy entertaining
and being entertained.

Little Gerry is in first grade. He's still shy around
strangers, but talking loads with family and friends. Gerry
and Margaret Ann both take time every day to do things
with him, and I see him one evening a week.

Edgar has bought a condominium and is moving in next
week. He has a girl and everyone says she is a lot like me
only not as bitchy or touchy as I was. He and I now have
an acceptable relationship, and we can both be comfortable
together at family functions, like Little Gerry's sixth
birthday. The times we do have problems to work out, we
act pretty rational.

One of the problems we've had to think about together
is Melissa. I tried setting limits and rules for her. At first
she lived within the limits. Then, one by one, she broke
each rule. Then she got worse than before we set up the
limits. I tried reasoning, then restricting her privileges and
cutting her allowance. It was all no good. I finally got a
belly full the afternoon I came home and found her passed
out cold, nude and unresponsive on the living room floor. I
told her she could either shape up and live by the house
rules or ship out. She chose to ship out. She tried to get
her boy friend to take her in. When he refused, she went to
Gerry and Margaret Ann. They refused, too. So she asked
Edgar and he agreed. She's enrolled in tenth grade and
living with her Dad in Tucson. She's been with him about
six weeks now and, when I call there, she's home, and the
two of them are busy decorating the new condo. She has
the opportunity to start fresh there. And she knows now
her Dad still loves and wants her, and I'm not sure she felt

that after he left. And she doesn't have to struggle so hard to let go from me.

She started coming home weekends and doing the same old stuff, and I told her that she was welcome to come here anytime she wanted to live by my rules, but I wasn't willing to provide a weekend home base for her to wheel and deal from, so now she doesn't think she wants to come here anymore.

My changes are not so dramatic, but evident. I like the relationships I have with Edgar, Gerry, Margaret Ann and Little Gerry. The situation with Melissa was difficult. I don't know if I did what was best for her, but what I was doing wasn't working and I couldn't just sit by and watch her go down the tube. I do know that when I get angry now I walk away until I feel calm instead of acting crazy. I'm Little Gerry's grandmother now, and Margaret Ann is his mother. And she's Gerry's wife, and most of the time I stay out of their business. Sometimes I slip, but mostly I catch myself and stop.

I'm still dating my friend, Joe, who is becoming more responsible. He gives me a lot of love and rarely puts me down.

I know there is hope for Melissa. Thank you for making us all feel better.

Love to you both,
Berenice


January 25, 1982

Dear Ruth:

These last three weeks have been a bitch for all of us, but I want to update you. Edgar died in a boating accident three weeks ago. Gerry, Margaret Ann, and Melissa handled all of the funeral arrangements themselves. Melissa and Gerry went through the condo and moved everything out. Margaret Ann and Melissa cleaned everything out of one of Margaret Ann and Gerry's bedrooms and helped Melissa set the room up with her things in it. Margaret Ann and Gerry went to a lawyer and are handling the estate. Melissa finished her semester at school and registered into a school in Gerry's district. I handled the transfer. I'm really proud of how adult Gerry has been and how the three of them are pulling together to work things out. I feel left out. I really want to charge in and tell everybody what they should do and how they should do it,—and I'm not. I'm just doing nothing and keeping my mouth shut, and that's the hardest thing I've ever done. I've lost my role of mother, role of wife, role of rescuer and role of persecutor, and though I frequently feel like the victim, I'm not laying a guilt trip on the kids. My task, at this point is—if I'm not any of those things I used to be and don't do any of those things I used to do, to do—who am I and what do I do?? I feel pretty empty and directionless and scared right now, but I'm also pretty proud of what my kids are doing. And what I'm not. Eventually, I'll figure out where I go from here. I haven't yet.

Thanks for being available.

> Love to you and Les,
> Berenice

July 4, 1982

Dear Ruth and Les:

Are you having a family workshop this summer? If so, please send me the details. Margaret Ann and I had a good talk today. She said that Gerry has made many changes since Lake Tahoe, but he's at an impasse now and is seeking help, but doesn't know who, in this area, has the potency that you two do. I thought maybe we could work something out if you've got something coming up. If Melissa is ready to move, I'd include her, too, but since I haven't discussed it with her, I don't know if she is or not.

Melissa is living with Gerry and Margaret Ann. She's finished tenth grade and has withdrawn from high school. She's signed up to take her High School equivalency exams next week and plans to enroll in Jr. College, for a computer programming course the end of August. She's broken off with the creep she was with and is dating a guy twenty-seven years old. (She's sixteen.) But this guy is college educated, good looking, well kept, well dressed, and highly intelligent. Melissa told Margaret Ann that she's never dated anyone before who she felt cared for her as a person rather than an object. She's not getting stoned or

drunk all the time anymore and her eyes sparkle again.
Well, there isn't *anything* about what she's doing that
would be my way for her, but she's doing it her way, and it
seems to be working for her. I'm just glad to hear her
giggle again.

Margaret Ann is pregnant. She plans to quit work and
to stay home and keep Gerry's and her current boss's books
when the baby comes. She looks fantastic and is relating to
Gerry very differently. She's a terrific lady, and I'm proud
of her.

Gerry has stopped doing illegal and overtly destructive
things to himself and is doing a great job with his repair
business and fixing up the house and yard. He is just great
with Melissa. She listens to him and hears him. But he's
still making himself physically ill and still goes on drinking
binges—but he realizes that this, too, is self-destructive
behavior. He wants to change and doesn't seem to be able
to. And he admits to needing help.

This last year has been a bitch for me. I've lost my role
as mother, lost my fantasy that Edgar would come back,
lost the financial security that he represented, lost the
strokes and status I got as a student and graduate
assistant. My roof leaked, and the house had termites in it,
and my job leaves me exhausted and drained. I've been too
overwhelmed to even know where to begin to start
rebuilding my life. I decided that the roof and termites
better have first priority, so I am in the process of
repairing and redecorating the house. Socially and
emotionally I'm stuck—not the person or place I used to be
and not really sure of who or what I want to be instead.
Not bound by any commitment or responsibility to anyone
other than myself, my options are limitless and all those
choices scare the hell out of me. It was a lot simpler and
safer when I was in my little cage trying to run everyone
else's life. A large part of me wants to crawl back there
and slam the door shut, but Edgar is dead, the kids have
cut loose, and I can't go back—and that's scarey too. I have
just enough faith in myself to know that sooner or later I'll
get tired of being in limbo and will get off my ass and do
something, but not enough faith to believe that I know, and
will do, what's best for me. Strange, isn't it, that for years
(and sometimes now, too) I thought I knew what was best
for everyone else.

What's happening with you two and how's the book

coming? I keep wondering how you can end a book based on the lives of ever-changing relationships. There doesn't seem to be a stopping place.

Let me know what and where your current workshop schedule is and don't be surprised if one or more Barkers show up, if you have the space.

Just realized I didn't mention Little Gerry. He's going to be seven in September. He finished first grade with flying colors and can read like a whiz. He's in a summer rec program with lots of activities and field trips. He visits me once or twice a month and I treasure the time we spend together. Melissa also visits me about once a month. While she's not wildly enthusiastic about it, she's not cold and rejecting anymore either.

Love to you both and thanks again for the good things you helped to have happen in our families.

Berenice

# THE DELLAPIETRAS

The Dellapietras never returned for the second workshop. They continued living together as a family. Dom contacted Ruth in March; Angela and Maria were fighting again and he was concerned. The fighting had begun almost exactly when Dom began drinking again.

Ruth and I saw the family for a two-hour session. I referred Maria to a therapist near her home. She was moody, not following through with her school work, and having difficulties with her friends. Marco's behavior was grown-up and appropriate for his age. He was trying hard to please his parents. School was going well for him. This change seemed to be throughly integrated into his behavior.

Dom had recently begun drinking again. He was only occasionally acting as a father—usually when he was sober. Neither Dom nor Angela knew why he was drinking again. I suggested that Angela and Dom seek couple's therapy and urged Dom to go back to AA.

Dom and Angela continued with therapy only briefly. They were doing even better parents and decided to do it on their own for that summer. Maria's therapist agreed.

Many months later Angela called me to say that she

was feeling depressed because of her grandmother's death and some interchange with her father. Angela reported it this way:

*My Dad's mother, my grandmother, died this last month. She asked for my father and, after tracking him from California to Louisiana, I finally got in touch with him in New York City. I told him that his mother was dying. He said not to bother him, that he might get out to see her, but that I should butt out. He never did come. I always had the idea that he would come back if I needed him and that he would care for his mother. Now I've stopped waiting for him.*

I worked with Angela until her depression cleared. Then, she again discontinued therapy.

Angela was continuing in school and enjoying it tremendously. She had begun school in the fall after the workshop. During that workshop, Angela had decided that she was not dumb or crazy. She had held with that decision even through the crisis with her father and through Dom's drinking. Maria and Marco were performing well at school and relating well to each other.

Just recently, Angela called for the last time. It had been a year since I had seen any of them. Angela arranged for her and the children to come up and see me. Dom's drinking had begun again and then gotten gradually worse. She was now ready to take the kids and leave. Several months earlier, she had asked Dom to leave, but he had refused to go. Angela reported that Dom was a different person now and that even his friends and colleagues no longer trusted or supported him. He had deteriorated significantly, particularly after the economic climate had harmed his business.

Angela herself was sad, but she was determined to take the best care possible of herself, Maria and Marco. Throughout everything she had continued her school and worked occasionally as a physical-therapy assistant. Angela continued to trust her own mind and her own worth even though she sought validation from me. Angela reported she had not "covered for Dom" since leaving the workshop several years ago. She said, "I've stuck by him, because he's a good person but I haven't covered up reality for him. What's real is real for us even when it's not pretty."

Maria was doing very well, both in school and in her piano. She and Marco continued to connect appropriately.

Maria sometimes gets anxious about getting and losing friends. Marco has grown up to his age, though he is still a performer.

In some ways, things seemed to be in the same place they were at the end of the workshop for this family. Dom was drinking and their marital relationship was bad. In reality, this family had traveled hundreds of miles down the road.

# 8

# Redecision Family Therapy and Intensive Multiple-Family Therapy/Theory

Since its inception, family therapy has been plagued by the lack of a theoretical base that simultaneously takes into account the history of individual members of the family, the history of the family unit, and the current interaction among family members. Without that theoretical base, it is almost impossible to define either normality or pathology in the family. Furthermore, it is extremely difficult to evaluate the success of family therapy, unless one strictly relates behavioral change to outcome. The lack of a broad paradigm also contributes to a division of opinion among practitioners who espouse any of the major epistomologies—systemic/behaviorist, experiential, or psychodynamic.

The theoretical framework that governs our work attempts just such an amalgam. We integrate these viewpoints into a cohesive model called *Redecision Family*

*Therapy.* \* Redecision therapy was conceived, developed, and polished by Robert and Mary Goulding of the Western Institute for Group and Family Therapy. We have integrated many of their basic formulations into our model of family therapy.

This theoretical model can be used in many different therapeutic structures, from long-term treatment to intensive multiple-family groups. Aside from giving direction and structure to the family treatment process, its greatest advantage is that it encourages many forms of psychotherapeutic intervention. An intervention technique's suitability is determined by its aims and style rather than its content.

Redecision Family Therapy follows a developmental-interactional paradigm. That is to say, one's personal history shapes one's perceptions of oneself and others and determines personal values and expectations, which in turn direct one's style of interaction. One's experience as a family member, together with one's unique personal makeup, determine the extent and flexibility of the strategies one uses to cope with and master different situations in the current environment.

Each individual enters the world carrying "biological givens." Each individual also enters a family that has "family givens." The child's early needs and the intensity with which they are experienced, the availability of the parents and family to respond to the child, and the time period over which responses are made, create the environment to which the child must adapt.

At the most basic level, the child must adapt in order to survive; at the next level, to feel the least pain; and, at the highest level, to feel pleasure. Over time and through the constant repetition of the parent–child–family interaction, the child builds an internal model of herself, her parents, and later the outside world. This early model of herself and others becomes the model she carries around with her. She brings it into every room she enters and into every relationship she forms. She chooses a partner whose model

---

\*"Redecision" is a service mark filed with the U.S. Commission of Patents and Trademarks by Robert L. Goulding and Mary McClure Goulding.

of the world and of himself will mesh with hers. In fact, his model will provide evidence that her model is correct and should be maintained.

The building blocks for this internal model are called early decisions. Newborn infants have their own temperaments and styles of expression. The families they are born into may have similar or dissimilar styles and temperaments. The infant and the family must, in some way, accommodate each other. This step-by-step process of accommodation or adaptation is called early decision-making. Early decisions become the fiber of the infant, the infant's model, as she develops her characteristic response to herself, her family, and the world. She "acts as if she decided long ago" the way she and others would be.

In choosing a partner, a person makes life as predictable as possible by choosing someone whose background, style, and early decisions allow for patterns of interacting that regulate the closeness so both partners can feel most comfortable. Much of people's daily interaction is a continual negotiation to obtain some measure of congruence between their inner experience of any situation and the perceived reality. These manifest patterns of interaction are the net result of each person attempting to negotiate the difference between inner and outer realities, between perceptions of self and others, and between different but interlocking life plans or scripts. When the patterns are limited in number, shallow in depth, and rigidly adhered to, we can predict that the family as a unit, or some of its members, will experience psychological or physical distress.

Systemic/behavioral therapists suggest that the patterns of interaction are the problem and that the solution is to change these patterns. These therapists often use what Chasin and Grunebaum have called the "ingenious" techniques. Other therapists focus on the "experience" of the family and take the position of a nurturing parent who helps the family to grow via restructuring new and different experiences. The dynamically oriented therapist, on the other hand, is more likely to focus on the individuals' character organization, defenses, or the quality of their object relationships.

Families are groups of people who share a common history, have an affectionate bond, and have a common purpose. As a unit, each family has a structure, a hierarchy of relationships, and some characteristic patterns of interaction. We think of the structure as the boundary between the various subgroups. It is also evident in the interactional patterns.

Redecision Family Therapy considers the boundaries to be very much like the superstructure of a building. The boundaries determine the family's strength and limits in terms of size and general shape. This does not describe what happens inside, nor does it indicate the number, shape, or size and form of the substructures. Nor does it tell us about purpose. If the superstructure is small, confined, and rigidly fixed, it severely limits the family's organization and flexibility.

As family therapists, we must know and understand the superstructure and its manifestations in the patterns of interaction. We must know where its strengths and weak points are and the points at which a small change can have a maximum effect. (Selvini Palazolli *et al.* refer to this as the nodal point.) Knowing this is only the first step in the procedure, however. Buildings and people do not automatically optimize themselves once their limits are extended. Our research and experience indicate that change is maximized when both the individual components and the system change.

Our view of the developmental-interactional paradigm is that current behavior (in the form of interactional patterns) and personal history (in the form of early decisions) operate in a reciprocal relationship. We might work first on one aspect and then the other, but dealing with both is essential to family therapy.

To help effect systemic and individual changes in an orderly fashion, we have divided our treatment model or structure into three stages. In the *systems stage,* we observe, evaluate, and intervene in the system. Then, in the *redecision stage,* we dissect out the individuals' characteristic responses from the interaction patterns at large. We trace the roots of these characteristic actions, the early decisions; and, through regressive techniques, we facilitate redecisions. Finally, in the *reintegration stage,* we focus on building a new family system that helps the family and its individuals maintain confidence in themselves and in their ability to resolve any normal developmental difficulties that might arise.

The systems stage is present-oriented and explores the current process. The redecision stage focuses on the archaic or intrapsychic past. The reintegration stage focuses on the present with an eye to the future.

Although we describe these stages as distinct entities, they are rarely clearly demarcated. While a family is involved in work in one stage, the work of other stages may be going on as well. Movement back and forth among the three stages is continual. A progression through the stages occurs during almost every interview and over the entire treatment process. In our workshops, as you may have noted while reading the stories, the initial individual work often starts on the second day, while the third afternoon takes us back for a different look at the system.

# STAGE ONE: THE SYSTEM

Whenever two or more people come together for any period of time, they form a specific unit. Depending on the length of time they are together, the commonality of their interests (through either work or kinship), and the strength of their bond, each unit or system develops a specific character of its own. The system has its own process, or way of functioning. It also has a structure and a set of rules that define its day-to-day operating style.

A basic understanding of how the family system works is shared, although usually not articulated, by the family members. This shared "culture" provides comfort and a sense of inclusion and belonging. It provides the safety that allows its members to grow and to learn to explore themselves and the outside world.

Under some circumstances, this system can also be detrimental to its members. A family such as the Barkers, for example, invariably turns inward in times of stress or uncertainty. They feel comforted by being part of a very caring network of family members. At other times, when no crisis is apparent, they experience a feeling of disloyalty if they turn outward. It is not surprising, then, that the Barkers reported that their family "seemed to create a crisis and live from crisis to crisis." This family rigidly adhered to its common "culture" and structure. As a result, they evolved very few options for resolving difficulties or for getting out.

A lack of options and a rigid adherence to old responses

often create the problem. One of the primary tasks of the family therapist is to increase the options of the family and its members.

### Creating the Environment

The first challenge for us is to create the environment in which family members will reveal themselves in their natural states. This is quite a task, since families usually restrict or distort their behaviors, thought, and feelings when outsiders are present. Much of family therapy is devoted to creating artificial environments—sculpts or tableaus, drawings, games, movement exercises, and the like—in which the family will show itself. One of our ways, and perhaps the most powerful, is to create the actual natural environment. Four families sitting at a community dinner table away from home have a hard time being other than as they are. We also pay constant attention to establishing an environmental structure within the therapy room and the living space that is safe and allows people to move, act, and be who they are.

### Assessment

After we create an environment that allows us to observe with some degree of accuracy how the family operates, we begin the assessment process. In assessing the family, we watch for what the flow of information looks like, the impediments to that flow, what happens to the expression of affect, how disagreements are handled, and a host of other similar variables. In other words, we note the events and their order. We also note what does not occur that might be expected to. Since each family has a unique way of managing itself and a characteristic pattern of information flow and expression of affect, we observe and note the recurrence of these patterns. Gerry's drive over the cliff on Thursday, which had the effect of reestablishing his centrality, is one example of recurrence in a pattern. Bette's hand on Bill's knee whenever he got emotional is another. Each of these examples stopped the flow of information or affect.

In this early part of the first stage, we also look at the structure of the family. We are particularly concerned with the hierarchy of relationships and the alliances and coalitions. The most functional family unit is one in which the hierarchy is understood by all. Adults who are parents are part of one alliance whose voice has more weight than children who are adolescents, who in turn have more weight (not value) than younger children. Yet each alliance has its place in the structure of the family, providing both a sense or order and belonging.

We use the concept of boundaries (as described by Berne, Minuchin, and others) to describe the structure of the family. We concern ourselves with three different boundary configurations. The first is the internal minor or self boundary. This is the set of characteristics by which individuals distinguish themselves from each other. In the absence of this boundary, people are not able to separate what is inside them from what is outside. Nor can they distinguish what is real from what is not. An accompanying rigidity excludes any contact with others. At the beginning of the workshop, for instance, Robin became exceedingly anxious whenever he was under Paula's unflinching gaze. He lost contact with his separateness and himself.

The internal major boundary, our second configuration of concern, separates leadership from nonleadership. Without clear and congruent leadership, the family's day-to-day life becomes chaotic, like the proverbial ship without a captain. The Dellapietras are a case in point. Dom and Maria formed a coalition that crossed the generational boundary and consequently invalidated and undermined Angela's attempts to be in charge, set limits, and lend direction to the family. It is no surprise that Angela's self-esteem was quite low.

The external boundary, that set of characteristics by which the family unit knows itself, is the third configuration. The therapist, who quite understandably begins from the position of an outsider, confronts this boundary first. When he becomes an insider who can maintain his own values in spite of the current family rules and norms, the therapist can then teach the family to tolerate, then accept, and ultimately welcome differences.

The external boundary of the Barker family was troublesome. "We are the Barkers" referred to not only all the people at the workshop, but also Rusty, who had died some years before, and Berenice's mother, Gertrude Mackay. The Barkers had a strong and relatively impermeable external boundary. It wasn't easy to become a member of the clan. Once you were in, it wasn't easy to get out.

In the early phase of therapy people demonstrate normal fears, self-protective reflexes, and both childlike trust and mistrust. The interventions we use in this phase allow families room to reveal themselves at their own pace and to feel some measure of trust in us and in the group. Very helpful at this point is the presence of other troubled families, which creates a sense of universality, of shared problems, of others being worse off. Having families with some previous group experience is also helpful.

We start by allowing people to identify themselves and then make contact with others. We encourage them to move away from their families at first, then to get back to the safety of their families as we structure topics for discussion. Families sometimes talk privately among themselves sometimes with the rest of the group listening. On occasion, we use games that are icebreakers but are also revealing. We might have families drawing murals as a combined project while we observe. To guide the pace of these early interventions, we pay attention to the tone of the group and the amount of pressure to reveal—or the resistance against revealing—information.

Once we assess the structure of the family, the repetitive patterns and their rigidity or flexibility, and the relative strengths and vulnerabilities of the individual family members, we are ready to move on to the formation of working contracts.

## Contracts

Clearly defined goals and working agreements that focus on resolving the underlying interpersonal and dynamic difficulties are an essential part of our work. These contracts facilitate the psychotherapeutic process by providing a goal-oriented structure that defines all deviations as a form of avoidance of solving the problem. In other words, contracts serve as a focal point for the work of psychotherapy as well as a reference point for digressions.

The contract is the agreement we reach with the family about defining the problem and the way to solve it. The contract considers the family's needs as well as its dysfunction. The contract also considers the needs of individual members.

A family comes to us with a problem that it or someone else wants fixed. If we accept them in therapy it is because we think, on the basis of our experience, that we can help them fix the problem. The family also comes with many unspoken and often unconscious expectations of us and of each other. These unconscious expectations reflect longstanding pain and a history of having tried and failed to solve their own problem.

We initially consider how the family's structure and process either helps or hinders the problem's resolution. We then consider the individual pain and struggles. Finally, we mutually develop the contract which, in effect, says: "If you as a family change in these ways, you will have the best chance of resolving your problem. Furthermore, as individuals you have each struggled with the problem in your own characteristic ways. If you resolve the individual *core* problem—if you change the model of yourself and the world that you carry around inside—you will eliminate your pain and prevent yourselves from getting into similar situations again."

The contract with the Dellapietras is a good example. Angela and Dom agreed with us that they each allowed and invited the kids to interfere with their relationship, to prevent problem-solving, and to distrupt the development of a clear parental alliance. To change this, Angela—who limited herself by her struggle to avoid contact with anyone, except for a brief period of time—and Dom—who continued to relive the multigenerational history of male camaraderie though bar-hopping and alcoholism—needed to confront themselves. Under the contract, the couple would work to form a stronger parental alliance, Angela would work to change her ability to make contact, and Dom would live without his association of maleness, friendship, and alcohol.

### Intervention for Change

Following contracts comes the design and execution of interventions that will change the structure of the family and the patterns of interaction. In the Barker family, the main structural defect was that three family units had been linked into one conglomerate. The mother–daughter unit, the father unit (he was effectively separated), and the son–his wife–their son unit were bound to each other through the maternal grandmother. Each person reacted to what he or she thought others felt and wanted, without regard to which unit the others belonged.

Our overall contract was to facilitate their separation

from each other. Since part of their entwinement was an expression of the emotional power of the maternal grandmother, we needed to examine the relevant dynamics and help the family view grandmother in a different light. Games, sculpts, and drawings underscored their togetherness and permitted them to voice whatever discomfort they felt about the enmeshment. We then deliberately worked separately with the natural subunits. We confronted the dynamics that inhibited each subunit from forming its own separate and cohesive unit. We helped the individuals redecide and maintain their own separation. This second-stage redecision work facilitated the first-stage separation work and vice versa.

A similar example from the Sarnon family demonstrates the use of interventions to resolve rigidly held patterns. Bill, Bette, and Nick were fused by Bette's touch and her belief that she knew what Bill was thinking and feeling, that she could finish his sentences, and that she should control Nick's intentions and actions. To interrupt these patterns, we decided to work separately with Bill and Bette, to treat them individually rather than as a couple, even when they were together.

Numerous intervention options are possible during the first stage. They may be direct or indirect, fast or slow, light or heavy. We choose different combinations to constantly maintain a balance between support and confrontation. This balance provides safety and facilitates progress.

It should be noted that some families will do first-stage work only. We accept this and work within the needs and requirements of the family. Individuals may not be good candidates for regressive work or may not want to invest the time, money, and emotional energy that second-stage work entails. In the intensive multiple family workshop, this is not usually a major problem. The residential character, time limit, and group dynamics contribute to most family members' decision to do individual intrapsychic work. Individuals often work indirectly or vicariously as they identify with other group members or as they look for and try on other role models.

Again, the special character and evolution of the multiple family group structure is important. During the first stage, we watch the group form into a cohesive unit. We next notice how the energy of the group often shifts from anticipatory and hopeful excitement to sluggish withdrawal. This usually signals the onset of resistance as people struggle with the question of whether to reveal their most private selves. The group senses the existence of long-kept "secrets" long before the secrets become known. We also experience a phase during which the energy becomes polarized with anger toward one or both of us. Recognizing and then facilitating the expression of this anger frees the group to begin the work of the second, or redecision, stage. These phases are quite similar to those described by Speck and Attneave in their work on family networks. In many senses, the multiple family structure creates a new family network.

## STAGE TWO: REDECISION

Redecisions are made when an individual's thinking, feeling, and being as a child are reexperienced as an adult, using that adult's competence, assets, and abilities. Knowing what she knows now, and being who she is now, the adult metaphorically becomes the child of three or seven or ten. Then, with the structure and guidance of the therapist and utilizing her current strengths and abilities, she is helped to perceive herself, the situation, and the other people differently. She recognizes her early decision and redecides based on updated or current information. Through the redecision process, she frees herself to think feel and behave differently in her current life.

### Recognizing Early Decisions

When we do redecision work with individuals, we ask them what they want to change and then help them explore, regress, and redecide. In other words, what they bring into the therapy room is always their choice.

This is not the case in our redecision work with families. We consider the potential impact of any individual change on the interpersonal process of the family and guide clients toward making those changes that will have the greatest impact on the family problem and the current dysfunctionality. We carefully locate those central behaviors and beliefs that are revealed in the present and that signal archaic decisions representative of the person's model of herself and the outside world. We can see the imprint of an early decision in a person's posture, demeanor, voice tone, choice of words, choice of job, choice of mate, as well as in every other area of activity. We can see the imprint through repetitive behaviors and absolute beliefs such as "always" and "never."

We then select the individuals who are likely to have the greatest impact on the family system or who are the most available for change through redecision work. Since parents are the "architects of the system" and the initial providers of safety, we most frequently begin redecision work with them. When the system is unlocked and the parents are different, it becomes safe, sensible, and more possible for the child to change her early decisions about how best to survive within the family. (A child's ability to redecide has a direct relationship with her age, incidentally. It is easier and safer for older children to change even if their parents don't than it is for younger children to change.)

### Contracts and Environment

After we recognize which early decisions are most significant in the family's problem, we help family members form contracts for individual change. Often, we simply ask people if they want to and are willing to change those aspects of themselves. Such a contract is most often entered into only after much thought and consideration. It is a contract for internal change and involves all the risks of confronting oneself.

We do redecision work with individuals within the family setting or within the different peer groups, depending on the individual issue. Sexual identification and growing-up problems for a mother such as Angela are best focused on within the women's group. Edgar realized his early decision regarding his father within the men's group, where he was with other fathers and separate from his wife, with whom he acted in predictable ways. And it was within the family group that Bill Sarnon decided to stop suffering in silence.

We arrange the groups with a purpose and a plan in mind. The sequence is based on who needs to or would be more available to do individual work. Then, when redecisions are made by an individual apart from her family, we help that person integrate both the information and her new self back into the family.

### Techniques for Facilitating Regressive Work

As we said, redecision work requires temporary emotional regression from the "here and now" to the "then and there." To get someone to regress, we have to either actively structure the setting or notice when the client regresses spontaneously and utilize that opportunity.

The specific regression technique we choose at any given time depends, as do all our intervention choices, on our assessment of the safest, easiest way of proceeding. Seriously disturbed people can regress quickly but without carrying their adult cognitive functions with them. We don't use regressive techniques with people who become confused easily. We might, for instance, use therapeutic structures such as a family sculpt where we maintained someone in the present as she looks at the picture of the past.

The technique we use most frequently is the progressive regression, or going back in steps. Noticing the repetitions of thinking and feeling in the present, we ask the person to stay with what he is thinking and feeling while he experiences the last time he felt and thought the same things. Then we ask him to remember the time before that, and the time before that, until the person moves himself to the earliest memory. Bill Sarnon worked in this way.

Another common technique for regressing is to separate the parts of a mental debate (the gestalt two-chair technique). A child can play his side of the argument he's having with his mother; then he can enact his mother's side. We did this with Nick by having him look at things as Bette would, and with Angela by having her talk to her absent mother and long-absent father. We also ask people to dramatize the voices of an internal struggle. "Be the two separate voices in your head [or the two separate people]." We help each person make the introjects real in the present, and then make the present as young as possible.

Frequently we use nonverbal techniques to enter the past. We ask people to choose a scene from their childhood and to draw a picture of it. Then we ask them to "get into the picture." As a variation on this approach, we sometimes ask clients to bring old photographs of themselves and their families.

Another nonverbal technique is to ask someone to set up a family sculpture. We used the family sculpt technique with Melissa and Berenice. Each of them stimulated her thinking and feeling from the past and then utilized the sculpture to identify her early decision. Each could then redecide. Berenice chose, for example, not to stay locked into the old MacKay family.

People often regress on their own. We are alert to the nonverbal signs of regression—posture and body or facial expressions, tone of voice, and the amount of time it takes someone to respond to us. We ask, "How old do you feel at this moment?" and then investigate what happened in their family of origin when they actually were that age.

### Making the Redecision

"Okay, now that I've helped someone be back there in the 'there and then,' what do I do?" This is a question others frequently ask us and one that we sometimes ask ourselves.

Our "working through" process is again based on the work of Bob and Mary Goulding. First, we help the person identify and clarify the original decision and its components. This clarification is essential and must be done from the individual's insides. We stay within the confines of the client's interpretation of the early decision and make sure that what is identified is "true" for the client. The components of that early decision include the person's sense of herself, her sense of the other, and her sense of what she must do and feel in relationship to herself and to others. We direct the work by helping her identify and recreate different aspects of the early scenes.

Once the early decision is clearly identified, we decide on the next step for resolving the early impasse. Resolution occurs between this person and someone originally outside herself (such as father and mother) or between this person's perceived parts of herself. The actual "working through" is accomplished when we reenact the early scene and stimulate the development of a new conclusion, a redecision. As part of playing out the scene, we use fantasies, other people in the room, or objects to represent the symbols of the past. We have toys and play materials available to help people experience being little. When the working through involves an early integration of parts of the self, using symbolic materials such as dreams or clay and drawing is effective.

Redecisions are emotionally, behaviorally, and intellectually integrated updates of a person's sense of himself and others. Frequently, redecisions are made piece by piece. Sometimes people return to the same scene time and again; at other times, they use different scenes to rework the same early decision from a different time or perspective in their lives.

### After the Redecision

After a person redecides, there is often a spontaneous snapping back to the "here and now" and a "wow" response to what she has just accomplished for herself. Sometimes, though, the person is too hard on herself and rejects the part of her that made the original decision. This is done, for instance, by labeling the early decision as dumb rather than self-protective. We stress that early decisions were made for survival or to get along in the home of her childhood. In this way, we help each person accept the child in herself and reframe the old experience.

Redecisions are best maintained over time when immediately grounded in the present by a "wow" experience or some other method. A grounding technique can be as simple as a gestalt exercise in "being here now," asking someone to be aware of her body, or asking questions that require here-and-now thinking responses.

# STAGE THREE: REINTEGRATION

A redecision, as we think of it, is equivalent to a change in a person's internal frame of reference. This is thrilling, but it is not the end of the process. Most important is implementing that redecision. As a next step, we ask people, in effect: "Now that you have made the change and decided that you are worth being here [or that you will grow up and be successful, etc.], what will you do differently in your life and how will you do it?" The work of our model's third stage consists first of clearly articulating a response to this question and then of helping the person and family reintegrate the new self. An individual who has redecided will be different with his family, creating an unavoidable change in family dynamics.

Life changed significantly for Cinderella's stepmother and stepsisters when she stopped cleaning the hearth and became a princess. Bill Sarnon decided not to suffer in silence any longer, and Berenice Barker decided to think.

Prior to these redecisions, each had been expecting other family members to respond in ways that accommodated the early decision. Following their redecisions, each changed his or her demeanor, behavior, motives, and thinking and, inevitably, his or her position in the family. The family then required some help adjusting to these changes.

In reintegration, we have several different tasks and directions. First in this stage are preparation and practice. We predict the different ways in which the family might try to restore the old familiar style and we prepare them to resist that temptation. Sometimes we just identify and talk about what might come up. Sometimes we suggest the kind of rehearsal and role-playing that Dom and Angela did with Maria and Marco. At other times, we initiate the role-playing of redecisions that family members need to make in the future. We outlined such with Bette.

The second task in stage three is education and practice. Education has two focuses for us—individual education and family education. Berenice, who did not know how to be a competent woman, needed to learn from other women by choosing new role models and finding different arenas in which to practice and get support. It's like a grownup who has watched people ski but never tried himself. To become a skier, he starts on the bunny slopes and then progresses to harder moves.

In addition to this individual education, family education is essential. Teaching families how functional systems operate is easy and fun at this stage. All that is needed is a conceptual framework for doing what they have already started doing as they relate differently. Important elements include talking about and practicing completing tasks and transactions; validating self and other for age, sex, and person; joint problem-solving; focusing on the here and now; and accepting a wide range of affect expressed within appropriate boundaries. On the last afternoon of the workshop, we used exercises and games in this regard.

Stage three's third component is stroking. Learning about positive feedback and establishing a comfort and ease with all of its aspects is integral to the maintenance of change. With the help of the trainees, workshop family members learn to give, receive, and ask for strokes. In this way, they begin to work with the positive aspects of self and other they explored during the week.

This very important third stage is often the least emphasized part of family therapy. Therapists are usually much more excited to be working with a family in crisis or during the redecision process than in directing the teaching process for getting along from day to day. Also, the requirements for a therapist are different in third stage. In the first stage, the therapist is an active, inventive transformer. In second stage, the therapist is active, involved, and empathetic. In the third stage, the therapist becomes more of a guide to the family.

Our approach in the third stage is more intellectual and more directed at the adult part of the client. We stand back and help the family learn and integrate the changes so that the new patterns are solidified.

# ENDING OUR WORK

All of our work ends with rituals that help people say goodbye in the psychological sense as well as in the social sense. We honor the gestalt principle that a person must finish in the present before moving on to the future. We choose in the workshop to have three ending ceremonies: a party, final rounds, and less formal goodbyes. We start with the stroking session, continue with a party, and end with a ritual summing up and personal goodbyes.

The stroking session brings the family together into an active and supportive unit. The party widens the sphere of fun, supportive contact. Most often families roast the therapists, salute each other, and finish with the last few loose ends. Often they exchange gifts.

Finally, the formal rounds on Saturday morning allow everyone to make the public statements that often clarify and further cement the work of the week. The ensuing final good-byes are personal. Each person has contact with each other person and finishes up for the time being.

As a final theoretical salute, we have several factors to consider as we summarize the overall impact of this approach and consider its value in this or any other format. The first is the question of outcome. We turn to Bader, who published one of the few good studies of outcome of family therapy and reported a significant benefit by families who took part in one of our multiple family workshops. Furthermore, she found that this benefit lasted over three months. While this period is less than the six-month post-experience period we would like to have seen, it nonetheless pointed to the value of the intensive multiple family group. Furthermore, Bader concluded that families in which members made significant redecisions generally did better than those in which no redecisions were made. This attests not only to the value of the group and the systemic work, but also to the importance of individual/redecision work within the family context.

Second is the question of casualties. Intensive group therapy for individuals, despite the initial enthusiasm and without regard for the model (religious/spiritual, educational, or evocative/confrontational), has been shown to have casualties when a casualty is defined as an individual requiring therapy and/or hospitalization within the six-week post-group time frame. In fact, casualty rates for any form of therapy are in the one to two percent range, and for encounter group therapy in the five to ten percent range. It is important to recognize the possibility of casualties and to prepare for them. We believe it best to make certain that families who are engaged in our process have, if they choose, a therapeutic environment to which they can return at the end of the workshop and that the therapist be sufficiently informed in order to be able to continue the work of the group.

Finally, we can best summarize our thinking about the elements that go into making the intensive multiple family group a successful and valuable modality by quoting from a previously published work of our own:
1. The family experience is a week away from home. Family members make considerable preparations to get to the workshop, and at significant expense. Motivation is usually high, although at the same time anxiety and resistance may also be high. In total there is usually a considerable amount of concerted energy to get something accomplished.
2. The experience of other families in difficulty provides the sense of universality and hopefulness that is common to all forms of group therapy.
3. The presence of other family members facilitates cross-family connections and separation of family members from one another.
4. The "group" experience permits rapid interpersonal connections and group cohesion.

5. The time-limited structure frames the working experience and hastens the work of the group.
6. The three-stage model requires that change be reintegrated into the larger family network, and that cognitive grounding be achieved.
7. The therapists' style of confrontation and support keeps the group at its tasks, and the pace is rapid.
8. The large number of people present allows for alternative social networks and for family members to find different role models.
9. Different subgroups can be formed to facilitate personal work and provide additional sources of feedback. Bader* referred to self-report questionnaires completed by participants who detailed their perceptions of the essential elements of the workshop. These elements were "the therapist, specific pieces of therapeutic work, the workshop format, and . . . the environment." These self-reports agree with out experience and with the generally accepted criteria for group therapy.

---

*Bader, E. Redecision in family therapy: A study of change in an intensive family therapy workshop. Dissertation Abstracts: Ann Arbor, Michigan, 1976. University No. 7625064.

# *Bibliography*

1. Bader, E. Redecision in family therapy: a study of change in an intensive family therapy workshop. Dissertation Abstracts: Ann Arbor, Michigan. 1976. University No. 7625064.

2. Berne, E. *The Structure and Dynamics of Organizations and Groups*. Philadelphia: J.B. Lippincott, 1963.

3. Chasin, R., and Grunebaum, H. A brief synopsis of current concepts and practices in family therapy. *In* Pearce, J.K., and Friedman, L.J. (ed): *Family Therapy, Combining Psychodynamic and Family Systems Approaches*. New York: Grune and Stratton, 1980.

4. Goulding, R. L., and Goulding, M. *Changing Lives Through Redecision Therapy*. New York: Brunner/Mazel, 1978.

5. Minuchin, S. and Fishman, C. H. *Family Therapy Techniques*. Cambridge: Harvard University Press, 1981.

6. Selvini Palazzoli, M.; Cecchin, G.; Prata, G.; Boscolo, L. *Paradox and Counterparadox*. New York: Jason Aronson, 1978.

7. Speck, R., and Attneave, C. *Family Networks*. New York: Pantheon Books, 1973.